AF674077

Educational Aspiration

ABOUT THE AUTHOR

PANNEER SELVAM is born in Salem - Valappady of Tamil Nadu. He started his career as school teacher in New Delhi in the year 1991. He joins as lecturer in DIET, perundurai of Erode in 2000. Bharathiyar University were gave the Philosophy in Doctorates in Language and Education. He is the seventh diploma holder from National University of Educational Planning and Administration (NUEPA), New Delhi in 2002. In 2005, the Tamil Nadu government was given the 'Excellence Award' for his unrivalled teaching activities and some organization also. He has published more than hundreds of Research Papers and books in the field of Education. At present he is working in the department of Education, Bharathidasan University, Tamil Nadu.

ABOUT THE BOOK

People of all age levels form peer groups of their own. However, here, peer groups among children and youth are considered. While the world of the very young child is largely that of the parents and the home, older children and youth love in the dual world of their peer and adults. While a child at the primary school level is strongly family- oriented, the higher secondary school student is much more influenced by his peer group. Boys are much more peer oriented than girls in the higher secondary school stage, a n d get free from the influence of their families, with regard to their opinions and attitudes. An Adolescent spends a great deal of time with their own age-group, and the values and attitudes of their own particular set of friends within the peer-group become an important influence on their behaviour. The reasons for the growing importance of peer relationships are varied but three major areas can be distinguished. Education is a process which makes an individual to adopt himself whole heartedly for the changing environment. Education also provides an individual opportunity to acquire skills for a better living. Education further enables a person to perceive a stimulus and respond in a positive manner.

Educational Aspiration

Dr. S.K. Panneer Selvam
Assistant Professor, Department of Education
Bharathidasan University, T.N.,India

AMIGA PRESS INC.

AMIGA PRESS INC.
H.O:- 28-A, Indra Park, St.No-9
Near-Chander Nagar, Krishna Nagar
Delhi: - 110051 (India)
Tel: - 011-22504028, +91-98736-57000
Email: - amigapress@gmail.com
info@amigapress.co.in
amigaeditorial@gmail.com
amigapub@gmail.com

Website: - www.amigapress.co.in

This edition is published by Amiga Press Inc.

ISBN: 978-93-84533-64-9

Copyright©Reserved

First Published 2020

All rights reserved, no part of this publication may be reproduced, stored in a retrieval system or transmitted in any form or by any means, electronic, mechanical, photocopying, recording or otherwise without the prior written permission of the publisher or the copyright holder.

This book contains information obtained from authentic and highly regarded sources. Reasonable efforts have been made to publish reliable data and information, but the author's, editor/s and publisher cannot assume responsibility for the validity of all materials or the consequences of their use. The author/s, editor/s and publishers have attempted to trace and acknowledge the copyright holders of all materials reproduced in this publication and apologize to copyright holders, if permission and acknowledgements to publish in the form have not been taken. If any copyright material has not been acknowledge please write and let us know so we may rectify it, in subsequent reprints.
Publisher Notice: - Presentations, Logos (the way they are written/ Presented), in this book are under the copyright of the publisher and hence, if copied/resembled the copier will be prosecuted under the law.

Printed and bound in India by Replika Press Pvt. Ltd.

Contents

❐

1

The Problems and its Perspectives

Socialization is the process by which a person develops from a mere biological organism, as at birth, to an adequate adult human person. Socialization means learning the ways of a culture. No one is regarded as fully-grown, in a psychological sense, until he learns to display a measure of the prevailing adult attitudes, values, beliefs and knowledge of the subculture to which he belongs.

Socialization requires moving through a series of age-related subcultures. At any given time in the life of a growing child or youth we may refer to the dominant thought patterns of his age mates as his peer culture. This statement should be qualified with the observation that until a child is old enough to become a member of neighbourhood play group, or a nursery school group, he has no true peer culture. During the first two or three years of life the only culture he knows is that part of the adult culture which his parents and adult relatives see fit to teach him, or the peer culture which older siblings transmit.

Man is aware of himself. He can objectify himself, stand apart from himself and, as it were, look at himself. He can think of himself. Biologically self-awareness is an evolutionary novelty. So the problem is how the neonate who has no awareness whatever develops into an adult with self-awareness.

SELF IMAGE

Self image is one's own idea about him, conception or mental image one has of oneself. Self image is how you perceive yourself. This self image can be very positive, giving a person confidence in their thoughts and action, or negative, marking a person doubtful of their capabilities and ideas.

DEFINITIONS OF SELF IMAGE

According to Oppenheiner Agnes, "self image is a person's mental picture."

According to Andrew M.Colman, "Self image is the idea or conception that once has of oneself in general".

According to Rogers-et-al, "Self image is the idea or conception, it is stored information and influence the way we think and remember, it is otherwise called as "Self Schema."

According to Jacques Lacan, "Self-image is the dimension of the imaginary idea ego".

CHARACTERISTICS OF SELF-IMAGE?

Self image can be explained with the help of following characteristics. Self image is,

- How one regards himself/herself.
- The mental picture of how he/she believes he appears to others.
- How one picture his/her physically self.
- How one believes others see him/her physically.
- One's idea (positive or negative, rational or irrational) of how he/she presented himself/herself to others and how he/she is subsequently judged by them.
- A personal assessment of one's character, personality, skills, abilities, and other attributes.
- A powerful internal mechanism influencing how one feels about himself/herself.
- An accumulation of scripts one has been given (consciously or otherwise) and has learned well.

CREATING A SELF IMAGE

One's self image is developed by how one assesses the following factors in his/her personhood:

- Physical appearance
- Shape of his/her body
- Accomplishments in academics
- Achievement in athletics
- Social skills
- Value system
- Skills, abilities and competencies
- Relationship with family, relatives, siblings, peer group and others.
- Behavior in social and professional situations
- Background and environment from which he/she came
- Roles played in life at school, home, and work and in the community.
- Jobs and job titles held
- Goals, ambitions and aspiration for the future.

INTER PERSONAL REALATIONSHIP AND SELF IMAGE

Self-image is to do with how people perceive you and this will affect how they relate to you, it will affect relationship either positively or negative, we many believe how we see ourselves is how others see us, this cannot be true. Our view of our self is shaped by our unique thoughts and beliefs and we will have a distorted view. We see our self in a positive or negative way and both will be biased, we may have negative view of our self and if so you are probably highly critical of our self.

PARENT AND PEER ATTACHMENT

Family Relations

The number of possible relationship within a family increases exponentially with the number of individual family members. In a four-person family, for example, there are 11 groupings of family members. (i.e. six dyads, four triads, and one tetrad). In addition, relations among relationship (e.g. between the couple and the parent-child system) must be taken into account, not to mention the relationships connecting the family and its sub-systems with other social units (e.g. extended family, peers). These complex patterns of relationships should be kept in mind as some of the major types of relationships within the family are briefly reviewed.

Parents-Child Relations

The care and socialization of children are among the most important societal tasks that, to a great extent, are entrusted to the family. Theoretical models to explore the determinants, concomitants and consequences of parenthood have increasingly become more complex by addressing not only specific parent child interactions but also by looking at contextual and systemic influences such as heredity, child temperament, the parents' personality and relationship history, couple relationship, workplace, social support and economic resources. In addition, theoretical advances, especially using attachment and social-learning approaches, have shown some convergence concerning the development of competent behaviour in children and adolescents.

The Responsibilities of the Parents

Family is very important because from it he/she inherits the cultural traditions. From this viewpoint family becomes more important for human. It is generally seen that if one is deprived of family protection, his development remains incomplete. Therefore for the desirable development of the child the family has to do certain responsibilities.

The child's first education begins in the family. The making or unmaking of his future life depends on his early experiences in the family. The mother influences the child immensely. After the mother, the father and sisters and brothers, guests, servants and casual visitors leave their impact on the child. The child has an inherent power to receive education consciously or unconsciously from the various aspects of his environment. Because of this conscious or unconscious learning the child is rightly regarded as the symbol of the interest, traditions, ideals and culture of his family. Thus when he comes to the school, he brings with his personality the traditions and culture of his family.

A child has an acute sense of curiosity. For fulfilling the same he is never tired of putting questions to the elders in the family. His questions must be answered in an appropriate manner and he must never be scolded for the style and contents of his questions. We must remember that the child is just in the process of growth.

Peer Groups

These are groups in which most members are of equal age and of similar social status. People of all age levels form peer groups of their own. However, here, peer groups among children and youth are considered. While the world of the very young child is largely that of the parents and the home, older children and youth love in the dual world of their peer and adults. While a child at the primary school level is strongly family-oriented, the higher secondary school student is much more influenced by his peer group. Boys are much more peer oriented than girls in the higher secondary school stage, and get free from the influence of their families, with regard to their opinions and attitudes. Peer group influences are encouraged by extracurricular activities, sports and other social influences. Peer groups develop certain status symbols which change from time to time. A status symbol establishes communication and relationship between peer group members, for example, long hair, blue jeans, striped shirts, and other fashions may become "the rage" for a while.

Importance of Peer Relationsips

During adolescence the need to belong to and identify with a group of individuals of the same age is stronger than it is at any other period. This tendency seems to hold in most contemporary societies. An Adolescent spends a great deal of time with their own age-group, and the values and attitudes of their own particular set of friends within the peer-group become an important influence on their behaviour. The reasons for the growing importance of peer relationships are varied but three major areas can be distinguished.

To begin with, relations with both same-and opposite-sex peers serve as prototypes (first examples) of adult social relationships. Adolescence is a period in which learning about interpersonal behaviour in a variety of situations-social, intimate, and work-oriented-speeds up and, as you will know from your own experience, even a short period of a year or eighteen months can produce a striking change in the social, intimate, and work-oriented-speeds up and, as you will know from your own experience, even a short period of a year or eighteen months can produce a striking change in the social maturity of the adolescent. Much of this social maturity is acquired in interactions with peers.

Peers also help the adolescent in defining his sense of himself. No longer a child, not yet an adult, the adolescent must prepare to meet the Demands his society makes of adult functioning in many spheres-social, sexual and vocational. The peer-group, members of which are facing similar choices, can help the adolescent in defining his sense of self and his expectations of the future.

FUNCTIONS OF PEER GROUPS

Peer groups are important to the young, in the development of the self and also in the learning of cultures. They help the young to become independent in their thoughts and decisions. Peer groups during adolescence are very significant, especially in western cultures. Such developmental tasks as learning to get along with companions and acquire a satisfactory sex role can be adequately achieved only through satisfactory peer relationships. Many of the attitudes of the teen-ager are a result of group influence and stimulation. The peer group represents a distinctive sub-culture in contemporary western society and even in Indian society to a lesser degree.

The peer group is primarily an activity group, which operates through social, recreational and vocational activities. The peer group provides sex-education in many cases. It assists the individual teen-ager in the process of self-identification and self-discovery. Social and emotional emancipation from the family is possible through the peer group. He acquires a status, which he cannot get in adult society. Thus the adolescent's personality develops through the important social agency known as "the peer group".

PEER RELATIONS AND DEVELOPMENT

A peer system refers to the interactions, relationships and group structures involving persons in a group of nearly the same developmental level. Age level is often used as an indicator for peer status. However, in many instances age mates are not peers. For example, in most school achievement domains mentally retarded persons are not peers of intellectually normal individuals. Furthermore, age mates may not be peers in every developmental domain. In athletics physically handicapped persons are not peers of non-handicapped individuals, although they may be peers in intellectual competence. Class group are often homogeneous on a number of characteristics, such as age level, achievement level, learning difficulties, and so on. The goal of this entry is to describe the relevance of peer relations in school classes for children's social, emotional, and personality development.

PEER COMPETENCE AND THE PEER SYSTEM

In a conceptual framework for the understanding of social relationships in groups, Hinde (1976) has distinguished three hierarchic levels: Interactions between individuals are seen as basic elements for social relationships. Relationships are the basis for group structure. Description of an interaction requires specification of the content, that is, what individuals are doing together (e.g., A does X to B and B responds with Y), and the equality of an interaction. An essential aspect of the quality of an interaction is its valence. Whether an interaction is positive/prosaically or negative/antisocial is an important determinant of the meaning of an interaction for a relationship.

PEER RELATIONS AND LEARNING

Children's communication with their peers has qualities that differ from the qualities of adult-child communication. For example, peer dialogues are usually more equal than conversations between adult and child: children usually listen more respectfully to adults than to peers for information and guidance. Such differences have serious implications for learning. Educators have become aware of these differences and have began to design classroom strategies that best exploit the learning opportunities provided by both peer and adult-child relations. This entry discusses contemporary methods for applying the special features of children's peer relations to their academic learning.

THREE TYPES OF PEER LEARNING

Although peer relations are generally more equal than adult-child relations, not all peer engagements are strictly alike. Peer relations themselves can be unequal to various extents. There are three main types of peer learning that have been introduced into classrooms by educational researchers. These have been called "peer tutoring," "cooperative learning," and "peer collaboration" (Damon and Phelps 1989). As in the contrast between adult-child and peer relations, the three district forms of peer learning offer different strengths and weakness for the educator.

Cooperative learning, also called "small group learning" or "group work", has been introduced into many schools because the available methods are relatively easy for teachers to adopt. The techniques can be integrated into the normal school day without disruptions in the regular classroom routine. Some cooperative learning programs require as little as an hour or two a week of classroom time.

There are a variety of cooperative learning techniques now in use. All begin by dividing classrooms into small "teams" of no more than four or five children. These teams are generally heterogeneous with respect to students' abilities. The teacher presents a task to the team, and the team sets out to master it. All cooperative learning methods rely on team solidarity and the motivation that it engenders. The assumption is that students will want to perform well for their team and that they will work for the success of their fellow team members and the team as a whole.

PEER TUTORING

In this approach, a child trains another child in skills and subject matter that the first child has mastered. Because the first child has greater information or competence than the second child, the two do not begin the relationship with equal status: rather, the first child is considered an expert and the second child a relative novice. Moreover, the unequal status of the two children is often compounded by other factors as well. Most attempts at peer tutoring pair an older child with a younger child or a bright child with an educationally disadvantaged one. Peer tutoring, in fact, is often called "cross-age5' tutoring, since the tutor is usually two or more years older than the tutee.

PEER COLLABORATION

In peer collaboration, a pair of novices work together to solve difficult tasks. This method differs from peer tutoring because the children begin at roughly the same levels of competence. It also differs from cooperative learning, because children work jointly on the same problem rather than individually on separate components of the problem. In actual practice, however, peer collaboration bears some resemblance to other types of peer learning. Even in peer collaboration, one child may assume the lead spontaneously; and the collaborators may separate for independent work.

EDUCATIONAL ASPIRATION

Education is a process which makes an individual to adopt himself whole heartedly for the changing environment. Education also provides an individual opportunity to acquire skills for a better living. Education further enables a person to perceive a stimulus and respond in a positive manner. Individual differences occur in learning and in the learning situation. This develops in the learner a particular way of learning which is called learning style. Information about learning style can help the faculty to become more aware of the students progress in academics. It can also serve as a guide in designing the learning experiences that match or mismatch student's styles depending on the teaching input. Knowledge of learning style helps to plan and organize the content systematically.

Every society has a concern for the younger generation and the education builds the character of the citizens. The task of developing the students is a balanced personality and competency for life skills rest in the teachers who mould the young minds. The teacher indirectly kindles the spirit of striving for the goal of the student's aspiration in their life. Aspiration is strong desires to reach something high or great young pupils' aspirations are guided by the teacher in the school setting. The school further provides an atmosphere to enable the students to prepare for adult life in the society.

Aspirations reflect individual's ideas of their "Possible selves" what they would like to become, what they might become, and what they do not wish to become. Realizing aspiration requires the investment of time, energy and resources, both from the young person and from others. The extent to which communities mobilize such support bears on the quality of life, both among students and among adults.

Due to the impact of aspiration on educational outcomes students' aspiration in school has become a major filed in educational research. Different goals can have dramatics impacts on achievement outcomes.

Even though a performance orientation emphasizes public recognition fir doing better than others on competition and gaining rewards and praises from others may be associated with achievement and an orientation to the mastery of concepts and the enjoyment of the students in an effort of meaningful learning tasks that is believed to be a major force for excellence. It would be unfortunate to learn that such tasks could drop during the years of schooling of the students.

DEFINITION OF EDUCATIONAL ASPIRATION

Aspiration strong desire to reach something high or great. Hence, educational aspiration is a desire to achieve high in education. Young people's aspirations guide what students learn in school, how they prepare for adult life and they eventually do (Walberg, 1989) this readers Digest report on educational aspirations of rural youth compared with students living elsewhere, and suggest ways communities can work together to raise the insights of their young people.

Frank (1935) defined level of aspiration as the future performance in a familiar task which an individual knowing his level of past performance in the task explicitly undertakes to reach.

Many investigators have considered aspiration as adequate approximation of the "action goal".

Aspiration in an individual can refer to the subject who always undertakes a task with certain demands which can change in the course of activity. The expectations goal setting or demands in connection with one's own future performance can be termed, as level of aspiration of the subject.

According to Guilford (1987) "Achievement is related to success or reaching a goal. Student's achievement depends upon their motivation, interest, academic input practice and the support from the home and the school setting.

LEVEL OF EDUCATIONAL ASPIRATION

The level of aspiration was first formulated by Dembo (1931) in course of an experimental investigation. Dembo's investigation discovered that when a require goal is too difficult the subject will set up an intermediate goal which is easier than the first or original goals so that he takes a step towards the required goal. The immediate goal is termed as the subjects' momentary level of aspiration.

The level of aspiration has roused keen interest and experimental. The technique is concerned with the effects of success or gratification and failure in a dynamic situation that has potential importance in both theoretical study of personality and in the field of clinical diagnosis and description. It its brad sense, the purpose of these series of studies is to analysis as far as possible some of the factors operating in the aspiration studies. Due to the dynamic nature this aspiration appears to be a useful method for the teachers and educationists. Aspiration has been applied to studies of motivation in school children, vocational choice, and academic success and personality traits.

According to Boyed (1982) level of aspiration is an individual ambition in a dynamic situation. Lewinkete (1980) considered that the level of aspiration is a choice is a psychological situation. The attitude with which a child enters a learning situation is dependent among other things, like on his previous success and failure experiences in similar situations.

The level of aspiration, which is a measure of the level of performance that an individual sets for himself and this, is based on success and failure experiences. Seas (1979) found that children who have consistently experienced success subjectively in their day school work and objectively in tests and school marks continue to set aspiration levels. However, when children have been consistently frustrated in their day to day learning efforts and disappointed in their marks, they set unrealistic aspiration levels, either too high or too low.

EDUCATIONAL ASPIRATION AND FAMILY ENVIRONMENT

Parents also have an effect on their children's level of aspiration. Weiner and Murry (1938) content that lower socio-economic parent have high level of aspiration for their children's education just as middle class parent do. The difference in the willingness to preserve the goals while removing the obstacles, and the difference between the reality and the ideal of these goals.

The family environment, as well as the schools that are economically disadvantaged and the student who are economically backward is also a factor for their poor academic preparation and may contribute to their high dropout rate. Family problem and the dialectal differences could also affect the academic development of the student.

RAISING ASPIRATION

Educational Institution plays a vital role in building and raising the educational aspiration of student at various levels. The resources available in the school along with the teacher's guidance and provide opportunities for achieving higher goals in life.

The society also has a part to play in raising the aspiration of the growing generation by way of allowing these students to build up a healthy competitive spirit, achieving goals set, encourage risk taking behaviors. Secondary schools need more relevant curricular so that students know themselves what is necessary for them. The Secondary school curriculum should stress the kinds of skills adults need, for example, working Co-operatively and solving.

Schools also should organize to address the social and emotional aspects of students. Matching small groups of students with a caring adult can provide students the coaching they need to jump all the hurdles that lie between them and high school graduation. Parent can raise their own expectation for their children's academic achievement. They should insist that teacher and student raise their expectations as well. Parents can also express their support for the children and help the schools to celebrate success.

Based on the above theoretical frame work of the study, an investigation is undertaken by the researcher to find the effect of self image and parent-peer attachment of first generation learners on their educational aspiration.

STATEMENT OF THE PROBLEM

The problem is stated as "An Investigation into Educational Aspiration of First Generation Learners in relation to their Self Image and Parent –Peer Attachment".

OPERATIONAL DEFINITIONS

Educational Aspiration

Educational aspiration purely depends upon success in completing a task and also enables the student to develop a positive attitude to fact any new task and complete it successfully. This kind of educational aspirations can be developed by the student depending upon the success experiences and the encouragement he receives from his parents as well as from the teachers. In the present study, it is measured by Educational Aspiration Questionnaire, constructed and standardized by the investigator and Dr.S.Devasahayam Selvakumar (2014).

Self Image

According to H.J. Kysenck, the famous psychologist self image begins with a survey of one's own life taking into account outwards stage and inner condition and enabling one to reach an undertaking of one's personal development and critical judgment of one's spiritual and intellectual existence.

In the present investigation, self image is assessed through Self Image Inventory constructed and validated by John Garlock (1983).

Parent- Peer Attachment

Parent-child relationships are characterized both in terms of friendship and in terms of an authority relationship. As a result, the parent-child relationship may be better thought of as a "mixed relationship", or a mixture of horizontal and vertical power relationship (laursen and collins, 1994).

Furthermore, evidence suggests a considerable amount of overlap in peer and parent relationships. Both parents' peers provide emotional support and intimacy during adolescence and in nomination tasks, parents and peers receive equal numbers of nominations as primary support figures throughout adolescence (freeman, 1997).

According to the view of the investigator, the term parent-peer attachment refers to the scores obtained from the Parent-Peer Attachment Inventory, constructed and standardized by investigator and Dr.S.Devasahayam Selvakumar (2014).

First Generation Learners

In the present study, the investigator means the students those studying in standard IX from their family as first persons.

NEED FOR THE STUDY

Education is a human enterprise. It is a process and kind of activity in relation to human beings. It is a continuous effort to develop all capacities of the students to control their neighboring environment and to fulfill their needs. Though education is a part of human life, it cannot help the pursuers unless they have the required amount of educational aspirations. Individuals will have aspirations, all stages of life people try for self enhancement. The aspirations during student's period influence their behavior. An individual's aspiration level represents him not only as he is at any particular moment, but also as he would like to be at same problem in the future. The aspiration level of an individual is an important motivating factor. It is a frame a reference involving self esteem or alternatively experiences, that is the feeling of failure or success.

The primary purpose of this study is to refine and expand our understanding of the educational aspirations of first generation learners, in doing so, refine and expand our understanding of education and status attainment processes.

Self image plays a major role in the life of every human being; its level differs from stages. Self image is once own idea about himself, conception or mental image one has of oneself. Self image can be very positive or negative, makes a person doubtful of his capabilities and idea. A person's self-image is the mental picture, generally of a kind that is quite resistant to change, that depicts not only details that are potentially available to objective investigation by others (height, weight, hair color, gender, I.Q. score, etc.), but also items that have been learned by that person about himself or herself, either from personal experiences or by internalizing the judgments of others. Like any schema, self-schemas store information and influence the way we think and remember. For example, research indicates that information which refers to the self is preferentially encoded and recalled in memory tests, a phenomenon known as "Self-referential encoding". Self-schemas are also considered the traits people use to define themselves; they draw information about the self into a coherent scheme.

Poor self-image may be the result of accumulated criticisms that the person collected as a child which have led to damaging their own view of themselves. Children in particular are vulnerable to accepting negative judgments from authority figures because they have yet to develop competency in evaluating such reports. Also, adolescents are highly targeted to suffer from poor body image issues. Individuals that already exhibit a low-sense of self-worth may be vulnerable to develop social disorders.

The chief characteristics of Educational aspiration are adjustment. According to Lore (1953) the greater the degree of successful adjustment, the greater will be the aspirations towards education of the individual. Lesser mental health will be the lesser adjustment and greater conflict. The healthy individual can interpret any new situation and adapt it to suit himself, to suit it. He maintains a healthy and benevolent attitude towards life. Langner (1963) states that an individual having well attachment with parents and peer is one who is himself satisfied, lives peacefully with his neighbors, makes healthy citizens of his children, and even after performing these fundamental duties has enough energy left to something to benefit to society. Possessing good attachment individual can adjust properly to his environment, and make the best efforts for his own, his family's and his society's progress and betterment.

In modern society the proper development of everyone's personality can take place only, if there is mutual co-operation. Social relationships are a part of everyone's life. The greater the balance of these social relationships and their greater simplicity the better will be the individuals Aspirations towards the education. According to Clausen (1966) an individual maintains good adjustment with social situation, and is engaged in some or the other projects intended to benefit society.

According to Hilliard and et al. (1971), an individual having well attachment with parents and peers is a productive person. That is, he has a quality of spontaneity in work and in social relations that we recognize as creative, as using his potentialities and powers. He is able to use endowments, whether meagre or sample, in productive activity.

OBJECTIVES OF THE STUDY

The following objectives have been set in the present investigation

1. To find the levels of educational aspiration / self image /parent-peer attachment along with its dimensions of first generation learners.
2. To find out whether the following presage variables have significant influence / association on self image / Parent- peer attachment along with its dimensions and educational aspiration of first generation learners.
    - Gender (Male/Female)
    - Type of management of schools (Government/Government aided/ Self finance)
    - Medium of Instruction (Tamil/English)
    - Birth order of students (first born/middle born/last born)
    - Nature of the Family (Nuclear/Joint)
3. To find whether there is any significant association between categories of self image and levels of educational aspiration among first generation learners.
4. To find whether there is any significant correlation between parent - peer attachment and educational aspiration among first generation learners.

LIMITATIONS OF THE STUDY

The present study had the following limitations:

1. The sample is limited to 298 first generation learners.
2. The sample is taken only from Thiruvannamalai district, Tamilnadu.
3. The sample is restricted to first generation learners only.

CONCLUSION

The problem of the present study has been briefly discussed in this chapter, bringing out the need for the study, objectives of the study, significance of the study and so on. A detailed discussion of related literature on the problem is presented in the following chapter.

❐

2

Review of Related Literature

The survey of related studies implies locating, studying and evaluating reports of relevant researches, study of published articles, going through related portions of Encyclopaedias' and research abstracts, study of pertinent pages out of comprehensive books on the subject and going through related manuscripts if any. For any worthwhile study in any field of knowledge the research worker needs and adequate familiarity with the work which has already been done in the area of his choice. He needs to acquire up-to-date information about what has been thought and done in the particular area. He has to build upon the accumulated and recorded knowledge of the past. He drawn maximum benefit from the previous investigations, utilizes the previous findings, takes many hints from the designs and procedures of previous researches, matches his conclusions with the conclusions drawn earlier and tries to add from his side a line or two the existing store of knowledge.

STUDIES RELATED TO EDUCAIONAL ASPIRAIONS

Paul Boxer et al., (2011), conducted a study on the topic "Educational Aspiration-Expectation Discrepancies: Relation to Socioeconomic and Academic Risk-Related Factors" the study examined whether disconnection between educational aspirations and expectations is associated with socioeconomic status, academic performance, academic risk-related behaviours and related psychosocial factors in an ethnically and economically diverse sample of early adolescents from a public middle school (N=761). Results suggest that students who aspire to achieve more than they expect to achieve also are likely to have more economically disadvantaged backgrounds and poorer academic performance. These students also show a variety of academic and social risks. Specifically, students whose aspirations exceeded their expectations reported lower levels of school bonding, higher levels of test performance anxiety, and elevated behavioural / emotional difficulties.

Miao wang et al., (2011) investigated a study on the topic "The effects of single Parenthood on Educational Aspiration: A Comparative Study of Children in the United Kingdom and Hong Kong." Using data collected by the Organization for Economic Co-Operation and Development's Program for International Student Assessment in 2003, this study examines the gap in the educational aspirations of children from single-parent families and two-parent families in the United Kingdom (UK) and Hong Kong. Consistent with previous research on the relationship between cultural orientation and academic motivation, the analysis shows that child in the UK has statistically significant lower levels of educational aspiration than those in Hong Kong. Moreover, children from single-parent families in the UK and Hong Kong are found to have statistically significant lower levels of educational aspirations than those from two-parent families. Further analyses indicate that family capital and school experience are important factors for understanding the negative effects of single parenthood. Finally, we observe that single parenthood has a less negative effect on educational aspiration in the UK than it does in Hong Kong, which can be explained by differences in government family policy and family capital between the two regions, Based on the outcomes from the current analysis, several policy and service recommendations were put forward for improving children's educational aspiration and enhancing family well-being.

Lionel Page et al., (2007) conducted a study on "Aspiration Levels and Educational Choices an Experimental Study." The explanation of social inequalities in education is still a debated issue in economics. Recent empirical studies tend to downplay the potential role of credit constraint. This study tested a different potential explanation of social inequalities in education specifically that social differences in aspiration level result in different educational choices. Having existed for a long time in the sociology of education, this explanation can be justified if aspiration levels are seen as reference points in a prospect theory framework. In order to test this explanation, this study applies the method of experimental economics to the issue of educational choice and behaviour. One hundred and twenty-nine individuals participated in an experiment in which they had to perform through the experiment, a minimum level of success was required at the end of each level, and participants could either choose to stop and rake their reward or to pay a cost to continue further in order to possibly receive higher rewards. To test the impact of aspiration levels, outcomes were either presented as gains or losses relative to an initial sum. In accordance with the theoretical predictions, participants, in the loss framing group choose to go further in the experiment. There was also a significant and interesting gender effect in the loss framing treatment, such hat males performed better and reached higher levels.

Jianjun wang et al., (2001) made a study on "the effects of Educational Productivity on career aspiration aiming United States High School Students." Using structural equation modelling and data on 10th grade students from the Longitudinal Study of American Youth, a model was developed to show the relationship to career aspiration of eight indicators of "educational productivity": mathematics achievement; motivation; instructional quality; home, class and peer environment; and mass media influences.

Jungeun Olivia Lee et al., (2012) conducted an investigation on "The Role of Educational Aspirations and Expectations in the Discontinuity of Intergenerational Low-Income status". This study investigated one potential mechanism mediating continuity and discontinuity in low-income status across generations: children's educational aspirations and expectations. Data were drawn from a community sample of 808 participants who were followed from age 10 to 30. Four trajectory groups of children's educational aspirations and expectations were identified from ages 10 to 18: "stable-high" group, "stable-low" group, "increaser" group, and "decreases" group. Among participants from low-income families, those in the stable-high group and the increaser group were equally likely to graduate from high school. High school graduation was positively associated with level of total household income at age 30. Findings suggest that social work efforts that support the development of high educational aspiration and expectations in children might serve to reduce the intergenerational continuity of low-income status.

J. Mathew Irvin et al., (2012) made a study on "Educational Barriers of Rural Students and Youth; Relation of Individual and Contextual Difference Variables." The purpose of this study was to examine the relation of several individual and contextual difference factors to the perceived educational barriers or rural youth. Data were from a border national investigation of students' postsecondary aspirations and preparation in rural high schools across the United States. The sample involved more than 7,000 rural youth in 73 high schools across 34 states. Results indicated that some individual (e.g., African American race ethnicity and contextual (e.g., parent education) difference factors were predictive while others were not. Extensions to, similarities, and variations with previous research are discussed. Implications, limitations, and suggestions for future research are also discussed. Soo-Yong Byun et al., (2012) made a study on "The Role of Social Capital in Educational Aspirations of Rural Youth." Drawing on a recent national survey of rural high school students, this study investigated the relationship between social capital and educational aspirations of rural youth. Results showed that various process features of family and school social capital were important for predicting rural youths' educational aspirations beyond socio demographic background. In particular, parents' and teachers' educational expectations for their child and student, respectively, were positively related to educational aspiration of rural youth. In addition, discussion with parents about college was positively related to educational aspirations of rural youth. On the other hand, there was little evidence to suggest that number of siblings and school proportions of students eligible for free lunch and minority students are related to educational aspirations of rural youth, after controlling for the other variables. We highlight unique features of rural families, schools, and communities that may combine to explain the complexity of the role of social capital in shaping educational aspirations of rural youth.

Gill Richards et al., (2012) conducted a study on "Aspiring Girls: Great Expectations or Impossible dreams?" This study explores girls' aspirations for their future. The context was an ex-coalmining area where concerns had been raised by the local authority about the levels of achievement. The focus of the research was the views of Years 6 girls as they prepared for their transition to secondary school and Year 11 girls as they prepared for their transition to post compulsory school life. Perspectives of their staff were also sought, focusing on the impact of school and its community on girls' aspirations. Findings indicated that while the aspirations of the primary school girls were similar, those of the secondary girls differed significantly. Staff viewed this as reflective of the local context and schools those. These responses offer a basis on which schools could build strategies to increase aspirations and provide support towards their achievement.

C. Brayan Hutchins et al., (2012) investigation on "Planning for the Future: An Investigation of Work-Bound Rural Youth". The purpose of this study was to explore the postsecondary educational and occupational expectations of work-bound rural youth. Three groups of work-bound youth were identified (work-bound, work-bound with future educational plans, and work-bound but unsure/undecided about postsecondary education), and each group was compared to college-bound rural youth using results from a recent national investigation of the educational and occupational aspirations or rural youth. Results indicated that the majority of rural youth in this study planned to continue their education after high school (56%), followed by 34% who planned to work and further their education. Results of logistic regression analysis indicated that family characteristics and students' schooling experiences were the strongest predictors of work-bound status. Work-bound youth were more likely to report greater family economic hardship, lower parental expectations for completing college, and more negative schooling experience than college-bound rural youth.

STUDIES RELATED TO SELF IMAGE

Reynolds, Thelora u (1992) tested adolescent's self-image. It assessed aspects of the adjustment of 233 secondary students in Jamaica. Students reported satisfaction in seven areas such as impulse control, emotional tone, body image, social relationship, sexual attitudes, mastery of the external world and superior adjustment. Students reported that dissatisfaction in the dimensions of, orals, educational goals, family relationships and emotional health.

Brown Patricia m (1993) determined change in self- image. Thirty nine individuals with developmental disabilities received individualized rehabilitation program's based on client choice and implemented in client approved home/community environments and received training in residential, resulted in improved self – awareness, self-confidence, community activity and independence, compared to control group individuals.

Orr emda, ben-eliahu (1993) examined the gender difference in idiosyncratic sex-typed self-image and self-esteem. Findings from two studies with 179 male and 158 female Israeli early adolescents and 97 male and 183 female Israeli University students self-esteem is predicted significantly by masculine self-image, female self-esteem is predicted by non stero typed self-image and feminine self-image, significantly predicts the self-esteem of neither gender.

Cooper, joanne-e (1994) conducted a study under the heading metaphoric -J.Journal keeping and self-image in administrative women, Participants were asked to generate the women choose metaphors suggestion that journal keeping was positive and regenerating journals were also educational in that they could help the women see and speak more clearly about lives.

Reves, thea; medgyes, peter (1994) conducted a study to explore the non-native English language (ESL/EFL), the majority of non-native speakers of English, considering their language attitudes and self-image. It was found that the higher the non-native teacher's proficiency level in English, the self-conscious, hesitant, insecure they felt in the class.

Swearingen, c jan(1994) investigated women's ways of writing or images, self-images and craven images. It asks how religious faith and spirituality function in the creative lives of peoples and makers and searchers. Describes a weeklong summer workshop called "women's space, exploring out creative and spiritual selves' considers the historical achievements of women as writers and thinkers and the recent recovery of such works.

Beaty, lee.a(1995) tested the effects of paternal absence on male adolescents, peer relations and self-image. A sample of 20 father's present and 20 father absent middle school boys rated each other on peer adjustment and self-image. Results indicated that father absent boys evidence a poor sense of masculinity as well as poorer inter-personal relationship than do father present boys.

Gans, Jennifer (1995) attempted to study the relation of self-image to academic placement and achievement in hearing impaired students. The relationship was studied with 1,072 Colorado students with hearing impaired students. It was found that students who are hearing impaired with good English language skills have a more positive self-image than those whose language skills are below average. The relation between language and communication skills and self-image changed with intensity of special education service. Self-image was significantly poorer in children receiving special services 1-2 hours daily compared to children either in more fully mainstreamed or in more intensive delivery service options.

Smith, delores e (1995) conducted a study on gender and age variations in the self-image of Jamaican adolescents by attending three secondary schools in Jamaica. Results revealed statistically significant effects for both gender and age. Gender significantly influenced morals, while age differences affected six other dimensions.

Wardle,francis (1995) conducted a study on building self image if suggests that child-care professionals play a vital role in the early development of children's strong and positive self-image.

Self-image is built on self-awareness and in turn to facilitates better self-expression, ability to make decisions, creativity, spirituality, cultural harmony and healthy inter-personal relationships [(Reynolds, thelora-u(1992) Brown-patricia.m (1993) Cooper, jonne-e(1994), Swearingen, c jan(1994)]

STUDIES RELATED TO PARENT ATTACHMENT

Jain Shikha (2012) conducted a study on child rearing practices, adolescence, cognitive ability and achievement. Students from VII, IX and X class, about 108 in number along with their mothers were interviewed. It was found that, parent who is consistent in disciplining the child was the factor which positively and significantly related with academic achievement. Further if the child is brought up in a restrictive home environment. It acts as a block towards the academic achievement.

Manual Bheema (1990) made a study on the impact of emotional maturity and prolonged deprivation on indiscipline behaviour among students in relation to their achievement. From the sample of 472 students it was found that emotion instability was due to home environment. Child rearing experience and interaction with parents are positively related to academic achievement.

Deb Modha Grewal and Hindai Pal (2010) investigated the relationship between study habits and academic achievement of under graduate home science final year students. The study was conducted on a sample of 90 students. It was observed that family environment of the students is significantly related to academic achievement.

Chandy and Sumi (2009) conducted a study on application of certain pupil deficit models to differential achievement in English in University of Leerala. About 1040, (538 boys and 507 girls) from 74 schools: The results show that positive family relations improve academic achievement of the students.

Arora Relta (2008) Carried out studies on parent child relationship, teacher - student relationship and achievement of higher secondary students. In his study it was said that there is no significant relationship between achievement and parent child relationship. Educational standards of teacher student relationship were significantly related. Parent child relationship and teacher student relationship are significantly related.

Padhi J (2007) studied problem of home environment, the parent child relationship and children's competence during adolescence. About 100 students from classes VII, IX and X formed the sample of study. Among them 50 were girls and 50 were boys. It was found that children with positive self-concept were found to be confident about positive perceptions of their peers and teachers. With regard to the children's peer- checked competence, it was found that parental withdrawal mediated the child's peer affiliation and indirectly helped to develop the child's competence and self reliance.

Shah, Beena (2006) investigated the effect of family climate on home adjustment of adolescent. The students of class IX of Garhwal, manual constitution was drawn randomly from 12 schools in two districts. The findings say that home adjustment of students having satisfactory family climate was found to be superior to that of those who had highly dissatisfactory family climate. But in the case of girls, family climate did not play an important role in determining the level of home adjustment.

Shukla, Kiran (2006) undertook a study to examine, whether parental behaviour and interaction influence the development of social competence of the children. On the basis of income, professional affiliation and material possession about 150 families from high SES and 150 families from low SES were selected. In addition, there being one son and one daughter in the age range 10-15 years in each family was considered. About 30 parentless boys in the above age range from the local orphanage were also part of this sample. Parental authority as well as peer interaction did reveal highly significant main effects on social competence. Both sons and daughters of the upper SES group were found to differ significantly compared to lower SES groups.

Diana (2011) studied the fostering as seen by the careers children. Examined attitudes about foster care of 75 birth children of foster parents: Found that most enjoy or at least tolerate being part of foster family, with many indicating that, despite the problems, it can give them a greater appreciation of their own family and an awareness of the difficulties some of their peers must cope with.

Hoffmann - John-P (2010) studied the Investigating the Age Effects of Family structure on Adolescent Marijuana use. Differences among younger and older adolescents in the influence of family structure, family relations, and peer relation on marijuana use were studied in the sample (n=l, 725) from the National Youth Survey, 1976-78. Relative effects of drug-using peers and family variables are identified for younger and older adolescents.

Smith, - Delores-E (2009) studied the relationship between Jamaican Adolescents Drinking Partners and self-image Examined relationship between drinking partner (adult versus peer) and self-image of Jamaican adolescents (n=176) who reported alcohol use. Found that adolescents who drank with adults had significantly higher self-evaluations, reported less emotional fluctuation, had better family relationship, had higher vocational/educational goals, were more socially conscious, and had better psychological adjustment.

Giordano, - Peggy - C (2008) studied the Family and Peer Relations of Black Adolescents. Hypothesized that, compared to white adolescents, African - American adolescents maintain more intimate stance toward family, whereas friendships are less intense, and that African Americans perceive lower levels of peer pressure and are more tolerant of behavioural differences in friendships. Data from personal interviews with 942 adolescents lend support to this alternative portrait.

Bullock, - Janis - R (2007) studied the children's loneliness and their relationships with family children's feeling of loneliness related to family and peer relationships have only recently been documented by researchers. These feelings are now being recognized, researched, and assessed in children as young as five years of age. Helping professionals need to understand short-and long-term consequences of children's loneliness as it relates to their personal well-being and self-esteem.

Yam blade, - Lise-M; Belsky, Jay (2006) examined the links between children's relationship with their parents at one and three years and their relationships with a friend at five years. Positive and secure parent-child relationships were associated with children positive friendship and negative family relationship with negative friendships several counterintuitive findings emerged.

Freckhall, Peter; Luks, Alan (2005) studied the An Evaluation of parental Assessment of the Big Brothers/Big sisters Program in New York City. Parents rated impact of Big Brother/Big Sister Program on children along variables of school attendance, grades, family relationship, friendship, self-esteem, staying out of trouble, being responsible, frequency of contact, and length of time in program. Although children were rated as benefiting significantly from program, children's frequency of contact did not have significant effect on outcome measures.

STUDIES RELATED TO PEER ATTACHMENT

Abuja (2010) made an effort to assess the effectiveness of peer tutoring as an instrument in developing the urban and spatial abilities of the students. The major findings of the study were the following. The peer tutoring is significant entirely on academic achievement of the students in the subjects. The teaching strategy was found to be more useful for low and average achieving and learning disabled students. Peer tutoring was helpful in developing a sense of accomplishment in the peer tutoring; the learners received feedback to their performance and get motivated.

Shukla (2010) conducted a study to find out whether peer interactions influence the development of the social competence of the children. The major findings were the following. Peer interactions did reveal highly of significant effects of social competence. The children liked peers have scored significantly higher jeans in all important competition, social tolerance. Social leadership and social respectability are the least liked peers.

Robertson (2009) conducted an action research on 12 New Zealand Primary School Principals working in partnership to develop their leadership. Findings indicate that peer assisted leadership development helped principals. First of all, it is to focus on their professional and school development goals. Secondly, it reduced their feelings of isolation. Thirdly, it facilitated reflective thinking that lead to proactive and transformative action. Fourthly, it leads to the realization of the wider picture of principal's practice in New Zealand.

Slavin (2011) found out the development of social skills and helping skills students learned to value each other and to concentrate on positive relationship. Throughout the year, as new students came into the classes, they were immediately integrated into the teams. Guided interaction around most reluctant teachers becomes actively engaged in learning. Guided peer relations can work wonders in the lives of young students was the most outstanding finding.

Rigby (2010) Who had conducted survey on more than 25 thousand students observed that in the course of anyone year as many as half of the students attending school experience painful and unjustified aggression from students who are physically, psychologically or numerically more powerful than they are. A substantial proportion of these students about 1 in 7, are bullied weekly of more often. Some of these students are very resilient and appear to be unaffected by the emotionally upset or depressed following repeated incidents of peer victimization.

Castor (2010) developed an educational project the peer leader implemented, and evaluated in a rural high school in Australia. Student Peer leaders, identified by social metric methods, volunteered to attend a six day training camp to learn about health and sexuality, to develop social and infer personal skills, and participate in outdoor education activities. On return to their schools, peer leaders, were monitored unobtrusively together with their identified members of their peer group members one month later semi structured interview were conducted with selected peer readers, members of their peer group, parents and teachers. A follow up interview was conducted eight weeks later. The major findings of the project were the following. It accelerated the process of the growth and maturation of the student leaders with regard to their leadership skills. There was a marked improvement in their social development and peer interaction.

Calivari (2009) conducted a study to find out the link between attachment to home and peer relations, attachment to schools and peer relations. A sample of 176 ninth and tenth graders at risk for academic difficulties participated in the study. Result suggested; peer relations influence teenager's satisfaction with school. Peer relations influence one's self-view. Experiences with peer in the school environment can affect one's success in society.

Giles (2008) conducted a study to find out how celebrities influence the younger generation and is related to their social networks. He studied the relationship between celebrity interest, attachment to parents and peer and emotional autonomy among a sample of 191 adolescent who worship celebrities for entertainment and social reasons had a high attachment to peer. They were group players. They were self-confident. Peer interaction is an important feature of celebrity attachment.

Elizabeth C.W. (2005) studied the Enhance social skills with peer - Recommended books. Discusses how teachers can aid young children in developing social skills in and outside the home through reading and discussing books that present characters and social situations with which children can identity. Discusses several such child-recommended book titles from "children's choice" and includes an annotated bibliography of additional titles dealing with relationships with family, friends, and the larger world.

CONCLUSION

The Survey of related literature has helped the investigator to have a clear perspective of the problem arose for the present investigation. The review of related research work has enabled the investigator for formulate relevant hypotheses for the present study. Further based in this review, a suitable methodology and a well planned procedure for the present investigation could be adopted.

❐

3

Design of the Study and the Method of Investigation

A research design is the arrangement of conditions for collection and analysis of data in a manner that aims to combine relevance to the research purpose with economy in procedure. Clair seltzer (1962).

Research is a more systematic activity that is directed towards discovery and the development of an organized body of the knowledge. It involves the information about the research work in view of the framework of the study; availability of various data, observation, sampling etc., Research design involves the structure in frame work. It may help the research to organize his ideas in particular form.

HYPOTHESES OF THE STUDY

The following hypotheses have been set in the present study.

1. The level of educational aspiration of first generation learners is average in nature.
2. The level of self-image of first generation learners is moderate in nature.
3. The levels of parent and peer attachment and its dimensions of first generation learners are average in nature.

4. There is no significant difference between the mean scores of educational aspiration of first generation learners with regard to
    - Gender (Male / Female)
    - Type of management of schools (Government /Government Aided / Self finance)
    - Medium of instruction (Tamil / English)
    - Order of birth (First born / Middle born / Last born)
    - Type of family (Joint / Nuclear)
5. There is no significant association between the categories of self image of first generation learners and
    - Gender (Male / Female)
    - Type of management of schools (Government / Government Aided / Self finance)
    - Medium of instruction (Tamil / English)
    - Order of birth (First born / Middle born / Last born)
    - Type of family (Joint / Nuclear)
6. There is no significant difference in the mean scores of parent - peer attachment of first generation learners with regard to
    - Gender (Male / Female)
    - Type of management of schools (Government / Government Aided / self finance)
    - Medium of instruction (Tamil / English)
    - Order of birth (First born / Middle born / Last born)
    - Type of family (Joint / Nuclear)
7. There is no significant difference in the mean scores of parent Trust - a dimension of parent - peer attachment of first generation learners with regard to
    - Gender (Male / Female)
    - Type of management of schools (Government / Government Aided / Self finance)
    - Medium of instruction (Tamil / English)
    - Order of birth (First born / Middle born / Last born)
    - Type of family (Joint / Nuclear)
8. There is no significant difference in the mean scores of parent communication - a dimension of parent - peer attachment of first generation learners with regard to
    - Gender (Male / Female)

- Type of management of schools (Government / Aided / Self finance)
- Medium of instruction (Tamil / English)
- Order of birth (First born / Middle born / Last born)
- Type of family (Joint / Nuclear)

9. There is no significant difference in the mean scores of parent alienation - a dimension of parent- peer attachment of first generation learners with regard to
   - Gender (Male / Female)
   - Type of management of schools (Government/Government Aided / Self finance)
   - Medium of instruction (Tamil / English)
   - Order of birth (First born / Middle born / Last born)
   - Type of family (Joint / Nuclear)
10. There is no significant difference in the mean scores of peer Trust – a dimension of parent - peer attachment of first generation learners with regard to
    - Gender (Male / Female)
    - Type of management of schools (Government / Government Aided / Self finance)
    - Medium of instruction (Tamil / English)
    - Order of birth (First born / Middle born / Last born)
    - Type of family (Joint / Nuclear)
11. There is no significant difference in the mean scores of peer communication - a dimension of parent - peer attachment of first generation learners with regard to
    - Gender (Male / Female)
    - Type of management of schools (Government / Government Aided / Self finance)
    - Medium of instruction (Tamil / English)
    - Order of birth (First born / Middle born / Last born)
    - Type of family (Joint / Nuclear)
12. There is no significant difference in the mean scores of peer Alienation - a dimension of parent- peer attachment of first generation learners with regard to
    - Gender (Male / Female)
    - Type of management of schools (Government/Government Aided / Self finance)

- Medium of instruction (Tamil / English)
- Order of birth (First born / Middle born / Last born)
- Type of family (Joint / Nuclear)

13. There is no significant association between levels of educational aspiration and categories of self-image among first generation learners.
14. There is no significant correlation between educational aspiration and parent-peer attachment along with its dimensions among first generation learners.

TOOLS AND TECHNIQUES USED

The following tools have been used in the study

1. Educational Aspiration Questionnaire standardized by the investigator and Dr.S.Devasahayam Selvakumar (2014).
2. Self Image Inventory by the John Garlock (1983).
3. Inventory of Parent -Peer Attachment constructed by the investigator and Dr.S.Devasahayam Selvakumar (2014).

EDUCATIONAL ASPIRATION QUESTIONNAIRE

Description

Educational Aspiration questionnaire was constructed by the investigator and Dr.S.Devasahayam Selvakumar (2014).

It consists of 39 statements, out of which 17 items are positive statements and the rest are negative statements. The positive items are 1,4,9,10,13,14,18,19,20,21,22,25,26,27,29,34, and 35. In the same way, the negative items are 2,3,5,6,7,8,11,12,15,16,17,23,24,28,30,31,32,33,36,37,38, and 39.

Administration

Before the administration of the test, the following instructions were given to the students. "The form has few statements. Please read each statement carefully and then indicate your opinion by putting the (√) mark in the space provided besides it. Please put (√) mark in only one column for each statement."

Scoring

For each positive statement, one mark is given if the student answered as Yes; zero mark is given, if the student answered as No. For negative statement, the scores is done in the reverse order.

SELF IMAGE INVENTORY

Description

Self image inventory (appendix-II) constructed and standardized by John Garlock (1983) was used to study the self image among the school students. This tool consists of 20 items. It has five options. Each item specifies how the students perceive themselves and about their behavior and personality.

Administration

Students were asked to sit comfortably. Even though there was no time limit to finish the questionnaire, students completed the questionnaire within 25 minutes. They were also told that their response will be kept confident and used strictly for the purpose of research only.

Scoring

Scoring was done based on the following table.

TABLE. 3.1: Showing the Scoring Key for Self Image Inventory

Categories	Score
A	+2
B	+1
C	0
D	-1
E	-2

TABLE. 3.2: Showing the Interpretation of Scoring of Self Image Inventory

Score	Interpretation
+14 to +15	High self image
+14 to -14	Moderate self image
-15 to -40	Low moderate

INVENTORY OF PARENT - PEER ATTACHMENT

Description

Parent-Peer Attachment Inventory (Appendix-III) constructed by the investigator and Dr.S.Devasahayam Selvakumar (2014). This tool consists of 50 items. It has five options. Each item specifies how the students perceive themselves. First 25 items deal with parents' attachment and the remaining with peer attachment.

TABLE. 3.3: Showing the Nature of Items of Parent-Peer Attachment and its Dimensions.

S. No.	Parent-peer attachment in toto and its dimensions	Positive statements	Negative statements
1	Parent trust	1,2,4,12,13,20,21,22	3,9
2	Parent communication	5,7,15,16,19,24,25	6,14
3	Parent alienation	-	8,10,11,17,18,23
4	Peer trust	31,33,37,38,39,40,44,45,46	-
5	Peer communication	26,27,28,32,41,42,49,50	30
6	Peer alienation	-	29,34,35,36,43,47,48

Administration of the Tools

Assessment of parent-peer attachment scale is administered to the High School students. Set of instructions was given prior to the questions.

The investigator distributed the copies of questionnaire and instructed the students to fill up the personal information data and then move on the set 50 questions.

The instruction given to the students were as follows:

1. This questionnaire contains certain practical situations, which they might have come across in their day-to-day life.
2. There are 50 items, followed by 5 alternatives for each questions. Please put (√) against the alternative in each question that is most appropriate to them.
3. Please mark only one alternative, out of the five responses given and don't omit any item.
4. Please give true information without hesitation. There is no right or wrong answers. Read every statement carefully and tick at the appropriate box whether it is Strongly Agree (SA), Agree (A), No Idea (NI), Disagree (DA) and Strongly Disagree (SA).
5. The information called for in the questionnaire is purely for research study only. This information will be kept confidential and will not be used for any purpose.

Scoring

All the 50 items are not scored in the same way in 5-point scale. The five different alternatives carry different scores based on the positive and negative statements.

1. In the case of positive statements, the scoring pattern as given below,
    - 'Strongly agree' earns 5 points
    - 'Agree' earns 4 points
    - 'No idea' earns 3points

- 'Disagree' earns 2 points
- 'Strongly disagree' earns 1 point.

2. In the case of negative statements, it is the reverse of the scoring pattern for positive statements as given below,
   - 'Strongly agree' earns 1 point
   - 'Agree' earns 2 points
   - 'No idea' earns 3 points
   - 'Disagree' earns 4 points
   - 'Strongly disagree' earns 5 point.

The total sum of the scores is taken into consideration, Maximum Score for Parents attachment is 125 and maximum score for Peer attachment is 125.

PILOT STUDY

Before finalizing the final form of the tools and collecting data for main study, a pilot study was done in October 2014. It was conducted among 50 students to establish reliability and validity of the tools used in the study.

ESTABLISHING RELIABLITY AND VALIDITY OF THE TOOLS USED

Reliability

Educational Aspiration Questionnaire

To compute the reliability of Educational Aspiration questionnaire, odd-even method was used and it was found to be 0.73, using the spearman Brown formula, indicating the tool is highly reliable.

Self Image Inventory

To compute the reliability of self image inventory, odd and even method was employed. The reliability was computed and it was found to be 0.69, using Spearman Brown formula. The tool is highly reliable.

Parent- Peer Attachment Inventory

It is a test conducted to measure parent-peer attachment the extent that it measures whatever it is measuring consistently. The inventory was shown to learn professors and educationists and their opinions were obtained. The items of the questionnaire were found to be adequate. The reliability of the tool is measured by the Chronbach reliability method. The reliability value for the assessment of Parents-Peer group attachment among High school students is 0.07. It is concluded that the tool is reliable.

Validity

Educational Aspiration Questionnaire

The validity of educational Aspiration Inventory was found out by computing the square root of the reliability co-efficient which worked out to be 0.85. It shows that the validity of the Educational Aspiration Questionnaire is high.

Self Image Inventory

The validity of self image inventory was found out by computing the square root of the reliability co-efficient, which worked out to be 0.83, indicating high validity of the inventory.

Parent- Peer Attachment Inventory

The content of the tool is tested in case of validity. The validity of the tool administered by the investigator for assessment of Parent-Peer attachment is 0.877, by calculating the square root of coefficient of reliability. It indicates that the tool is highly valid.

SAMPLE FOR THE STUDY

TABLE. 3.4: Showing the Distribution of the Sample for the Present Study

S. No.	Name of the School	Management of the School	Boys	Girls	Total
1	Government high school, karikalampadi, Thiruvannamalai district, Pin 604 755.	Government school	17	18	35
2	Government higher secondary school, Mangalam, Thiruvannamalai Dt-606 752.	Government school	20	25	45
3	Government higher secondary school, kulathur, Thiruvannamalai Dt-606 755.	Government school	12	13	25
4	Government higher secondary school, kilpenathur, Thiruvannamalai Dt-604 601.	Government school	23	17	40
5	St. Antony's high school, Virudhuvilanginan, Thiruvannamalai Dt- 606 804.	Government -aided school	18	12	30
6	St.xavier's high school, zamin Gudalore, Thiruvannamalai Dt-606 755.	Government -aided school	20	15	35
7	St.mary's higher secondary school, Vettavalam, Thiruvannamalai Dt-606 754.	Government -aided school	25	20	45
8	P.S.A higher secondary school, Pavithiram, Thiruvannamalai Dt-606 806.	Self finance school	15	28	43
	Total		**150**	**148**	**298**

MAIN STUDY

The validated tools were used for the main study in November 2014 to collect the necessary data through survey method. The study was carried out among first generation learners in Thiruvannamalai district, Tamilnadu. In this investigation, the main purpose is to study educational aspiration, self image and parent –peer attachment among first generation learners.

STATISTICAL TECHNIQUES USED

(a) Mean

$$\text{Mean } \left(\bar{X}\right) = A + \frac{\sum fd}{\sum f} \times i$$

Where,

A = Assumed mean

f = frequency

d = deviation from the assumed mean

i = Class interval

(b) Standard Deviation

$$\text{Standard Deviation, } SD(\sigma) = \sqrt{\frac{\sum fd^2}{N} - \left[\frac{\sum fd}{N}\right]^2} xi$$

Where,

f = Frequency

d = Deviation from the assumed mean

I = Class interval

N = Total frequency

(c) 't' TEST

To continue the significance of difference between means of various measures test is used:'t' ratio is calculated from the relation.

$$\text{'t'-ratio} = \frac{M_1 \sim M_2}{\sqrt{\frac{\sigma_1^2}{N_1} + \frac{\sigma_1^2}{N_2}}} = \frac{M_1 \sim M_2}{S \in D}$$

Where,

= Means of the groups

SED = Standard Error Deviation

(d) F-TEST

F- ratio = Variance between the group / Variance within the group

Correction term

$$C = \frac{\sum r_1 + \sum r_3 + \sum x_3}{N}$$

(e) CHI- SQUARE TEST

$$\text{Equation } X^2 = \frac{\sum (f_o - f_e)^2}{f_e}$$

Where as f_o - Observed frequency

f_e - Expected frequency

CONCLUSION

This chapter outlines the design of the present study, the procedure followed and the nature of the sample selected. It describes the hypotheses to be tested, the tools used and the method of administration and scoring. The next chapter presents analysis and discussion in the light of the hypotheses formulated.

❐

4

Statistical Analysis and Interpretation of the Data

Research consists of systematic observation and description of the characteristics of properties of discovering relationships, starts with the description of the measures of the variables and goes on to the higher levels of statistical analysis. The data collected is carefully edited, systematically classified and tabulated, scientifically analysed and interpreted and rationally concluded.

Thus, in the present study, the data were collected with regard to educational aspiration, self image and parent-peer attachment. The data have been subjected to the following statistical analysis, namely percentile, descriptive, differential, correlation and association. The results of the statistical analysis have been summarized and tabulated.

For the investigator, analysis of collected data turns out to be a very important task. The information collected through the tools has been quantified as detailed in the following tables. For analysing the Educational aspiration of first generation learners in relation to their self image and parent-peer attachment, the following tables were prepared.

CATEGORISATION OF THE SAMPLE BASED ON THE VARIABLES OF THE STUDY

Categories of the Sample Based on the Educational Aspiration

The sample has been classified on the basis of their Educational aspiration of first generation learners into their three categories (low/ moderate / high), as indicated in the following table.

TABLE. 4.1: Showing the level of Educational Aspiration of First Generation Learners

Variable	Number of sample	Range	Level	Frequency	Percentage
Educational aspiration	298	0-34	Low	216	72.5
		35-37	Moderate	35	11.7
		3 8 - high	High	47	15.8

INFERENCE

From the table, it is clear that the level of educational aspiration among of first generation learners is low in nature.

Hence hypothesis- 1 stating that "The level of educational aspiration of first generation learners is average in nature" is rejected.

Categories of the Sample Based on the Self-Image

The sample has been classified on the basis of their Self Image of first generation learners into three categories (low/ moderate / high) as indicated in the following table.

TABLE.4.2: Showing the Level of Self Image Among First Generation Learners

Variable	Number of sample	Range	Level	Frequency	Percentage
Self-Image	298	0-34	Low	181	60.7
		35-37	Moderate	59	19.9
		38-high	High	58	19.5

INFERENCE

From the table, it is clear that the level of Self Image of first generation learners is low in nature.

Hence hypothesis – 2 stating that "The level of Self Image of first generation learners is moderate in nature" is rejected.

Categories of the sample based on Parent –Peer attachment along with its dimensions

The first generation learners have been classified on the basis on their parent- peer attachment along with its dimensions into three categories (low/ Moderate/high), as indicated in the table given below.

TABLE. 4.3: Showing the Levels of Parent-Peer Attachment among First Generation Learners along with its Dimensions

Variable		No. of Sample	Range	Level	Frequency	Percentage
Parent- Peer Attachment		298	Below 69	Low	74	24.8
		Between 70 and 83	Moderate	98	32.9	
		Above 84	High	126	42.3	
Dimensions of Parent -Peer Attachment	Parent Trust	298	Below 18	Low	121	40.6
			Between 19 and 20	Moderate	116	38.9
			Above 21	High	61	20.5
	Parent Communication	298	Below 18	Low	180	60.4
			Between 19 and 22	Moderate	5	1.7
			Above 23	High	113	37.9
	Parent Alienation	298	Below 9	Low	83	27.9
			Between 10 and 11	Moderate	93	31.2
			Above 12	High	122	40.9
	Peer Trust	298	Below 15	Low	82	27.5
			Between 16 and 18	Moderate	157	52.7
			Above 19	High	59	19.8
	Peer Communication	298	Below 17	Low	137	46.0
			Between 18 and 19	Moderate	76	25.5
			Above 20	High	85	28.5
	Peer Alienation	298	Below 14	Low	91	30.5
			Between 15 and 17	Moderate	90	30.2
			Above 18	High	117	39.3

INFERENCE

From the above table, it is found that Parent-peer attachment in toto and its dimension –Parent Alienation are high in nature, peer trust is moderate in nature and parent trust, parent communication, peer communication and Peer Alienation are low in nature.

Hence the hypothesis- 3 stating that "The levels of parent-peer attachment and its dimensions of first generation learners are average in nature" is partially verified.

INFLUENCE OF GENDER ON EDUCATIONAL ASPIRATION

The scores related to educational aspiration based on gender (males/ females) of first generation learners have been computed and details are furnished in the following table.

TABLE.4.4: Showing the Significant Difference between the mean Scores of Educational Aspiration of First Generation Learners with Respect to Gender

Variable	Gender	Number of cases	Mean	Standard Deviation	Critical Ratio	Level of Significance
Educational Aspiration	Males	150	34.5933	2.720	3.44	0.01
	Males	148	33.6959	1.669		

INFERENCE

From the above table, it is observed that the obtained CR value (3.44) is higher than the table value (2.58) at 0.01 level. Therefore there is significant difference between the mean scores of educational aspiration of first generation learners with regard to gender.

It is also noted that male first generation learners have exhibited significantly higher educational aspiration than their counterparts.

Hence the Hypothesis – 4(a) stating that "There is no significant difference between the mean scores of educational aspiration of first generation learners with regard to gender" is rejected.

INFLUENCE OF TYPE OF MANAGEMENT OF SCHOOLS ON EDUCATIONAL ASPIRATION

The scores of educational aspiration of first generation learners with regard to type of management of schools (government/government aided/self finance) have been analysed and the details are furnished in the following table.

TABLE. 4.5: ANOVA Showing the Significant Difference between the mean Scores of the Educational Aspiration of First Generation Learners with Respect to Type of Management of Schools.

Variable	Type of Management of Schools	Mean	SSb	SSw	df	Calculated 'F' value	LS
Educational Aspiration	Government	34.1827	4.4433	1567.0601	2	0.4182	NS
	Government Aided	3.9138					
	Self finance	34.3023			295		

INFERENCE

From the above table, the obtained 'F' value (0.4182) is lower than the table (3.03) at 0.05 level. Therefore there is no significant difference between the mean scores of Educational Aspiration of first generation learners with regard to type of management of schools.

Hence the hypothesis – 4(b) stating that "There is no significant between the mean scores of educational aspiration of first generation learners with regard to type of management of schools" is accepted.

INFLUENCE OF MEDIUM OF INSTRUCTION ON EDUCATIONAL ASPIRATION

The scores of educational aspiration based on medium of instruction (Tamil/English) of first generation learners have been computed and details are furnished in the following table below.

TABLE. 4.6: Showing the Significant Difference between the mean Scores of Educational Aspiration among First Generation Learners with Respect to Medium of Instruction

Variable	Medium of Instruction	Number of cases	Mean	Standard Deviation	Critical Ratio	Level of Significance
Educational Aspiration	Tail	163	34.7362	2.764	5.37	**0.01**
	English	135	33.4370	1.250		

INFERENCE

From the table, the obtained CR value (5.37) is higher than the table value (2.58) at 0.01 level. Therefore there is significant difference between the mean scores of educational aspiration of first generation learners with regard to medium of instruction.

It is also noted that Tamil medium students have exhibited significantly higher educational aspiration of first generation learners than their counterparts.

Hence Hypothesis – 4(c) stating that "There is no significant difference between the mean scores of educational aspiration of first generation learners with regard to medium of instruction" is rejected.

INFLUENCE OF ORDER OF BIRTH ON EDUCATIONAL ASPIRATION

The scores of educational aspiration of first generation learners with regard to order of birth (first born/middle born/last born) have been analysed and the details are furnished in the following table.

TABLE. 4.7: ANOVA Showing the Significant Difference between the mean Scores of the Educational Aspiration among the First Generation Learners with Respect to Order of Birth.

Variable	Order of Birth	Mean	SSb	SSw	df	Calculated 'F' value	LS
Educational Aspiration	First born	33.7185	933.111	638.2922	2	215.6515	0.01
	Middle born	37.0000					
	Last born	32.3218			295		

INFERENCE

From the above table, it is obtained that the 'F' value (215.6515) is greater than the table (4.68) at 0.01level. Therefore there is significant difference between the mean scores of Educational Aspiration among first generation learners with regard to order of birth.

Mover over, middle born students have significantly higher educational aspiration than first born and last born students.

Hence the hypothesis – 4(d) stating that "There is no significant difference between the mean scores of educational aspiration of first generation learners with regard to order of birth" is rejected.

INFLUENCE OF TYPE OF FAMILY ON EDUCATIONAL ASPIRATION

The scores of educational aspiration of first generation learners with regard to type of family (joint/nuclear) have been analysed and the details are furnished in the following table.

TABLE. 4.8: Showing the Significant Difference between the mean Scores of Educational Aspiration among the First Generation Learners with Respect to Type of Family.

Variable	Type of Family	Number of cases	Mean	Standard Deviation	Critical Ratio	Level of Significance
Educational Aspiration	Joint	175	34.5143	2.654	3.64	**0.01**
	Nuclear	123	33.6260	1.539		

INFERENCE

From the above table, it is observed that the obtained CR value (3.64) is higher than the table value (2.58) at 0.01 level. Therefore there is significant difference between the mean scores of educational aspiration among first generation learners with regard to type of family.

It is also noted that Joint family first generation learners have exhibited significantly higher educational aspiration than their counterparts.

Hence the Hypothesis – 4 (e) stating that "There is no significant difference between the mean scores of educational aspiration of first generation learners with regard to type of family" is rejected.

ASSOCIATION BETWEEN SELF IMAGE AND GENDER

Association between self image and gender (males/females) of first generation learners has been computed and presented in the following table.

TABLE. 4.9: Showing Chi-Square test Revealing the Extent of Association between the Self Image and Gender

Self Image	Gender		Total	LS
	Males	Females		
Low	90 (91.10)	91 (89.89)	181	NS
Moderate	30 (29.69)	29 (29.30)	59	
High	30 (29.19)	28 (28.80)	58	
Total	**150**	**148**	**298**	

df=2 chi-square value=0.7802

Comparing the obtained value of chi-square (0.7802) with that of table value (5.991) at 0.05 level, we find that self image and gender of first generation learners are not significantly associated.

Hence hypothesis-5a stating that, "There is no significant association between the categories of self image of first generation learners and gender" is accepted.

ASSOCIATION BETWEEN SELF IMAGE AND TYPES OF MANAGEMENT OF SCHOOLS

Association between self image and type of management of schools (government/government aided/self finance) of first generation learners has been computed and presented in the following table.

TABLE. 4.10: Showing Chi-Square Test Revealing the Extent of Association between the Self Image and Type of Management of Schools

Self Image	Type of management of schools			Total	LS
	Government	Government Aided	Self finance		
Low	118 (119.65)	37 (35.22)	26 (26.11)	181	NS
Moderate	41 (105.11)	8 (11.48)	10 (8.51)	59	
High	38 (38.34)	13 (11.28)	7 (26.11)	58	
Total	**197**	**58**	**43**	**298**	

df=4 chi-square value=2.01737

Comparing the obtained value of chi-square (2.01737) with that of table value (9.488) at 0.05 level, we find that self image and type of management of schools of first generation learners are not significantly associated.

Hence hypothesis-5b stating that, "There is no significant association between the categories of self image of first generation learners and type of management of schools" is accepted.

ASSOCIATION BETWEEN SELF IMAGE AND MEDIUM OF INSTRUCTION

Association between self image and medium of instruction (Tamil/ English) of first generation learners has been computed and presented in the following table.

TABLE. 4.11: Showing Chi-square Test Revealing the Extent of Association between the Self Image and Medium of Instruction

Self image	Medium of instruction		Total	LS
	Tamil	**English**		
Low	101 (99.00)	80 (81.99)	181	NS
Moderate	30 (32.27)	29 (26.72)	59	
High	32 (31.72)	26 (26.27)	58	
Total	**163**	**135**	**298**	

df=2 chi-square value=0.44718

Comparing the obtained value of chi-square (0.44718) with that of table value (5.991) at 0.05 level, we find that self image and medium of instruction (Tamil/English)of first generation learners are not significantly associated.

Hence hypothesis-5c stating that, "There is no significant association between the categories of self image of first generation learners and medium of instruction" is accepted.

ASSOCIATION BETWEEN SELF IMAGE AND ORDER OF BIRTH

Association between self image and order of birth (first born/middle born/last born) of first generation learners has been computed and presented in the following table.

TABLE. 4.12: Showing Chi-Square Test Revealing the Extent of Association between the Self Image and Order of Birth

Self Image	Order of birth			Total	LS
	First born	Middle born	Last born		
Low	83 (81.99)	37 (46.16)	61 (52.84)	181	0.05
Moderate	28 (26.72)	21 (15.04)	10 (17.22)	59	
High	24 (26.27)	18 (14.79)	16 (16.93)	58	
Total	**135**	**76**	**87**	**298**	

df=4 chi-square value=9.51

Comparing the obtained value of chi-square (9.51) with that of table value (9.51) at 0.05 level, we find that self image and order of birth of first generation learners are significantly associated.

Hence hypothesis-5d stating that, "There is no significant association between the categories of self image of first generation learners and order of birth" is rejected.

ASSOCIATION BETWEEN SELF IMAGE AND TYPE OF FAMILY

Association between self image and type of family (joint/nuclear) of first generation learners has been computed and presented in the following table.

TABLE. 4.13: Showing Chi-Square Test Revealing the Extent of Association between the Self Image and Type of Family

Self Image	Type of family		Total	LS
	Joint	Nuclear		
Low	109 (106.29)	72 (39.8)	181	NS
Moderate	33 (34.64)	26 (24.35)	59	
High	33 (34.06)	25 (23.93)	58	
Total	**175**	**123**	**298**	

df=2 chi-square value=0.43697

Comparing the obtained value of chi-square (0.43697) with that of table value (5.991) at 0.05 level, we find that self image and type of family of first generation learners are not significantly associated.

Hence hypothesis-5e stating that, "There is no significant association between the categories of self image of first generation learners and type of family" is accepted.

INFLUENCE OF GENDER ON PARENT-PEER ATTACHMENT

The scores of parent-peer attachment of first generation learners with regard to gender (males/females) have been analysed and the details are furnished in the following table.

TABLE. 4.14: Showing the Significant Difference between the Mean Scores of the Parent-Peer Attachment Among the First Generation Learners with Respect to Gender.

Variable	Gender	Number of cases	Mean	Standard Deviation	Critical Ratio	Level of Significance
Parent -peer attachment	Males	150	87.0867	11.346	15.56	**0.01**
	Females	148	66.7432	11.227		

INFERENCE

From the above table, it is obtained CR value (15.56) is higher than the table value (2.58) at 0.01 level. Therefore there is significant difference between the mean scores of parent-peer attachment among first generation learners with regard to gender.

It is also noted that Male first generation learners have exhibited significantly higher parent-peer attachment than their counterparts.

Hence the Hypothesis – 6(a) stating that "There is no significant difference between the mean scores of parent-peer attachment of first generation learners with regard to gender" is rejected.

INFLUENCE OF TYPE OF MANAGEMENT OF SCHOOLS ON PARENT-PEER ATTACHMENT

The scores of parent-peer attachment of first generation learners with regard to management of schools (government/government aided/self finance) have been analysed and the details are furnished in the following table.

TABLE.4.15: ANOVA Showing the Significant Difference between the mean Scores of the Parent-Peer Attachment among the First Generation Learners with Respect to Management of Schools.

Variable	Type of Management of Schools	Mean	SSb	SSw	df	Calculated 'F' value	LS
Parent-Peer attachment	Government	6.8782	6.4623	68534.4538	2		
	Government Aided	77.2069			295	0.0139	**NS**
	Self finance	77.1628					

INFERENCE

From the above table, it is obtained that the 'F' value (0.0139) is lower than the table (3.03) at 0.05level. Therefore there is no significant difference between the mean scores of parent-peer attachment among first generation learners with regard to type of management of schools.

Hence the hypothesis – 6 (b) stating that "There is no significant difference in the mean scores of parent-peer attachment of first generation learners with regard to type of management of schools" is accepted.

INFLUENCE OF MEDIUM OF INSTRUCTION ON PARENT-PEER ATTACHMENT

The scores of parent-peer attachment of first generation learners with regard to medium of instruction (Tamil/English) have been analysed and the details are furnished in the following table.

TABLE. 4.16: Showing the Significant Difference between the mean Scores of the Parent-Peer Attachment among the First Generation Learners with Respect to Medium of Instruction.

Variable	Medium of Instruction	Number of cases	Mean	Standard Deviation	Critical Ratio	Level of Significance
Parent- peer attachment	Tamil	163	87.7055	10.683	21.78	**0.01**
	English	135	64.0370	8.052		

INFERENCE

From the above table, it is obtained CR value (21.78) is higher than the table value (2.58) at 0.01 level. Therefore there is significant difference between the mean scores of parent-peer attachment among first generation learners with regard to medium of instruction.

It is also noted that Tamil medium first generation learners have exhibited significantly higher parent-peer attachment than their counterparts. Hence the Hypothesis – 6 (c) stating that "There is no significant difference between the mean scores of parent-peer attachment of first generation learners with regard to medium of instruction" is rejected.

INFLUENCE OF ORDER OF BIRTH ON PARENT-PEER ATTACHMENT

The scores of parent-peer attachment of first generation learners with regard to order of birth (first born/middle born/last born) have been analysed and the details are furnished in the following table.

TABLE. 4.17: ANOVA Showing the Significant Difference between the mean Scores of the Parent-Peer Attachment among the First Generation Learners with Respect to Order of Birth.

Variable	Order of Birth	Mean	SSb	SSw	Df	Calculated 'F' value	LS
Parent-Peer attachment	First born	64.97	41944.84	26596.07	2	232.62	0.01
	Middle born	80.23			295		
	Last born	92.77					

INFERENCE

From the above table, it is obtained that the 'F' value (232.6232) is higher than the table (4.68) at 0.01 level. Therefore there is significant difference between the mean scores of Parent-Peer attachment among first generation learners with regard to order of birth.

Mover over, last born students have shown significantly higher parent-peer attachment than first born and middle born students.

Hence the hypothesis – 6 (d) stating that "There is no significant difference in the mean scores of parent-peer attachment of first generation learners with regard to order of birth" is rejected.

INFLUENCE OF TYPE OF FAMILY ON PARENT-PEER ATTACHMENT

The scores of parent-peer attachment of first generation learners with regard to type of family (joint/nuclear) have been analysed and the details are furnished in the following table.

TABLE. 4.18: Showing the Significant Difference between the mean Scores of Parent-peer Attachment of First Generation Learners with Respect to Type of Family.

Variable	Type of Family	Number of cases	Mean	Standard Deviation	Critical Ratio	Level of Significance
Parent -peer attachment	Joint	175	84.9429	12.369	14.07	0.01
	Nuclear	123	65.6585	11.110		

INFERENCE

From the above table, it is observed that the obtained CR value (14.07) is higher than the table value (2.58) at 0.01 level. Therefore there is significant difference between the mean scores of Parent-Peer attachment of first generation learners with regard to type of family.

It is also noted that joint family first generation learners have exhibited significantly higher parent-peer attachment than their counterparts.

Hence the Hypothesis – 6 (e) stating that "There is no significant difference in the mean scores of parent-peer attachment of first generation learners with regard to type of family" is rejected.

INFLUENCE OF GENDER ON PARENT TRUST- A DIMENSION OF PARENT-PEER ATTACHMENT

The scores of parent trust- a dimension of parent-peer attachment of first generation learners with regard to gender (males/females) have been analysed and the details are furnished in the following table.

TABLE. 4.19: Showing the Significant Difference between the mean Scores of Parent Trust - a Dimension of Parent-Peer Attachment of First Generation Learners with Respect to Gender.

Variable	Gender	Number of cases	Mean	Standard Deviation	Critical Ratio	Level of Significance
Parent Trust	Males	150	18.3333	1.230	8.23	**0.01**
	Females	148	19.7770	1.479		

INFERENCE

From the above table, it is obtained CR value (8.23) is higher than the table value (2.58) at 0.01 level. Therefore there is significant difference in the mean scores of Parent trust- a dimension of Parent-Peer first generation learners with regard to gender.

It is also noted that female first generation learners have exhibited significantly higher parent trust- a dimension of parent-peer attachment than their counterparts.

Hence the Hypothesis – 7 (a) stating that "There is no significant difference in the mean scores of Parent trust- a dimension of parent-peer attachment of first generation learners with regard to gender" is rejected.

INFLUENCE OF TYPE OF MANAGEMENT OF SCHOOLS ON PARENT TRUST- A DIMENSION OF PARENT-PEER ATTACHMENT

The scores of parent trust- a dimension of parent-peer attachment of first generation learners with regard to type of management of schools (government/ government aided/self Finance) are analysed and tabulate in the following table.

TABLE. 4.20: ANOVA Showing the Significant Difference between the mean Scores of the Parent Trust- a Dimension of Parent-Peer Attachment of First Generation Learners with Respect to Type of Management of Schools.

Variable	Type of Management of Schools	Mean	SSb	SSw	df	Calculated 'F' value	LS
Parent Trust	Government	19.0254	0.3843	829.8607	2	0.0683	NS
	Government Aided	19.0862			295		
	Self finance	19.1163					

INFERENCE

From the above table, it is obtained that the 'F' value (0.0683) is lower than the table (3.03) at 0.05level. Therefore there is no significant difference between the mean scores of the Parent trust- a dimension of Parent-Peer attachment of first generation learners with regard to type of management of schools.

Hence the hypothesis – 7 (b) stating that "There is no significant difference in the mean scores of parent trust – a dimension of parent - peer attachment of first generation learners with regard to type of management of schools" is accepted.

INFLUENCE OF MEDIUM OF INSTRUCTION ON PARENT TRUST - A DIMENSION OF PARENT-PEER ATTACHMENT

The scores of parent trust -a dimension of parent-peer attachment of first generation learners with regard to medium of Instruction (Tamil/English) have been analysed and the details are furnished in the following table.

TABLE. 4.21: Showing the Significant Difference between the mean Scores of Parent Trust - a Dimension of Parent-Peer Attachment of First Generation Learners with Respect to Medium of Instruction.

Variable	Medium of Instruction	Number of cases	Mean	Standard Deviation	Critical Ratio	Level of Significance
Parent Trust	Tamil	163	18.2515	1.229	10.36	**0.01**
	English	135	20.0148	1.630		

INFERENCE

From the above table, it is obtained CR value (10.36) is higher than the table value (2.58) at 0.01 level. Therefore there is significant difference between the mean scores of parent trust -a dimension of parent-peer attachment of first generation learners with regard to medium of instruction.

It is also noted that English medium first generation learners have exhibited significantly higher parent trust-a dimension of parent-peer attachment than their counterparts.

Hence the Hypothesis – 7 (c) stating that "There is no significant difference in the mean scores of parent trust -a dimension of parent-peer attachment of first generation learners with regard to medium of instruction" is rejected.

INFLUENCE OF ORDER OF BIRTH ON PARENT TRUST - A DIMENSION OF PARENT-PEER ATTACHMENT

The scores of parent trust- a dimension of parent-peer attachment of first generation learners with regard to order of birth(first born/middle born/last born) have been analysed and the details are furnished in the following table.

TABLE. 4.22: ANOVA Showing the Significant Difference between the mean Scores of Parent Trust -a Dimension of Parent-Peer Attachment of First Generation Learners with Respect to Order of birth.

Variable	Order of Birth	Mean	SSb	SSw	df	Calculated 'F' value	LS
Parent Trust	First born	19.92			2		
	Middle born	17.63					
	Last born	18.93	257.7153	572.5297	295	66.3948	**0.01**

INFERENCE

From the above table, it is obtained that the 'F' value (66.3948) is higher than the table (4.68) at 0.01 level. Therefore there is significant difference between the mean scores of parent trust a dimension of parent-peer attachment with regard to order of birth.

Movers over first born students have shown significantly higher parent trust than middle born and last born students.

Hence the hypothesis –7 (d) stating that "there is no significant in the mean scores of Parent trust -a dimension of parent-peer attachment of first generation learners with regard to order of birth" is rejected.

INFLUENCE OF TYPE OF FAMILY ON PARENT TRUST -A DIMENSION OF PARENT-PEER ATTACHMENT

The scores of parent trust- a dimension of parent-peer attachment of first generation learners with regard to type of family (joint/nuclear) have been analysed and the details are furnished in the following table.

TABLE. 4.23: Showing the Significant Difference between the mean Scores of Parent Trust- a Dimension of Parent-Peer Attachment of First Generation Learners with Respect to Type of Family.

Variable	Type of Family	Number of cases	Mean	Standard Deviation	Critical Ratio	Level of Significance
Parent Trust	Joint	175	18.4286	1.328	8.16	0.01
	Nuclear	123	19.9350	1.717		

INFERENCE

From the above table, it is obtained CR value (8.16) is higher than the table value (2.58) at 0.01 level. Therefore there is significant difference between the mean scores of parent trust- a dimension of parent-peer attachment of first generation learners with regard to type of family.

It is also noted that nuclear family first generation learners have exhibited significantly higher parent trust- a dimension of parent-peer attachment than their counterparts.

Hence the Hypothesis – 7 (e) stating that "There is no significant difference in the mean scores of parent trust- a dimension of parent-peer attachment of first generation learners with regard to type of family" is rejected.

INFLUENCE OF GENDER ON PARENT COMMUNICATION - A DIMENSION OF PARENT-PEER ATTACHMENT

The scores of parent communication-a dimension of parent-peer attachment of first generation learners with regard to gender (males/females) have been analysed and the details are furnished in the following table.

TABLE. 4.24: Showing the Significant Difference between the mean Scores of Parent Communication- a Dimension of Parent-Peer Attachment of First Generation Learners with Regard to Gender.

Variable	Gender	Number of cases	Mean	Standard Deviation	Critical Ratio	Level of Significance
Parent communication	Males	150	15.5067	0.502	22.86	0.01
	Females	148	23.4257	4.185		

INFERENCE

From the above table, it is obtained CR value (22.86) is higher than the table value (2.58) at 0.01 level. Therefore there is significant difference in the mean scores of Parent communication- a dimension of parent-peer attachment of first generation learners with regard to gender.

It is also noted that female first generation learners have exhibited significantly higher of parent communication - a dimension of parent-peer attachment than their counterparts.

Hence the Hypothesis – 8 (a) stating that "There is no significant difference in the mean scores of Parent communication-a dimension of parent-peer attachment of first generation learners with regard to gender" is rejected.

INFLUENCE OF TYPE OF MANAGEMENT OF SCHOOLS ON PARENT COMMUNICATION - A DIMENSION OF PARENT-PEER ATTACHMENT

The scores of parent communication-a dimension of parent-peer attachment of first generation learners with regard to type of management of schools (government/government aided/self finance) have been analysed and the details are furnished in the following table.

TABLE. 4.25: ANOVA Showing the Significant Difference in the mean Scores of Parent Communication-a Dimension of Parent-Peer Attachment of First Generation Learners with Respect to Type of Management of Schools.

Variable	Type of Management of Schools	Mean	SSb	SSw	Df	Calculated 'F' value	LS
Parent Communication	Government	19.43	3.40	7280.01	2 295	0.0689	NS
	Government Aided	19.60					
	Self finance	19.23					

INFERENCE

From the above table, it is obtained that the 'F' value (0.0689) is lower than the table (3.03) at 0.05 level. Therefore there is no significant difference between the mean scores of Parent communication- a dimension of Parent-Peer attachment of first generation learners with regard to type of management of schools.

Hence the hypothesis – 8(b) stating that "There is no significant difference in the mean scores of parent communication - a dimension of parent - peer attachment of first generation learners with regard to type of management of schools" is accepted.

INFLUENCE OF MEDIUM OF INSTRUCTION ON PARENT COMMUNICATION- A DIMENSION OF PARENT-PEER ATTACHMENT

The scores of Parent communication- a dimension of parent-peer attachment of first generation learners with regard to medium of instruction (Tamil/English) have been analysed and the details are furnished in the following table.

TABLE. 4.26: Showing the Significant Difference between the Mean Scores of Parent Communication- a Dimension of Parent-Peer Attachment among First Generation Learners with Respect to Medium of Instruction.

Variable	Medium of Instruction	Number of cases	Mean	Standard Deviation	Critical Ratio	Level of Significance
Parent Commu nication	Tamil	163	15.4785	0.501	29.17	**0.01**
	English	135	24.2222	3.453		

INFERENCE

From the above table, it is obtained CR value (29.17) is higher than the table value (2.58) at 0.01 level. Therefore there is significant difference between the mean scores of parent communication- a dimension of parent-peer attachment of first generation learners with regard to medium of instruction.

It is also noted that English medium first generation learners have exhibited significantly higher parent communication- a dimension of parent-peer attachment than their counterparts.

Hence the Hypothesis – 8(c) stating that "There is no significant difference in the mean scores of parent communication - a dimension of parent-peer attachment of first generation learners with regard to medium of instruction" is rejected.

INFLUENCE OF ORDER OF BIRTH ON PARENT COMMUNICATION - A DIMENSION OF PARENT-PEER ATTACHMENT

The scores of parent communication- a dimension of parent-peer attachment of first generation learners with regard to order of birth(first born/ middle born/last born) have been analysed and the details are furnished in the following table.

TABLE. 4.27: ANOVA Showing the Significant Difference between the mean Scores of Parent Communication - a Dimension of Parent-Peer Attachment of First Generation Learners with Regard to Order of Birth.

Variable	Order of Birth	Mean	SSb	SSw	df	Calculated 'F' value	LS
Parent Commun ication	First born	24.15	5529.67	1753.73	2	465.080	**0.01**
	Middle born	15.00			295		
	Last born	16.00					

INFERENCE

From the above table, it is obtained that the 'F' value (465.080) is higher than the table (4.68) at 0.01 level. Therefore there is significant difference between the mean scores of parent communication -a dimension of parent-peer attachment of first generation learners with regard to order of birth.

Moreover, first born students have shown significantly higher parent communication than middle born and last born students.

Hence the hypothesis – 8 (d) stating that "There is no significant in the mean scores of parent communication - a dimension of parent-peer attachment of first generation learners with regard to order of birth" is rejected.

INFLUENCE OF TYPE OF FAMILY ON PARENT COMMUNICATION - A DIMENSION OF PARENT-PEER ATTACHMENT

The scores of parent communication -a dimension of parent-peer attachment of first generation learners with regard to type of family (joint/ nuclear) have been analysed and the details are furnished in the following table.

TABLE.4.28: Showing the Significant Difference between the mean Scores of Parent Communication - a Dimension of Parent-Peer Attachment of First Generation Learners with Respect toType of Family.

Variable	Type of Family	Number of cases	Mean	Standard Deviation	Critical Ratio	Level of Significance
Parent communication	Joint	175	16.3714	2.843	17.93	**0.01**
	Nuclear	123	23.8049	3.931		

INFERENCE

From the above table, it is obtained CR value (17.93) is higher than the table value (2.58) at 0.01 level. Therefore there is significant difference between the mean scores of parent communication- a dimension of parent-peer attachment of first generation learners with regard to type of family.

It is also noted that nuclear family first generation learners have exhibited significantly higher parent communication - a dimension of parent-peer attachment of first generation than their counterparts.

Hence the Hypothesis – 8 (e) stating that "There is no significant difference in the mean scores of parent communication - a dimension of parent-Peer attachment of first generation learners with regard to type of family" is rejected.

INFLUENCE OF GENDER ON PARENT ALIENATION- A DIMENSION OF PARENT-PEER ATTACHMENT

The scores of parent alienation -a dimension of parent-peer attachment of first generation learners with regard to gender (males/females) have been analysed and the details are furnished in the following table.

Table. 4.29: Showing the Significant Difference between the mean Scores of Parent Alienation-a Dimension of Parent-Peer Attachment of First Generation Learners with Respect to Gender.

Variable	Type of Family	Number of cases	Mean	Standard Deviation	Critical Ratio	Level of Significance
Parent alienation	Males	150	10.6200	1.500	1.31	NS
	Females	148	10.8100	0.950		

INFERENCE

From the above table, it is obtained CR value (1.31) is lower than the table value (1.96) at 0.05 level. Therefore there is no significant difference between the mean scores of parent alienation -a dimension of parent-peer attachment of first generation learners with regard to gender.

Hence the Hypothesis – 9(a) stating that "There is no significant difference in the mean scores of parent alienation -a dimension of parent-Peer attachment of first generation learners with regard to gender" is accepted.

INFLUENCE TYPE OF MANAGEMENT OF SCHOOLS ON PARENT ALIENATION- A DIMENSION OF PARENT-PEER ATTACHMENT

The scores of parent alienation- a dimension of parent-peer attachment of first generation learners with regard to type of management of schools (government/government aided/self finance) have been analysed and the details are furnished in the following table.

TABLE. 4.30: ANOVA Showing the Significant Difference between the mean Scores of the Parent Alienation- a Dimension of Parent-Peer Attachment of First Generation Learners of Students with Respect to Type of Management of Schools.

Variable	Type of Management of Schools	Mean	SSb	SSw	df	Calculated 'F' value	LS
Parent Alienation	Government	10.6650	4.6566	466.0984	2 295	1.4736	NS
	Government Aided	.9655					
	Self finance	0.6047					

INFERENCE

From the above table, it is obtained that the 'F' value (1.4736) is lower than the table (3.03) at 0.05 level. Therefore there is no significant difference between the mean scores of the parent alienation- a dimension of Parent-Peer attachment of first generation learners with regard to Type of management of schools.

Hence the hypothesis – 9 (b) stating that "There is no significant difference in the mean scores of parent alienation – a dimension of parent - peer attachment of first generation learners with regard to Type of management of schools." is accepted.

INFLUENCE OF MEDIUM OF INSTRUCTION ON PARENT ALIENATION -A DIMENSION OF PARENT-PEER ATTACHMENT

The scores of parent alienation- a dimension of parent-peer attachment of first generation learners with regard to medium of instruction (Tamil/English) have been analysed and the details are furnished in the following table.

TABLE. 4.31: Showing the Significant Difference in the mean Scores of the Parent Alienation - a Dimension of Parent-Peer Attachment of First Generation Learner's of Students with Respect to Medium of Instruction.

Variable	Medium of Instruction	Number of cases	Mean	Standard Deviation	Critical Ratio	Level of Significance
parent alienation	Tamil	163	10.5828	1.502	2.10	**0.05**
	English	135	10.8741	0.859		

INFERENCE

From the above table, it is obtained CR value (2.10) is higher than the table value (1.96) at 0.05 level. Therefore there is significant difference between the mean scores of the parent alienation- a dimension of parent-peer attachment of first generation learners of students with regard to medium of instruction.

It is also noted that English medium first generation learners of have exhibited significantly higher parent alienation- a dimension of Parent-Peer attachment than their counterparts.

Hence the Hypothesis – 9 (c) stating that "There is no significant difference in the mean scores of the parent alienation - a dimension of parent-peer attachment of first generation learners with regard to medium of instruction" is rejected.

INFLUENCE OF ORDER OF BIRTH ON PARENT ALIENATION - A DIMENSION OF PARENT-PEER ATTACHMENT

The scores of parent alienation- a dimension of Parent-peer attachment of first generation learners with regard to order of birth (first/middle/last birth) have been analysed and the details are furnished in the following table.

TABLE. 4.32: ANOVA Showing the Significant Difference between the mean Scores of the Parent Alienation - a Dimension of Parent-Peer Attachment of First Generation Learners with Respect to Order of Birth.

Variable	Order of Birth	Mean	SSb	SSw	df	Calculated 'F' value	LS
Parent Alienation	First born	10.6741	292.6747	178.0803	2 295	242.4160	**0.01**
	Middle born	9.3158					
	Last born	12.0000					

INFERENCE

From the above table, it is obtained that the 'F' value (242.4160) is higher than the table (4.68) at 0.01 level. Therefore there is significant difference between the mean scores of parent alienation- a dimension of Parent-peer attachment of first generation learners with regard to order of birth.

More over, last born students have shown significantly higher parent alienation than first born and middle born students.

Hence the hypothesis – 9 (d) stating that "There is no significant in the mean scores of parent alienation - a dimension of Parent-peer attachment of first generation learners with regard to order of Birth" is rejected.

INFLUENCE OF TYPE OF FAMILY ON PARENT ALIENATION -A DIMENSION OF PARENT-PEER ATTACHMENT

The scores of parent alienation - a dimension of parent-peer attachment of first generation learners with regard to type of family (joint/nuclear) have been analysed and the details are furnished in the following table.

TABLE. 4.33: Showing the Significant Difference between the mean Scores of Parent Alienation - a Dimension of Parent-Peer Attachment of First Generation Learners with Respect to Type of Family.

Variable	Type of Family	Number of cases	Mean	Standard Deviation	Critical Ratio	Level of Significance
Parent alienation	Joint	175	10.6514	1.450	1.12	**NS**
	Nuclear	123	10.8049	0.920		

INFERENCE

From the above table, it is obtained CR value (1.12) is lower than the table value (1.96) at 0.05 level. Therefore there is no significant difference between the mean scores of parent alienation - a dimension of Parent-Peer attachment of first generation learners with regard to type of family.

Hence the Hypothesis – 9 (e) stating that "There is no significant difference in the mean scores of parent alienation - a dimension of Parent-Peer attachment of first generation learners with regard to type of family" is accepted.

INFLUENCE OF GENDER ON PEER TRUST-A DIMENSION OF PARENT-PEER ATTACHMENT

The scores of peer trust-a dimension of Parent-peer attachment of first generation learners with regard to gender (males/females) have been analysed and the details are furnished in the following table.

TABLE. 4.34: Showing the Significant Difference between the mean Scores of Peer Trust - a Dimension of Parent-Peer Attachment of First Generation Learners with Respect to Gender.

Variable	Gender	Number of cases	Mean	Standard Deviation	Critical Ratio	Level of Significance
Peer Trust	Males	150	16.7733	3.090	0.53	NS
	Females	148	16.9324	1.930		

INFERENCE

From the above table, it is obtained CR value (0.53) is lower than the table value (1.96) at 0.05 level. Therefore there is no significant difference between the mean scores of peer trust - a dimension of parent-peer attachment of first generation learners with regard to gender.

Hence the Hypothesis – 10(a) stating that "There is no significant difference in the mean scores of Peer Trust - a dimension of Parent-Peer attachment of first generation learners with regard to gender" is accepted.

INFLUENCE OF TYPE OF MANAGEMENT OF SCHOOLS ON PEER TRUST-A DIMENSION OF PARENT-PEER ATTACHMENT

The scores of peer trust- a dimension of Parent-peer attachment of first generation learners with regard to type of management of schools (government/ government aided/self finance) have been analysed and the details are furnished in the following table.

TABLE. 4.35: ANOVA Showing the Significant Difference between the mean Scores of the Peer Trust - a Dimension of Parent-Peer Attachment of First Generation Learners with Respect to Type of Management of schools.

Variable	Type of Management of Schools	Mean	SSb	SSw	Df	Calculated 'F' value	LS
Peer Trust	Government	16.7970	1.7872	1969.7162	2	0.1338	NS
	Government Aided	16.9655			295		
	Self finance	6.9535					

INFERENCE

From the above table, it is obtained that the 'F' value (0.1338) is lower than the table (3.03) at 0.05 level. Therefore there is no significant difference between the mean scores of peer trust -a dimension of parent-peer attachment of first generation learners with regard to type of management of schools.

Hence the hypothesis – 10 (b) stating that "There is no significant difference in the mean scores of peer trust - a dimension of parent and peer attachment of first generation learners with regard to Type of management of schools" is accepted.

INFLUENCE OF MEDIUM OF INSTRUCTION ON PEER TRUST - A DIMENSION OF PARENT-PEER ATTACHMENT

The scores of peer trust- a dimension of parent-peer attachment of first generation learners with regard to medium of instruction (Tamil/English) have been analysed and the details are furnished in the following table.

TABLE. 4.36: Showing the Significant Difference between the mean Scores of Peer Trust - a Dimension of Parent-Peer Attachment of First Generation Learners with Respect to Medium of Instruction.

Variable	Medium of Instruction	Number of cases	Mean	Standard Deviation	Critical Ratio	Level of Significance
Peer Trust	Tamil	163	16.8030	3.041	0.37	NS
	English	135	16.9111	1.879		

INFERENCE

From the above table, it is obtained CR value (0.37) is lower than the table value (1.96) at 0.05 level. Therefore there is no significant difference between the mean scores of peer trust -a dimension of parent-peer attachment of first generation learners with regard to medium of instruction.

Hence the Hypothesis – 10(c) stating that "There is no significant difference between the mean scores of Peer Trust - a dimension of Parent-Peer attachment of first generation learners with regard to Medium of Instruction" is accepted.

INFLUENCEOF ORDER OF BIRTH ON PEER TRUST -A DIMENSION OF PARENT-PEER ATTACHMENT

The scores of peer trust-a dimension of parent-peer attachment of first generation learners with regard to order of birth (first born/middle born/last born) have been analysed and the details are furnished in the following table.

TABLE. 4.37: ANOVA Showing the Significant Difference between the mean Scores of Peer Trust - a Dimension of Parent-Peer Attachment of First Generation Learners with Respect to order of Birth.

Variable	Order of Birth	Mean	SSb	SSw	df	Calculated 'F' value	LS
Peer Trust	First born	16.8296	601.6674	1369.8359	2 295	64.758	**0.01**
	Middle born	14.8158					
	Last born	18.6667					

INFERENCE

From the above table, it is obtained that the 'F' value (64.758) is higher than the table (4.68) at 0.01 level. Therefore there is significant difference between the mean scores of peer trust -a dimension of parent-peer attachment of first generation learners with regard to order of birth.

More over, last born students have shown significantly higher peer trust than first born and middle born students.

Hence the hypothesis – 10(d) stating that "There is no significant difference in the mean scores of Peer Trust -a dimension of Parent-Peer attachment of first generation learners with regard to order of birth" is rejected.

INFLUENCEOF TYPE OF FAMILY ON PEER TRUST- A DIMENSION OF PARENT-PEER ATTACHMENT

The scores of peer trust-a dimension of parent-peer attachment of first generation learners with regard to type of family (joint/nuclear) have been analysed and the details are furnished in the following table.

TABLE. 4.38: Showing the Significant Difference between the mean Scores of Peer Trust - a Dimension of Parent-Peer Attachment of First Generation Learners with Respect to Type of Family.

Variable	Type of Family	Number of cases	Mean	Standard Deviation	Critical Ratio	Level of Significance
Peer Trust	Joint	175	16.7771	2.989	0.65	NS
	Nuclear	123	16.9593	1.844		

INFERENCE

From the above table, it is obtained CR value (0.65) is lower than the table value (1.96) at 0.05 level. Therefore there is no significant difference between the mean scores of peer trust -a dimension of parent-peer attachment of first generation learners with regard to type of family.

Hence the Hypothesis – 10 (e) stating that "There is no significant difference in the mean scores of peer trust - a dimension of parent-peer attachment of first generation learners with regard to type of family" is accepted.

INFLUENCE OF GENDER ON PEER COMMUNICATION - A DIMENSION OF PARENT-PEER ATTACHMENT

The scores of peer communication- a dimension of parent-peer attachment of first generation learners with regard to gender (males/females) have been analysed and the details are furnished in the following table.

TABLE. 4.39: Showing the Significant Difference between the Mean Scores of Peer Communication - a Dimension of Parent-Peer Attachment of First Generation Learners with Respect to Gender.

Variable	Gender	Number of cases	Mean	Standard Deviation	Critical Ratio	Level of Significance
Peer Comm unication	Males	150	17.4333	1.383	8.90	**0.01**
	Females	148	19.0135	1.666		

INFERENCE

From the above table, it is obtained CR value (8.90) is higher than the table value (2.58) at 0.01 level. Therefore there is significant difference between the mean scores of peer communication- a dimension of parent-peer attachment of first generation learners of students with regard to gender.

It is also noted that female first generation learners has exhibited significantly higher peer communication- a dimension of parent-peer attachment than their counterparts.

Hence the Hypothesis – 11(a) stating that "There is no significant difference in the mean scores of peer communication - a dimension of parent-peer attachment of first generation learners with regard to gender" is rejected.

INFLUENCE OF TYPE OF MANAGEMENT OF SCHOOLS ON PEER COMMUNICATION - A DIMENSION OF PARENT-PEER ATTACHMENT

The scores of peer communication- a dimension of parent-peer attachment of first generation learners with regard to type of management of schools (government/government aided/self finance) have been analysed and the details are furnished in the following table.

TABLE. 4.40: ANOVA Showing the Significant Difference between the mean Scores of the Peer Communication - a Dimension of Parent-Peer Attachment of First Generation Learners Students with respect to Type of Management of Schools.

Variable	Type of Management of Schools	Mean	SSb	SSw	df	Calculated 'F' value	LS
Peer Communication	Government	18.25	3.74	875.07	2	0.6313	NS
	Government Aided	18.00			295		
	Self finance	18.34					

INFERENCE

From the above table, it is obtained that the 'F' value (0.6313) is lower than the table (3.03) at 0.05level. Therefore there is no significant difference between the mean scores of the peer communication -a dimension of parent-peer attachment of first generation learners with regard to type of management of schools.

Hence the hypothesis – 11(b) stating that "There is no significant difference in the mean scores of peer communication - a dimension of parent-peer attachment of first generation learners with regard to type of management of schools" is accepted.

INFLUENCE OF MEDIUM OF INSTRUCTION ON PEER COMMUNICATION - A DIMENSION OF PARENT-PEER ATTACHMENT

The scores of peer communication- a dimension of parent-peer attachment of first generation learners with regard to medium of instruction (Tamil /English) have been analysed and the details are furnished in the following table.

TABLE. 4.41: Showing the Significant Difference between the mean Scores of Peer Communication - a Dimension of Parent-Peer Attachment of First Generation Learners with Respect to Medium of Instruction.

Variable	Medium of Instruction	Number of cases	Mean	Standard Deviation	Critical Ratio	Level of Significance
Peer Commun cation	Tamil	163	17.5031	1.429	8.74	0.01
	English	135	19.0815	1.648		

INFERENCE

From the above table, it is obtained CR value (8.74) is higher than the table value (2.58) at 0.01 level. Therefore there is significant difference between the mean scores of peer communication- a dimension of parent-peer attachment of first generation learners with regard to medium of instruction.

It is also noted that English medium first generation learners have exhibited significantly higher peer communication- a dimension of parent-peer attachment than their counterparts.

Hence the Hypothesis – 11(c) stating that "There is no significant difference in the mean scores of Peer Communication - a dimension of Parent-Peer attachment of first generation learners with regard to medium of instruction" is rejected.

INFLUENCEOF ORDER OF BIRTH ON PEER COMMUNICATION - A DIMENSION OF PARENT-PEER ATTACHMENT

The scores of peer communication -a dimension of parent-peer attachment of first generation learners with regard to order of birth (first born/middle born/ last born) have been analysed and the details are furnished in the following table.

TABLE. 4.42: ANOVA Showing the Significant Difference between the mean Scores of Peer Communication - a Dimension of Parent-Peer Attachment of First Generation learners with Respect to Order of Birth.

Variable	Order of Birth	Mean	SSb	SSw	df	Calculated 'F' value	LS
Peer Comm unication	First born	19.23	368.75	510.07	2 295	106.6337	0.01
	Middle born	18.26					
	Last born	16.59					

INFERENCE

From the above table, it is obtained that the 'F' value (106.6337) is higher than the table (4.68) at 0.01 level. Therefore there is significant difference between the mean scores of peer communication- a dimension of parent-peer attachment of first generation learners with regard to order of birth.

More over, first born students have shown significantly higher peer communication than middle born and last born students.

Hence the hypothesis – 11(d) stating that "There is no significant in the mean scores of peer communication - a dimension of parent-peer attachment of first generation learners with regard to order of birth" is rejected.

INFLUENCEOF TYPE OF FAMILY ON PEER COMMUNICATION- A DIMENSION OF PARENT-PEER ATTACHMENT

The scores of peer communication- a dimension of parent-peer attachment of first generation learners with regard to type of family (joint/nuclear) have been analysed and the details are furnished in the following table.

TABLE. 4.43: Showing the Significant Difference between the mean Scores of Peer Communication - a Dimension of Parent-Peer Attachment of First Generation Learners with Respect to Type of Family.

Variable	Type of Family	Number of cases	Mean	Standard Deviation	Critical Ratio	Level of Significance
Peer Comm-unication	Joint	175	17.6286	1.495	7.57	**0.01**
	Nuclear	123	19.0569	1.676		

INFERENCE

From the above table, it is obtained CR value (7.57) is higher than the table value (2.58) at 0.01 level. Therefore there is significant difference between the mean scores of peer communication -a dimension of parent-peer attachment of first generation learners with regard to type of family.

It is also noted that nuclear family first generation learners have exhibited significantly higher Peer Communication - a dimension of Parent-Peer attachment than their counterparts.

Hence the Hypothesis – 11(e) stating that "There is no significant difference in the mean scores of peer communication - a dimension of parent-peer attachment of first generation learners with regard to type of family" is rejected.

INFLUENCE OF GENDER ON PEER ALIENATION - A DIMENSION OF PARENT-PEER ATTACHMENT

The scores of peer alienation- a dimension of parent-peer attachment of first generation learners regard to gender (males/females) have been analysed and the details are furnished in the following table.

TABLE. .44: Showing the Significant Difference between the mean Scores of Peer Alienation - a Dimension of Parent-Peer Attachment of First Generation Learners with Respect to Gender.

Variable	Gender	Number of cases	Mean	Standard Deviation	Critical Ratio	Level of Significance
Peer Alienation	Males	150	15.2933	2.197	7.39	**0.01**
	Females	148	17.2027	2.265		

INFERENCE

From the above table, it is obtained CR value (7.39) is higher than the table value (2.58) at 0.01 level. Therefore there is significant difference between the mean scores of peer alienation- a dimension of parent-peer attachment of first generation learners with regard to gender.

It is also noted that female first generation learners have exhibited significantly higher Peer Alienation- a dimension of Parent-Peer attachment than their counterparts.

Hence the Hypothesis – 12 (a) stating that “There is no significant difference in the mean scores of peer alienation - a dimension of parent-peer attachment of first generation learners with regard to gender” is rejected.

INFLUENCE OF TYPE OF MANAGEMENT OF SCHOOLS ON PEER ALIENATION - A DIMENSION OF PARENT-PEER ATTACHMENT

The scores of peer alienation- a dimension of parent-peer attachment of first generation learners with regard to type of management of schools (government/government aided/self finance) have been analysed and the details are furnished in the following table.

TABLE. 4.45: ANOVA Showing the Significant Difference between the mean Scores of the Peer Alienation - a Dimension of Parent-Peer Attachment of First Generation Learners with Respect to Type of Management of Schools.

Variable	Type of Management of Schools	Mean	SSb	SSw	df	Calculated 'F' value	LS
Peer Alienation	Government	16.38	20.36	1724.24	2	1.7417	NS
	Government Aided	16.20			295		
	Self finance	15.62					

INFERENCE

From the above table, it is obtained that the 'F' value (1.7417) is lower than the table (3.03) at 0.05level. Therefore there is no significant difference between the mean scores of the peer alienation -a dimension of parent-peer attachment of first generation learners with regard to type of management of schools.

Hence the hypothesis – 12 (b) stating that "There is no significant difference in the mean scores of peer alienation - a dimension of parent - peer attachment of first generation learners with regard to type of management of schools" is accepted.

INFLUENCE OF MEDIUM OF INSTRUCTION ON PEER ALIENATION - A DIMENSION OF PARENT-PEER ATTACHMENT

The scores of peer alienation- a dimension of parent-peer attachment of first generation learners with regard to medium of instruction (Tamil/English) have been analysed and the details are furnished in the following table.

TABLE. 4.46: Showing the Significant Difference between the mean Scores of Peer Alienation-a Dimension of Parent-Peer Attachment of First Generation Learners of Students with Respect to Medium of Instruction.

Variable	Medium of Instruction	Number of cases	Mean	Standard Deviation	Critical Ratio	Level of Significance
Peer Alienation	Tamil	163	15.3374	2.270	7.79	**0.01**
	English	135	17.3333	2.144		

INFERENCE

From the above table, it is obtained CR value (7.79) is higher than the table value (2.58) at 0.01 level. Therefore there is significant difference between the mean scores of peer alienation -a dimension of parent-peer attachment of first generation learners with regard to medium of instruction.

It is also noted that English medium first generation learners have exhibited significantly higher Peer Alienation -a dimension of Parent-Peer attachment than their counterparts.

Hence the Hypothesis – 12(c) stating that "There is no significant difference in the mean scores of peer alienation -a dimension of parent-peer attachment of first generation learners with regard to medium of instruction" is rejected.

INFLUENCEOF ORDER OF BIRTH ON PEER ALIENATION-A DIMENSION OF PARENT-PEER ATTACHMENT

The scores of peer alienation -a dimension of parent-peer attachment of first generation learners with regard to order of birth (first born/middle born/ last born) have been analysed and the details are furnished in the following table.

TABLE. 4.47: ANOVA Showing the Significant Difference between the mean Scores of Peer Alienation - a Dimension of Parent-Peer Attachment of First Generation Learners with Respect to Order of Birth.

Variable	Order of Birth	Mean	SSb	SSw	df	Calculated 'F' value	LS
Peer Alienation	First born	17.31	302.97	1441.62	2 295	30.9994	**0.01**
	Middle born	15.73					
	Last born	15.02					

INFERENCE

From the above table, it is obtained that the 'F' value (30.9994) is higher than the table (4.68) at 0.01 level. Therefore there is significant difference between the mean scores of peer alienation- a dimension of parent-peer attachment of first generation learners with regard to order of birth.

Moreover, first born students have shown significantly higher peer alienation than middle born and last born students.

Hence the hypothesis – 12(d) stating that "There is no significant difference in the mean scores of peer alienation - a dimension of parent - peer attachment of first generation learners with regard to order of birth" is rejected.

INFLUENCEOF TYPE OF FAMILY ON PEER ALIENATION-A DIMENSION OF PARENT-PEER ATTACHMENT

The scores of peer alienation-a dimension of parent-peer attachment of first generation learners with regard to type of family (joint/nuclear) have been analysed and the details are furnished in the following table.

TABLE. 4.48: Showing the Significant Difference between the mean Scores of Peer Alienation - a Dimension of Parent-Peer Attachment of First Generation Learners with Respect to Type of Family.

Variable	Type of Family	Number of cases	Mean	Standard Deviation	Critical Ratio	Level of Significance
Peer Alienation	Joint	175	15.5829	2.330	5.95	**0.01**
	Nuclear	123	17.1789	2.247		

INFERENCE

From the above table, it is obtained that the CR value (5.95) is higher than the table (2.58) at 0.01 level. Therefore there is significant difference between the mean scores of peer alienation- a dimension of parent-peer attachment of first generation learners with regard to type of family.

It is also noted that nuclear family first generation learners have exhibited significantly higher peer alienation -a dimension of parent-peer attachment than their counterparts.

Hence the hypothesis – 12 (e) stating that "There is no significant in the mean scores of peer alienation - a dimension of parent-peer attachment of first generation learners with regard to type of family" is rejected.

ASSOCIATION BETWEEN LEVELS OF EDUCATIONAL ASPIRATION AND CATEGORIES OF SELF IMAGE

Association between levels of educational aspiration and categories of self image First generation learners has been computed and presented in the following table.

TABLE. 4.49: Showing Chi-Square Test Revealing the Extent of Association between Levels of Educational Aspiration and Categories of Self Image

Educational Aspiration	Self Image			Total	LS
Low	137 (131.19)	38 (42.76)	3 (42.04)	216	NS
Moderate	21 (21.25)	8 (6.92)	6 (6.81)	35	
High	23 (28.54)	13 (9.30)	11 (9.14)	47	
Total	**181**	**59**	**58**	**298**	

df=4 chi-square value=3.99875

Comparing the obtained value of chi-square (3.99875) with that of table value (9.488) at 0.05 level, we find that levels of educational aspiration and categories of self image first generation learners are not significantly related.

Hence hypothesis-13 stating that, "There is no significant association between levels of educational aspiration and categories of self image among first generation learners" is accepted.

CORRELATION BETWEEN EDUCATIONAL ASPIRATION AND ARENT-PEER ATTACHMENT ALONG WITH ITS DIMENSIONS AMONG FIRST GENERATION LEARNERS

The correlation between educational aspiration and parent-peer attachment along with its dimensions among first generation learners are calculated and the details are tabulated in the following table.

TABLE. 4.50: Showing the Correlation between Educational Aspiration and Parent –Peer Attachment along with its Dimensions among First Generation Learners.

Parent –Peer Attachment and its dimensions	Educational Aspiration 'r'value	Level of Significance
Parent Trust	0.4423	**0.01**
Parent Communication	0.365	**0.01**
Parent Alienation	0.6876	**0.01**
Peer Trust	0.4463	**0.01**
Peer Communication	0.1288	**0.01**
Peer Alienation	0.5189	**0.01**
Parent-Peer Attachment in Totol	0.478	**0.01**

INFERENCE

From the above table, we infer that Parent-Peer attachment along with its dimensions and Educational Aspiration of First Generation Learners are significantly and positively correlated

Hence the hypothesis – 14 stating that "There is no significant correlation between educational aspiration and parent-peer attachment along with its dimensions among first generation learners" is rejected.

CONCLUSION

This chapter summarizes the analysis of data, testing of hypotheses, description and inference of the tables. A brief report of the research study together with the major findings and conclusion along with their educational implications has been presented in the succeeding chapter.

❐

5

Summary, Findings and Conclusion

In this chapter, after presenting briefly the statement of the problem and the description of the procedure used in the investigation, the findings and the conclusions are presented. In the light of the findings of the present study, suggestions have been proposed at the end of the chapter for further research in this field.

STATEMENT OF THE PROBLEM

The problem is stated as follows, "An Investigation into Educational Aspiration of First Generation Learners in relation to their Self Image and Parent - Peer attachment".

OPERATIONAL DEFINITIONS

Educational Aspiration

Educational aspiration purely depends upon success in completing a task and also enables the student to develop a positive attitude to fact any new task and complete it successfully. This kind of educational aspirations can be developed by the student depending upon the success experiences and the encouragement he receives from his parents as well as from the teachers.

In the present study, it is measured by Educational Aspiration Questionnaire, constructed and standardized by the investigator and Dr.S.Devasahayam Selvakumar (2014).

Self Image

According to H.J. Kysenck, the famous psychologist, self image begins with a survey of one's own life taking into account outwards stage and inner condition and enabling one to reach an undertaking of one's personal development and critical judgment of one's spiritual and intellectual existence.

In the present investigation, self image is assessed through Self Image Inventory constructed and validated by John Garlock (1983).

Parent- Peer Attachment

Parent-child relationships are characterized both in terms of friendship and in terms of an authority relationship. As a result, the parent-child relationship may be better thought of as a "mixed relationship", or a mixture of horizontal and vertical power relationship (laursen and collins, 1994). Furthermore, evidence suggests a considerable amount of overlap in peer and parent relationships. Both parents' peers provide emotional support and intimacy during adolescence and in nomination tasks, parents and peers receive equal numbers of nominations as primary support figures throughout adolescence (freeman, 1997).

According to the view of the investigator, the term parent-peer attachment refers to the scores obtained from the Parent-Peer Inventory constructed and standardized by investigator and Dr.S.Devasahayam Selvakumar (2014).

FIRST GENERATION LEARNERS

In the present study, the investigator means the students who are studying in standard IX from their family as first persons.

OBJECTIVES OF THE STUDY

The following objectives have been set in the present investigation

1. To find the levels of educational aspiration / self image /parent-peer attachment along with its dimensions of first generation learners.
2. To find out whether the following presage variables have significant influence / association on self image / Parent- peer attachment along with its dimensions and educational aspiration of first generation learners.

- Gender (Male/Female)
- Type of management of schools (Government/Government aided/ Self finance)
- Medium of Instruction (Tamil/English)
- Birth order of students (first born/middle born/last born)
- Nature of the Family (Nuclear/Joint)

3. To find whether there is any significant association between categories of self image and levels of educational aspiration among first generation learners.
4. To find whether there is any significant correlation between parent - peer attachment and educational aspiration among first generation learners.

HYPOTHESES OF THE STUDY

The following hypotheses have been set in the present study:

1. The level of educational aspiration of first generation learners is average in nature.
2. The level of self-image of first generation learners is moderate in nature.
3. The level of parent and peer attachment and its dimensions of first generation learners are average in nature.
4. There is no significant difference between the mean scores of educational aspiration of first generation learners with regard to
    - Gender (Male / Female)
    - Type of management of schools (Government /Government Aided / Self finance)
    - Medium of instruction (Tamil / English)
    - Order of birth (First born / Middle born / Last born)
    - Type of family (Joint / Nuclear)
5. There is no significant association between the categories of self image of first generation learners and
    - Gender (Male / Female)
    - Type of management of schools (Government / Government Aided / Self finance)
    - Medium of instruction (Tamil / English)
    - Order of birth (First born / Middle born / Last born)
    - Type of family (Joint / Nuclear)
6. There is no significant difference in the mean scores of parent - peer attachment of first generation learners with regard to Gender (Male / Female)

- Type of management of schools (Government / Government Aided / self finance)
- Medium of instruction (Tamil / English)
- Order of birth (First born / Middle born / Last born)
- Type of family (Joint / Nuclear)

7. There is no significant difference in the mean scores of parent Trust - a dimension of parent - peer attachment of first generation learners with regard to

    - Gender (Male / Female)
    - Type of management of schools (Government / Government Aided / Self finance)
    - Medium of instruction (Tamil / English)
    - Order of birth (First born / Middle born / Last born)
    - Type of family (Joint / Nuclear)

8. There is no significant difference in the mean scores of parent communication - a dimension of parent - peer attachment of first generation learners with regard to

    - Gender (Male / Female)
    - Type of management of schools (Government / Government Aided / Self finance)
    - Medium of instruction (Tamil / English)
    - Order of birth (First born / Middle born / Last born)
    - Type of family (Joint / Nuclear)

9. There is no significant difference in the mean scores of parent alienation - a dimension of parent- peer attachment of first generation learners with regard to

    - Gender (Male / Female)
    - Type of management of schools (Government / Government Aided / Self finance)
    - Medium of instruction (Tamil / English)
    - Order of birth (First born / Middle born / Last born)
    - Type of family (Joint / Nuclear)

10. There is no significant difference in the mean scores of peer Trust - a dimension of parent - peer attachment of first generation learners with regard to

    - Gender (Male / Female)
    - Type of management of schools (Government / Government Aided / Self finance)

- Medium of instruction (Tamil / English)
- Order of birth (First born / Middle born / Last born)
- Type of family (Joint / Nuclear)

11. There is no significant difference in the mean scores of peer communication - a dimension of parent - peer attachment of first generation learners with regard to
    - Gender (Male / Female)
    - Type of management of schools (Government / Government Aided / Self finance)
    - Medium of instruction (Tamil / English)
    - Order of birth (First born / Middle born / Last born)
    - Type of family (Joint / Nuclear)
12. There is no significant difference in the mean scores of peer Alienation - a dimension of parent- peer attachment of first generation learners with regard to
    - Gender (Male / Female)
    - Type of management of schools (Government / Government Aided / Self finance)
    - Medium of instruction (Tamil / English)
    - Order of birth (First born / Middle born / Last born)
    - Type of family (Joint / Nuclear)
13. There is no significant association between levels of educational aspiration and categories of self-image among first generation learners.
14. There is no significant correlation between educational aspiration and parent-peer attachment along with its dimensions among first generation learners.

SAMPLE OF THE STUDY

Random sampling technique was adopted for the selection of sample. The schools selected for the study were divided into different management namely Government, Government Aided and Self finance schools. The sample of 298 school students of first generation learners were taken for the study. 145 first generation learners from Government Schools, 110 first generation learners from Government aided Schools, 43first generation learners from Self finance Schools were chosen for the study.

TOOLS USED IN THIS STUDY

The following tools have been used in the study

1. Educational Aspiration Questionnaire standardized by the investigator and Dr.S.Devasahayam Selvakumar (2014).
2. Self Image Inventory by John Garlock (1983).
3. Inventory of Parent - Peer Attachment constructed by the investigator and Dr.S.Devasahayam Selvakumar (2014).

COLLECTION OF DATA

Each of the printed copies of answer sheets consisted of a personal data sheet. Educational Aspiration questionnaire, Self Image Inventory and Inventory of Parent - peer attachment which were distributed to the students and the data was collected personally by the investigator.

ANALYSIS OF DATA

After the data was collected, it was subject to statistical tests of significance for testing the hypotheses formulated by the investigator.
The methods of analysis used were,

1. Percentile Analysis.
2. Differential Analysis.
    - Critical Ration
    - ANOVA
3. Correlation Analysis
4. Chi-square Test

MAJOR FINDINGS OF THE STUDY

The present investigation has led to the following major findings:

1. The level of educational aspiration among of first generation learners is low in nature.
2. The level of Self Image of first generation learners is low in nature.
3. Parent-peer attachment in toto and its dimension –Parent Alienation are high in nature, peer trust is moderate in nature and parent trust, parent communication, peer communication and Peer Alienation are low in nature.
4. There is significant difference between the mean scores of educational aspiration of first generation learners with regard to gender. Male first generation learners have exhibited significantly higher educational aspiration than their counterparts.

5. There is no significant difference between the mean scores of Educational Aspiration of first generation learners with regard to type of management of schools.
6. There is significant difference between the mean scores of educational aspiration of first generation learners with regard to medium of instruction. Tamil medium students have exhibited significantly higher educational aspiration of first generation learners than their counterparts.
7. There is significant difference between the mean scores of Educational Aspiration among first generation learners with regard to order of birth. Middle born students have significantly higher educational aspiration than first born and last born students.
8. There is significant difference between the mean scores of educational aspiration among first generation learners with regard to type of family. Joint family first generation learners have exhibited significantly higher educational aspiration than their counterparts.
9. Self image and gender of first generation learners are not significantly associated.
10. Self image and type of management of schools of first generation learners are not significantly associated.
11. Self image and medium of instruction (Tamil/English) of first generation learners are not significantly associated.
12. Self image and order of birth of first generation learners are significantly associated.
13. Self image and type of family of first generation learners are not significantly associated.
14. There is significant difference between the mean scores of parent-peer attachment among first generation learners with regard to gender. Male first generation learners have exhibited significantly higher parent-peer attachment than their counterparts.
15. There is no significant difference between the mean scores of parent-peer attachment among first generation learners with regard to type of management of schools.
16. There is significant difference between the mean scores of parent-peer attachment among first generation learners with regard to medium of instruction. Tamil medium first generation learners have exhibited significantly higher parent-peer attachment than their counterparts.
17. There is significant difference between the mean scores of Parent-Peer attachment among first generation learners with regard to order of birth. Last born students have shown significantly higher parent-peer attachment than first born and middle born students.

18. There is significant difference between the mean scores of Parent-Peer attachment of first generation learners with regard to type of family. Joint family first generation learners have exhibited significantly higher parent-peer attachment than their counterparts.
19. There is significant difference in the mean scores of Parent trust- a dimension of Parent-Peer attachment of first generation learners with regard to gender. Female first generation learners have exhibited significantly higher parent trust - a dimension of parent-peer attachment than their counterparts.
20. There is no significant difference between the mean scores of the Parent trust - a dimension of Parent-Peer attachment of first generation learners with regard to type of management of schools.
21. There is significant difference between the mean scores of parent trust -a dimension of parent-peer attachment of first generation learners with regard to medium of instruction. English medium first generation learners have exhibited significantly higher parent trust -a dimension of parent-peer attachment than their counterparts.
22. There is significant difference between the mean scores of parent trust - a dimension of parent-peer attachment with regard to order of birth. First born students have shown significantly higher parent trust than middle born and last born students.
23. There is significant difference between the mean scores of parent trust - a dimension of parent-peer attachment of first generation learners with regard to type of family. Nuclear family first generation learners have exhibited significantly higher parent trust - a dimension of parent-peer attachment than their counterparts.
24. There is significant difference in the mean scores of Parent communication - a dimension of parent-peer attachment of first generation learners with regard to gender. Female first generation learners have exhibited significantly higher of parent communication - a dimension of parent-peer attachment than their counterparts.
25. There is no significant difference between the mean scores of Parent communication - a dimension of Parent-Peer attachment of first generation learners with regard to type of management of schools.
26. There is significant difference between the mean scores of parent communication - a dimension of parent-peer attachment of first generation learners with regard to medium of instruction. English medium first generation learners have exhibited significantly higher parent communication- a dimension of parent-peer attachment than their counterparts.

27. There is significant difference between the mean scores of parent communication - a dimension of parent-peer attachment of first generation learners with regard to order of birth. First born students have shown significantly higher parent communication than middle born and last born students.
28. There is significant difference between the mean scores of parent communication - a dimension of parent-peer attachment of first generation learners with regard to type of family. Nuclear family first generation learners have exhibited significantly higher parent communication - a dimension of parent-peer attachment of first generation than their counterparts.
29. There is no significant difference between the mean scores of parent alienation - a dimension of parent-peer attachment of first generation learners with regard to gender.
30. There is no significant difference between the mean scores of the parent alienation - a dimension of Parent-Peer attachment of first generation learners with regard to Type of management of schools.
31. There is significant difference between the mean scores of the parent alienation - a dimension of parent-peer attachment of first generation learners of students with regard to medium of instruction. English medium first generation learners of have exhibited significantly higher parent alienation- a dimension of Parent-Peer attachment than their counterparts.
32. Therefore there is significant difference between the mean scores of parent alienation - a dimension of Parent-peer attachment of first generation learners with regard to order of birth. Last born students have shown significantly higher parent alienation than first born and middle born students.
33. There is no significant difference between the mean scores of parent alienation - a dimension of Parent-Peer attachment of first generation learners with regard to type of family.
34. There is no significant difference between the mean scores of peer trust - a dimension of parent-peer attachment of first generation learners with regard to gender.
35. There is no significant difference between the mean scores of peer trust -a dimension of parent-peer attachment of first generation learners with regard to type of management of schools.
36. There is no significant difference between the mean scores of peer trust -a dimension of parent-peer attachment of first generation learners with regard to medium of instruction.

37. There is significant difference between the mean scores of peer trust - a dimension of parent-peer attachment of first generation learners with regard to order of birth. Last born students have significantly higher peer trust than the first born and middle born students.
38. There is no significant difference between the mean scores of peer trust -a dimension of parent-peer attachment of first generation learners with regard to type of family.
39. There is significant difference between the mean scores of peer communication - a dimension of parent-peer attachment of first generation learners of students with regard to gender. Female first generation learners have exhibited significantly higher peer communication - a dimension of parent-peer attachment than their counterparts.
40. There is no significant difference between the mean scores of the peer communication -a dimension of parent-peer attachment of first generation learners with regard to type of management of schools.
41. There is significant difference between the mean scores of peer communication - a dimension of parent-peer attachment of first generation learners with regard to medium of instruction. English medium first generation learners have exhibited significantly higher peer communication- a dimension of parent-peer attachment than their counterparts.
42. There is significant difference between the mean scores of peer communication - a dimension of parent-peer attachment of first generation learners with regard to order of birth. First born students have shown significantly higher peer communication than middle born and last born students.
43. There is significant difference between the mean scores of peer communication - a dimension of parent-peer attachment of first generation learners with regard to type of family. Nuclear family first generation learners have exhibited significantly higher Peer Communication - a dimension of Parent-Peer attachment than their counterparts.
44. There is significant difference between the mean scores of peer alienation - a dimension of parent-peer attachment of first generation learners with regard to gender. Female first generation learners have exhibited significantly higher peer alienation than their counter parts.
45. There is no significant difference between the mean scores of the peer alienation - a dimension of parent-peer attachment of first generation learners with regard to type of management of schools.

46. There is significant difference between the mean scores of peer alienation -a dimension of parent-peer attachment of first generation learners with regard to medium of instruction. English medium first generation learners have exhibited significantly higher Peer Alienation -a dimension of Parent-Peer attachment than their counterparts.
47. There is significant difference between the mean scores of peer alienation - a dimension of parent-peer attachment of first generation learners with regard to order of birth. First born students have significantly higher peer alienation than middle born and last born students.
48. There is significant difference between the mean scores of peer alienation - a dimension of parent-peer attachment of first generation learners with regard to type of family. Nuclear family first generation learners have exhibited significantly higher peer alienation -a dimension of parent-peer attachment than their counterparts.
49. Levels of educational aspiration and categories of self image first generation learners are not significantly related.
50. Parent-Peer attachment along with its dimensions and educational aspiration of first generation learners are significantly and positively correlate

EDUCATIONAL IMPLICATIONS

- The importance of Self image and its awareness should be given to the first generation learners, irrespective of the type of schools.
- Only those students who make their life and education self image of first generation learners achieve high position in life.
- The potentials and dreams of first generation learners are to be actualized. It is essential to give them every opportunity to excel, to dream and realize those dreams, to live full and healthy lives, enriched with stable and meaningful relationship. If the first generation learners do not grow up with proper self- image, it affects their personality causing poor academic performance. They feel lonely, unable to interact with other persons in the school, at home and in society. This may cause in extreme causes ending their life too.
- Very frequently schools criticize parents for sending children to them who are untrained and parents in turn criticize schools for not doing a good adjustment. Negative blaming is not useful in raising children.
- Cooperation between the home and the school can greatly benefit all concerned. When a partnership exits between teachers and parents and if they use similar successful methods then

children prepare for life and their academic achievement will be meritorious. Hence, the most important educational implication is that of cooperation and mutual support and encouragement between teachers and parents.

- Adjustment behaviour can be fostered among school children by ensuring unthreatening and liberal school climate in educational institutions.
- The inter-personal relationship between the teachers and the learners as well as among the learners should be warm and cordial marked by dignity and mutual concern.
- Tutorial system could be restored back in schools, particularly in higher secondary schools so that a teacher can be put in charge of 15 to 20 first generation learners. The tutorial teacher can provide the necessary personal and emotional guidance by developing intense interaction with the students under his charge, even outside the classrooms like the homes of students.
- In the classroom teaching techniques, methods involving group dynamics like discussion, seminar symposium etc. could be increasingly put into use whereby maximum students' participation in the teaching-learning process to be ensured in an unthreatening situation.
- Educational and vocational counselling sessions could be arranged periodically to minimize the anxiety of first generation students, paving the way for better adjustment in behaviour.

LIMITATIONS

The present study had the following limitations:

1. The sample is limited to 298 first generation learners.
2. The sample is taken only from Thiruvannamalai district, Tamilnadu.
3. The sample is restricted to first generation learners only.

SUGGESTIONS FOR FURTHER STUDY

A number of problems were raised in the course of discussion of the findings in the present study. Following are some of the suggestions given by the investigator for the undertaking further research.

- This study is confined to only 298 first generation learners of Thiruvannamalai district. Further studies can be conducted on other districts.
- This study can be extended by adding few more variables related to first generation learners.

- A detailed analysis can be under taken to study the effect of self-image of first generation learners to increase the levels of educational aspiration of their performance.
- This study can be extended to cover the first generation learners of lower classes and also at U.G. and P.G. levels.
- The study could also be conducted in Tribal areas also

CONCLUSION

This chapter gives an overall picture of the thesis work, which consists of the major findings, summary, suggestions for further research and educational implications of the study, which is the goal to be reached. The present study is sure to provide some insight into the field of educational research and the findings of the study can serve a database for further research.

❐

6

The Problem and its Perspectives

Trait forgiveness stems from the interpersonal nature of such traumata which often involves the harming or killing of another (Occult, Pickett, & Pope, 2005). Possession of a dispositional response style of forgiveness toward persons (including oneself) responsible for inflicting harm may act as a mechanism of healing and resilience following traumatic combat exposure.

That is, a general disposition to forgive could aide combat soldiers in breaking the negative bond which keeps them cognitively attached to the debilitating aspects of their traumatic combat experiences (e.g., intrusive thoughts of powerlessness, victimization, sadness, and anger; Orcutt et al., 2005; Snyder & Heinze, 2005). The present study operationalizes trait forgiveness within this framework seeing it as a framing mechanism in which a negative attachment to a seeming transgression can be decreased (Thompson, Snyder, et al., 2005).

Just as trait forgiveness has been operationalized in a number of ways; it has also been measured in a number of ways. The present study will use a measure of trait forgiveness designed to assess a respondent's self-appraisal of his or her general disposition to forgive.

Quality of life is more subjective and intangible. The United Nations' Universal Declaration of Human Rights, adopted in 1948, provides an excellent list of factors that can be considered in evaluating quality of life. It includes many things that citizens of the United States and other developed countries take for granted, but that are not available in a significant number of countries around the world.

- freedom from slavery and torture
- equal protection of the law
- freedom from discrimination
- freedom of movement
- freedom of residence within one's home country
- presumption of innocence unless proved guilty
- right to marry
- right to have a family
- right to be treated equally without regard to gender, race, language, religion, political beliefs, nationality, socioeconomic status and more
- right to privacy
- freedom of thought
- freedom of religion
- free choice of employment
- right to fair pay
- equal pay for equal work
- right to vote
- right to rest and leisure
- right to education
- right to human dignity

Forgive them, and you will be set free."- These were not exactly the words R. T. Kendall had hoped to hear during a painful situation when he had been terribly wronged! However, these words cut into his heart. He knew he couldn't ignore them and also be healed. When everything in you wants to hold a grudge, point a finger and remember the pain, God wants you to lay it all aside. You can avoid spiritual quicksand and experience the incredible freedom found in total forgiveness. Is total forgiveness easy? Of course not...but this book will give you a game plan...and the encouragement to cast out areas of un forgiveness that have kept you from enjoying the best God has to offer you. Learn what forgiveness is and what is is not. Uncover the physical, emotional and spiritual consequences of un forgiveness, and see why God adamantly encourages you to forgive others.

These thematic articles deal with important aspects of quality of life. However, one of the challenges of a multidimensional approach to quality of life is ultimately to produce a synthesis of the question. We attempt this here by considering 9 aspects of quality of life, for which statistics are already available: material living conditions, financial risks to which people are exposed, their health, their level of education, working conditions, involvement in public life, contacts with others, economic security and physical security (Appendix). Most of the corresponding indicators are calculated on the basis of data from the SRCV survey (Insert 2). For most of these dimensions, our analysis is in line with the "StiglitzSenFitoussi" Commission recommendations, and for most of them, their effect on quality of life is fairly intuitive. For example, level of education affect's quality of life, over and above it effecting professional careers and future in come. Social connection shave direct bearing on quality of life, as they are usually a source of satisfaction, but they also constitute are source that can be mobilized in most aspects of life. Studies on well-being also stress that uncertainty surrounding one's future economic situation has a negative effect on the quality of life of those concerned. Theoretically, risk concerns all factors that can lead to a sudden loss of income or status in the future, in other words, for working people this can be illness, mater- nifty and unemployment, or for working and retired people alike, uncertainties hanging over the pension systems. For the moment, the only measurement used here is that of the risk of finding oneself unemployed in the coming year.

Lastly, the Commission highlight ted the fact that the nature of daily activities can have a considerable effect on people's personal well-being. However, bringing together the "quality" of activities of daily life into a single indicator is difficult to achieve. To a certain extent, people's taste for activities is a personal matter which varies considers a person to another, and therefore applying a standard across the board makes little sense. On the other hand, regardless of individual likes or dislikes, the nature of activities practiced does depend on where people are in their life cycle, their family situation, and their profession- nil activity, etc. So it is difficult to find an indicator to measure the quality of personal activities which is applicable to everyone and is relevant to each individual. For the working population, measuring the "quality" of their job in terms of working conditions would seem logical, given the importance of this activity in their lives. What is more, quality of employment has been considered in previous studies and so the fruits of earlier work could be used. However, by making this choice, the quality of personal activities is then on measured for people who are in work. A possible extension in future would be to extend the measurement of this dimension to other people.

VARIABLES CHOSEN FOR THE STUDY

- Trait Forgiveness
- Quality of Life

DESCRIPTION OF VARIABLES

Trait Forgiveness

Trait Forgiveness and Personality My research has shown that forgiveness-seeking depends on the severity of the act and on the perpetrator's personality (comparing introverts and extraverts). When an offending act was severe, most summary of Findings Concerns that motivate a perpetrator to seek forgiveness include: Damaged self-worth, justice, impression management, the victim and others, the relationship, religion/God.Perpetrators followed a similar sequence of forgiveness-seeking – they first reflected and sought to gain trait forgiveness before they asked forgiveness from others, and this was true for both introverts and extraverts. However, in low and moderate guilt/severity situations, extraverts were more likely to immediately seek forgiveness from their victim (interpersonal forgiveness- seeking) while introverts were more likely to first turn inwards to try and soothe the self and forgive the self (intrapersonal forgiveness-seeking) before seeking forgiveness from others. The next step of the research is to explore the reasons why both turn inward in high severity situations, and also, whether or not both types of forgiveness-seeking are required for resolution. It may be that once extraverted perpetrators receive forgiveness from their victims, they are able to move on from the situation and do not need to seek forgiveness from themselves.

What Factors Motivate Forgiveness Seeking? Why do perpetrators ask forgiveness? There are a number of reasons that may be of importance, including avoiding punishment, atoning for earlier actions, improving the lot of the victim, and responding to moral or ethical concerns. To explore these reasons, we developed a forgiveness seeking questionnaire that asks about perpetrators' concerns that underlie the motivation for asking for forgiveness. Preliminary results have shown that there exist 6 major areas of concern for a perpetrator once he/she has transgressed: Damaged self- worth, justice, impression management, the victim and others (friends and family), the relationship with the victim, and God. In addition, preliminary results also show that a perpetrator's concerns vary depending on the severity of the situation (we have assessed low, moderate and high severity transgressions). In addition a perpetrator's concerns immediately following the transgression are often quite different than concerns in the longer term (in order to eventually move on from the situation).

How Do Perpetrators Ask for Forgiveness? We have also examined what behaviors perpetrators use in order to seek forgiveness. Results have shown the existence of four categories of forgiveness- seeking behaviors that we have termed: Approach behaviors (e.g. calling the victim), avoidance behaviors (e.g.

giving the victim some space), denying and hiding behaviors (e.g. blaming someone else), and groveling behaviors (e.g. doing whatever it takes for however long it takes). As with the concerns, preliminary results show that the forgiveness-seeking behaviors a perpetrator engages in after a transgression vary depending on the severity of the situation and the time frame (immediately following the transgression or in the longer term).

QUALITY OF LIFE

The field of quality of life outcomes in health has been developed in a relative vacuum, which can be seen as oneof its major weaknesses. The field could benefit from a consideration of the convergence of knowledge and consequent insights from such diverse research areas as adapt- nation, positive psychology, and genetics. Althoughdisparate, these areas of research have in common that they provide new insights into the changeability of qualityof life (i.e., research on adaptation and positive psychology) versus its stability (i.e., genetic research). The objective of this paper is to highlight recent advances in these areas of research insofar as they support a state (i.e., environmental) and trait (i.e., genetic) conceptualization of quality of life and to start discussing their implications for quality-of-life research in health. As a caveat, we would like to note that the choice of these distinct research areas is not intended to be comprehensive and that we cannot and do not claim to pay credit to the depth and richnessof these research fields. Our ultimate aim is to stimulate thinking and discussion about these and other implications of the state-trait conceptualization to further the field of quality-of-life outcomes in health.

Quality of experiences at school can affect students' attitudes and behaviours. Positive ideas about school, tasks during class and teachers are regarded important for students' psychological health. Positive views can develop other behaviours related to school and learning. On the other hand, having negative views regarding school can result in unsatisfactory daily experiences at school and hamper learning (Johnson and Johnson, 1993). In this context, it can be argued that quality of school life has an important place in the development of students academically and in other areas.

RELATIONSHIPS BETWEEN TRAIT FORGIVENESS AND QUALITY OF LIFE

Physically, forgiveness creates a higher quality of life, a healthier body, and a more positive attitude. Dr. Enright has scientifically proven these and other therapeutic benefits of forgiveness through his experimental studies (with Randomized Experimental and Control Groups). In every one of Dr. Enright's studies, those in the experimental group showed better emotional health (reduced anger, anxiety, depression, and/or PTSD symptoms with increased hopefulness about the future, self-esteem, and/or willingness to forgive) than those in the control group. For more information, read the text of all the journal articles related to Dr. Enright's research projects.

According to the respected health website WebMD.com, if you can bring yourself to forgive, you are likely to enjoy lower blood pressure, a stronger immune system, and a drop in the stress hormones circulating in your blood. Back pain, stomach problems, and headaches may disappear. And you'll reduce the anger, bitterness, resentment, depression, and other negative emotions that accompany the failure to forgive.While refusing to forgive may not directly cause disease, according to WebMD, the negative impact of holding on to painful memories and past wounds can weaken the immune system and make you more susceptible to illness including cancer. In fact, forgiveness therapy is now an integral part of treatment at Cancer Treatment Centers of America. Watch a video interview with Rev. Michael Barry, director of pastoral care at the Cancer Treatment Centres of America in Philadelphia. "It's important to treat emotional wounds or disorders because they really can hinder someone's reactions to the treatments — even someone's willingness to pursue treatment," said Dr. Steven Sandyford, chief of surgery at Cancer Treatment Centres of America.

Watch a short video about the amazing power forgiveness has had on one woman's life and her battle with cancer. "If I hadn't learned to forgive," Jayne Valera says, "I may not even be alive today." Watch the video here. According to Duke University, Univ. of Tennessee, and Stanford University, "Holding onto hurts, grudges, annoyances, pet peeves or old wounds hurts the body, especially when the memories are triggered by current life events." They confirmed a physiological link between negative emotional states like revengeful thinking and actions and how it produces stress on the body. They found that stress from revenge or hateful thoughts also lowers the immune system, leaving you more vulnerable to illness and asserts that, "People who are able to forgive can actually modify their heart rate, lower their blood pressure, decrease physical pain and even relieve their depression." Read the story in Psychology Today. Harvard Women's Health Watch also reported findings on how forgiveness instead of hate or holding on to grudges can benefit your mental and physical health. Read What Does Forgiveness Have to Do With Depression?

Spiritually, forgiveness affirms what our faith usually requires of us and, therefore, helps us live a quality of life of integrity. Forgiveness has a common theme across Hebrew, Confucian, Buddhist, Christian, Muslim, and Hindu writings. Many people forgive because their God asks them to do so. They forgive as an act of love toward God. They forgive because they know that it is a morally good thing to do. Socially, forgiveness reduces anger and resentment and often leads to an improvement in personal relationships with family, friends and community. Forgiveness has a way of cutting through our anger, disappointment and resentment to give everyone involved a fresh start. As you forgive, you are set free from the prison of resentment. Forgiving liberates us. Only forgiveness liberates us from a painful past to a brand-new future. At the same time, those around us benefit because we are less likely to carry our anger into other situations. We are less likely to displace our anger onto those who don't deserve such treatment.

"Forgiveness has no downside according to Dr. Peter Breggin. "A renewal of our capacity to forgive can only improve our inner quality of life and empower us in every activity we undertake. Think about Mother Teresa, Gandhi, Mandela, and Martin Luther King Jr. It is no coincidence that each of these spiritual and political leaders advocated forgiveness. Each found in forgiveness an empowering attitude toward their personal lives as well as toward their political work in the world." Peter R. Breggin, M.D. is a Harvard-trained psychiatrist and the author of more than 20 books and dozens of peer-reviewed scientific articles, many in the field of psychopharmacology. Read his insightful blog "How Forgiveness Can Change Your quality of Life" in the Jan. 2, 2013 Huffington Post. For a list of the beneficial aspects of forgiveness that other researchers have quantified, see Research Facts behind Forgiveness on quality of life.

DEFINITION OF TRAIT FORGIVENESS

Forgiveness is the overcoming of negative affect and judgment toward the offender, not by denying ourselves the right to such affect and judgment, but by endeavoring to view the offender with benevolence, compassion, and even love, while recognizing that he or she has abandoned the right to them. The important parts of this definition are as follows: a) one who forgives has suffered a deep hurt, thus showing resentment; b) the offended person has a moral right to resentment but overcomes it nonetheless; c) a new response to the other accrues, including compassion and love; d) this loving response occurs despite the realization that there is no obligation to love the offender (Subkoviak, Enright, Wu, Gassin, Freedman.

They elaborate further that forgiveness involves the affective, cognitive and behavioral systems, that is, how a person forgiving another feels, thinks and behaves toward him or her. The psychological response that is forgiveness includes the absence of negative effect, judgment, and behavior, toward the perpetrator and the presence.

Other definitions of forgiveness from a psychological perspective include aspects of the Enright definition. Gorsuch and Hao (1993) would add that a truly comprehensive definition of forgiveness would need to integrate not only the cognitive, affective and behavioral components, but also the volitional, motivational, spiritual, religious and interpersonal aspects of forgiveness. They do not specify what these additional components of forgiveness would look like and some of their categories overlap with the affective, behavioral and cognate definition.

Pingleton (1989) agrees that the spiritual dimension of forgiveness is an important component of forgiveness as well as the volitional element. Monbourquette (1992) adds that while the volitional dimension of forgiveness plays an important role, all of our faculties are mobilized in forgiving another person: compassion, heart, intellect, judgment and imagination.

Gartner (1988) contends that mature forgiveness is definitively not the replacement of negative hateful feelings with loving feelings and thus would appear to be in disagreement with the affective dimension of the Enrich definition of forgiveness. He defines mature forgiveness from an object relations perspective, as an integrated realistic view that contains both good and bad aspects of self and others. In the case of a survivor of sexual abuse, for instance, Gartner would contend that in being able to keep both the good and bad aspects of the perpetrator in view, forgiveness would allow the survivor to absorb the full evil of the abuse that was committed while not losing sight of the humanity of the perpetrator.

Canale (1990) views forgiveness as a therapeutic agent in psychotherapy and considers the cognitive dimension of forgiveness. He understands forgiveness in the context of the cognitive restructuring that complements the emotive aspects of dealing with hurt and resentment.

Studzinski (1986) defines forgiveness as a willful process in which the forgiver chooses not to retaliate but rather respond to the offender in a loving way. Walters (1984) also sees forgiveness as a voluntary process that usually requires courage and multiple acts of the will to complete. He views forgiveness as an essential process due to the destructiveness of not forgiving and asserts that to forgive is to give up all claim on the offender, including letting go of the emotional consequences of the hurt. In Walters' view, the person who has been hurt has two alternatives: to be destroyed by resentment which leads to death, or to forgive which life.

Forgiveness is further described in the psychological literature as: a powerful therapeutic intervention and as an intellectual exercise in which the patient makes a decision to forgive (Fitzgibbons, 1986); a voluntary act and a decision and choice about how one deals with the past (Hope, 1987); a letting-go of a record of wrongs and a need for vengeance and releasing associated negative feelings such as bitterness and resentment (DiBlasio, 1992); the accomplishment of mastery over a wound and the process through which an injured person first fights off, then embraces, then conquers a situation that nearly destroyed him (Flanigan, 1992).

In defining forgiveness, the psychological literature tends to focus on the benefits of forgiveness for the forgiver and the role of forgiveness in the therapeutic and healing process. Rowe, Halling, Davies, Leifer, Powers & van Bronkhorst (1989) are among the few researchers from a predominantly psychological perspective to acknowledge and emphasize, based on their research, that the experience of forgiveness is spiritual or transpersonal as well as interpersonal. In their view, because forgiveness has qualities that transcend one's relationship with the person being forgiven and opens the forgiver to herself and the world in new ways, it has more than a purely interpersonal quality. In this regard, they speak of the experience of forgiving another in terms of its qualities of gift and grace. It may be because of this aspect of grace that is inherent to forgiveness that it has been described as a bridge between psychology and theology.

DEFINITION OF QUALITY OF LIFE

The best way of approaching quality of life measurement is to measure the extent to which people's 'happiness requirements' are met - ie those requirements which are a necessary (although not sufficient) condition of anyone's happiness - those 'without which no member of the human race can be happy.'

Quality of life may be defined as subjective well-being. Recognising the subjectivity of quality of life is a key to understanding this construct. Quality of life reflects the difference, the gap, between the hopes and expectations of a person and their present experience. Human adaptation is such that life expectations are usually adjusted so as to lie within the realm of what the individual perceives to be possible. This enables people who have difficult life circumstances to maintain a reasonable quality of life.

Quality of Life is tied to perception of 'meaning'. The quest for meaning is central to the human condition, and we are brought in touch with a sense of meaning when we reflect on that which we have created, loved, believed in or left as a legacy.

There are essentially two perspectives taken in quality of life research: socialindicators research which considers the elites' valuation of what the people need, and conventional quality of life research which studies what people want, in order to improve their quality of life.

OPERATIONAL DEFINITION

Within the perspective of this study undertaken,

QUALITY OF LIFE

Quality of Life may be defined as the qualitative difference between the standard of living that a person dreams of and the standards which he has been able to attain at present.

TRAIT FORGIVENESS

Trait Forgiveness may be defined as a reaction that an individual develops towards forgiving the mistakes of others through empathy, mercy and benevolence.

NEED OF THE STUDY

Because researchers have mainly focused on forgiveness as a response to interpersonal transgressions, differences in people's disposition to forgive have gone largely unstudied (e.g., Emmons, 2000; McCullough, 2000). At the dispositional level, forgiveness is conceptualized as a ten- deny to forgive transgressions over time and across a wide variety interpersonal circumstances (Berry, Worthington, Parrott, O'Connor, &Wade,2001; Brown,2003; Emmons,2000; Mullet, Houdbine, Laumonier, & Girard, 1998). Trait forgiveness has been emphasized as a basis for re- spouses of forgiveness to specific transgressions (cf. Roberts, 1995). An important initial question in studying trait forgiveness is whether it simply reflects the Big Five personality taxonomy (John & Srivastava, 1999).Some research has begun to see delight on personality correlates of trait forgiveness, particularly the Big Five personality factors (for re- views see McCullough & Witvliet, 2002; Mullet, Neto, & Rivière, 2005). For example, Berry et al. (2001) reported that trait forgiveness is positively related to agreeableness (r = .33) and conscientiousness (r = .24). Individuals high in agreeableness tend to thrive in the interpersonal realm and experience less interpersonal conflicts. Several studies have demonstrated that highly agreeable people tend to score higher on trait forgiveness than their less agreeable counterparts (e.g., Ashton, Paunonen, Helmes, & Jackson, 1998; Brown, 2003). By contrast, trait forgiveness is negatively related to extraversion and neuroticism. For example, Walker and Gorsuch (2002) showed that trait

Forgiveness is negatively related to three facets of neuroticism, namely anxiety, emotionality, and distrust, and positively to emotional stability as the converse of neuroticism. Several studies show that emotionally stable individuals score higher on trait forgiveness (e.g., Berry et al., 2001; McCullough & Hoyt, 2002). Although related to the Big Five, forgiveness appears to be more than the mere expression of these personality traits. Research on trait forgiveness has not focused exclusively on associations with the Big Five personality factors. For instance, Ashton et al. (1998) reported that altruistic individuals show than less altruistic individuals. There is a loans association between trait gratitude and trait forgiveness (McCullough, Emmons, & Tsang, 2002). People who indicated that they tended to experience gratitude reported higher trait forgiveness. Further, people high in trait forgiveness are less ruminative than people low in trait forgiveness (Kilpatrick, &Johnson, 2001).It appears that ruminative tendencies sinter- free with people's tendency to forgive interpersonal transgressions. In addition, people high in trait forgiveness tended to report less vengeful attitudes and behaviors (Brown, 2003). Finally, people who consider the selves to be highly religious tend to value forgiveness more highly and report higher trait forgiveness than those who consider themselves less religious (McCullough & Worthington, 1999).

Research with older persons and children faces the challenge of incorporating normal developmental changes into evaluations of the quality of life. Particularly with these populations, it is necessary to distinguish age-related patterns of quality of life from quality of life patterns attributable to mental disorders (Gurland & Katz, 1997). This issue is further complicated by ambiguity in the concept of quality of life at different ages. Before gains can be made in this field, research must clarify the concept of quality of life across the life span. At present, these inquiries lack age-related, longitudinal, population-based information on quality of life issues as individual's age. A few studies have evaluated normative quality of life in older persons, but no studies are available with children. More normative data are needed to better understand quality of life constructs in children and older persons.

Several studies have examined the impact of dementia and the impact of depression on older persons' quality of life (Gurland & Katz, 1992; Gurland et al., 1997). A number of instruments have been developed to measure functional abilities of older patients with dementia; many of them consisting of interviews with an informant or behavioral observation of the patient with dementia (see Kluger & Ferris, 1991). In light of these methods, the subjective experience of the patient tends to be overlooked. Researchers who use these instruments compare quality of life with population norms, premorbid performance of the individual, or defined stages of impairment associated dementia (Gurland & Katz, 1997). There is a focus on the patient's ability to perform basic activities of daily living; however, there needs to be a greater emphasis on mobility, self-care, and home management in quality of life concerns. Gurland and Katz (1997) have developed a comprehensive framework for conceptualizing quality of life in older persons. They proposed that quality of life be considered across 19 domains, with each domain representing a challenge to adaptation and sets of responses an older person may make to meet this challenge. They suggested different grades of functioning based on the severity of impairment but have not yet developed a standardized quality of life instrument based on their framework.

To date, research on quality of life in children has been limited to illnesses thought to have psychosomatic components (e.g., allergies and asthma) and to cancer (for a review, see Ivan & Glazer, 1994; Pal, 1996). There is no well-established quality of life instrument that measures the impact of mental health problems on children's life circumstances (Schmeck & Poustka, 1997). As with older persons or individuals with severe mental illness, there exists some concern regarding children's report of life circumstance information. Children with mental disorders frequently participate in treatment at the request of their parents and may deny problems in quality of life. Moreover, children's reports may not be stable over time because of normal limitations in children's cognitive abilities and experience of time. By virtue of questions regarding the reliability and validity of youth reports, it appears necessary to clarify the life picture with the inclusion of parent and teacher reports. Given the influence of the family environment on child and adolescent functioning, an understanding of family functioning is also important in evaluating a child's quality of life (Schmeck & Poustka, 1997). These factors complicate attempts to design a simple, straightforward method of measuring quality of life in this population.

OBJECTIVES OF THE STUDY

1. To know the levels of trait forgiveness on quality of life among the higher secondary students.
2. To find out the impact of gender on trait forgiveness on quality of life among the higher secondary students.
3. To find out the impact of type of family on trait forgiveness and quality of life among the higher secondary students.
4. To find out the impact of father occupation on trait forgiveness and quality of life among the higher secondary students.
5. To find out the impact of mother occupation on trait forgiveness and quality of life among the higher secondary students.

SAMPLE

Selection of the sample in this research is convenient random sampling technique. A total of 300 students are selected from three different schools in thiruvannamalai district. The investigator selected totally 300 higher secondary students for the present investigation. 100 Student's from government school, and 100 students from government Aided school and 100 students from private school are chosen for the study. Each school has 50 boys and 50 girls.

LIMITATIONS OF THE STUDY

1. The sample is restricted to 300 Students
2. The study is restricted to higher secondary Students only.
3. The study is limited to Thiruvannamalai district.

CONCLUSION

The first chapter high lights the introduction of the problem and its statement, operational definitions of the terms, Need for the study, objectives and limitations of the study. A review of related literature design of the study, analysis and interpretations of the data and summary of the results are dealt with in the chapter that follows.

❐

7

Review of Related Literature

Jeremy regrets cheating on his girlfriend. Lisa feels guilty for eating an entire pepperoni pizza and ruining her diet. Will is disappointed with himself for playing so many video games instead of going to class. Based on this limited information, who might be the most likely to forgive themselves? Also, what factors determine those who are able to forgive themselves right away, and who needs more time? There are a number of factors that can affect whether or not self-forgiveness occurs, and research is just beginning to identify and understand them. This research aims to extend the current forgiveness literature by identifying important correlates of self-forgiveness for interpersonal and intrapersonal transgressions reviews related to quality of life.

FORGIVINGNESS, VENGEFULRUMINATION, AND AFFECTIVE TRAITS

Trait forgivingness is the disposition to forgive interpersonal transgressions over time and across situations. We define forgiveness as the replacement of negative unforgiving emotions with positive, other-oriented emotions. Rumination has been suggested as a mediator between forgivingness and emotional outcomes; however, we suggest that different content of rumination leads to different outcomes after transgressions. In four studies of 179, 233, 80, and 66 undergraduate students, trait forgivingness was negatively correlated with trait anger, hostility, neuroticism, fear, and vengeful rumination and was positively correlated with agreeableness, extraversion, and trait empathy. The disposition to ruminate vengefully mediated the relationship between trait forgivingness and (1) anger-related traits and (2) both revenge motivations and state anger following a specific recent transgression, but it did not mediate between forgivingness and (1) fearfulness and (2) avoidance motivations following a specific transgression. Self-hate statements, a proxy for depressive rumination, mediated the relationship between forgivingness and both depression and fearfulness but not the relationship between forgivingness and trait anger. Future research should distinguish the contents of mental rumination following interpersonal transgressions. Berry Jw et.al. (2005)

"TRAIT FORGIVENESS AND HELTH RELATED OUTCOMES AMONG PEOPLE WITH SPINAL CORD INJURY"

As motor vehicle accidents and violence cause the majority of spinal cord injuries (SCI) sustained in the USA and people with SCI will likely struggle with emotional issues related to the offender, the purpose of this exploratory study was to examine potential salutary effects of forgiveness among people with SCI incurred traumatically. Specifically, we hypothesized that forgiveness would have positive associations with health-related outcomes. A community-based sample of 140 adults (19-82 years of age) with SCI completed a self-report survey regarding dispositional forgiveness of self and others, health behaviour, health status, and life satisfaction. Hierarchical multiple regression analyses were employed to examine the relationships in question. After controlling for demographic variables, forgiveness of self was significantly associated with health behaviour and life satisfaction (uniquely accounting for 7% and 13% of the variance, respectively) and forgiveness of others was significantly associated with health status (uniquely accounting for 9% of the variance). Results suggest that forgiveness may play a role in the health and life satisfaction of people with traumatic SCI, with the benefit depending on the type of forgiveness offered. Webb, J. R. et.al (2011)

TRAIT EMOTIONAL INTELLIGENCE, FORGIVENESS, AND GRATITUDE IN CAPE VERDEAN AND PORTUGUESE STUDENTS

Trait emotional intelligence, forgiveness, and gratitude in Cape Verdean and Portuguese students Trait emotional intelligence, forgiveness, and gratitude are assumed to be theoretically linked with important implications for psychological and social well-being. This study examined the emotional and behavioural dispositional profile of Cape Verdeans and Portuguese by combining together for the first time trait emotional intelligence, emotional intelligence, forgiveness, and gratitude. The sample comprised 327 participants, of whom 119 were Cape Verdean and 208 were Portuguese. The results showed that trait emotional intelligence, willingness to forgive, and gratitude were higher for Cape Verdean compared to Portuguese participants. Lasting resentment was lower among the Cape Verdeans than among the Portuguese. Overall, data suggested that cultural differences might exist across the three constructs examined. Daniela C Wilks et.al (2015)

THE ROAD TO FORGIVENESS

Forgiveness has received widespread attention among psychologists from social, personality, clinical, developmental and organizational perspectives alike. Despite great progress, the forgiveness literature has witnessed few attempts at empirical integration. Toward this end, we Meta-analyse results from 175 studies and 26,006 participants to examine the correlates of interpersonal forgiveness (i.e., forgiveness of a single offender by a single victim). A tripartite forgiveness typology is proposed, encompassing victims' (a) cognitions, (b) affect, and (c) constraints following offense, with each consisting of situational and dispositional components. We tested hypotheses with respect to 22 distinct constructs, as correlates of forgiveness that have been measured across different fields within psychology. We also evaluated key sample and study characteristics including gender, age, time, and methodology as main effects and moderators. Results highlight the multifaceted nature of forgiveness. Variables with particularly notable effects include intent ($\bar{r}$ = -.49), state empathy ($\bar{r}$ = .51), apology ($\bar{r}$ = .42), and state anger ($\bar{r}$ = -.41). Consistent with previous theory, situational constructs are shown to account for greater variance in forgiveness than victim dispositions, although within-category differences are considerable. Sample and study characteristics yielded negligible effects on forgiveness, despite previous theorizing to the contrary: the effect of gender was non-significant, $\bar{r}$ = .01 and the effect of age was negligible, $\bar{r}$ = .06. Preliminary evidence suggests that methodology may exhibit some moderating effects. Scenario methodologies led to enhanced effects for cognitions; recall methodologies led to enhanced effects for affect Fehr, Michele J. et.al (2007)

EFFECTS OF A GROUP FORGIVENESS INTERVENTION ON FORGIVENESS, PERCEIVED STRESS, AND TRAIT-ANGER

The goal of this study was to evaluate the effects of a 6-week forgiveness intervention on three outcomes: (a) offense-specific forgiveness, (b) forgiveness-likelihood in new situations, and (c) health-related psychosocial variables, such as perceived stress and trait-anger. Participants were 259 adults who had experienced a hurtful interpersonal transgression from which they still felt negative consequences. They were randomized to a forgiveness-training program or a no-treatment control group. The intervention reduced negative thoughts and feelings about the target transgression 2 to 3 times more effectively than the control condition, and it produced significantly greater increases in positive thoughts and feelings toward the transgressor. Significant treatment effects were also found for forgiveness self-efficacy, forgiveness generalized to new situations, perceived stress, and trait-anger. S. Harris et.al (2006)

FORGIVINGNESS, VENGEFUL RUMINATION, AND AFFECTIVE TRAITS

Trait forgivingness is the disposition to forgive interpersonal transgressions over time and across situations. We define forgive- ness as the replacement of negative unforgiving emotions with positive, other-oriented emotions. Rumination has been suggested as a mediator between forgivingness and emotional outcomes; however, we suggest that different content of rumination leads to different outcomes after transgressions. In four studies of 179, 233, 80, and 66 undergraduate students, trait forgivingness was negatively correlated with trait anger, hostility, neuroticism, fear, and vengeful rumination and was positively correlated with agreeableness, extraversion, and trait empathy. The disposition to ruminate vengefully mediated the relationship between trait forgivingness and (1) anger-related traits and (2) both revenge motivations and state anger following a specific recent transgression, but it did not mediate be- tween forgivingness and (1) fearfulness and (2) avoidance motivations following a specific transgression. Self-hate statements, a proxy for de- pressive rumination, mediated the relationship between forgivingness and both depression and fearfulness but not the relationship between forgivingness and trait anger. Future research should distinguish the contents of mental rumination following interpersonal transgressions Jack W. Berry (2005)

FORGIVENESS FOR INTIMATE PARTNER VIOLENCE:

We examined victim and offender correlates of forgiveness for intimate partner violence. Participants were from couples (133 women, 76 men) in which males were convicted of intimate partner violence and court-ordered into an intervention program. In women, empathy and general religiousness positively related to forgiveness, but attributions of blame were unrelated to forgiveness. Several dispositional variables in men were associated with forgiveness in women. Men who were more dominant were more likely to be forgiven, but men with more psychological problems were less likely to be forgiven. Many offender effects were mediated by women's state empathy. Joann Tsang, Ph.D et.al (2007)

TESTING UNDERLYING MECHANISMS OF FORGIVENESS: NEED FOR CLOSURE AND ACCESSIBILITY

Although the ability to forgive transgressions has been linked to overall relationship satisfaction, the mechanisms that mediate this association have not been established. We propose that the tendency to forgive a romantic partner increases relationship satisfaction via increased relational effort and decreased negative conflict. In two studies, we used structural equations modeling to examine these variables as potential mechanisms that drive this association. In Study 1 (N = 523) and Study 2 (N = 446) we found that these variables significantly mediated the association between forgiveness and relationship satisfaction. The findings were robust when examined concurrently and longitudinally, across multiple measures of forgiveness, and when accounting for baseline relationship satisfaction and interpersonal commitment. These two mechanisms parallel theorized positive and negative dimensions of forgiveness and the motivational transformation that is said to underlie forgiveness. Theoretical implications and implications for intervention are discussed. Mary Kate Law Parker, et.al (2008)

VALIDATION OF FORGIVENESS SCALE AND A SURVEY ON THE RELATIONSHIP OF FORGIVENESS AND STUDENTS' MENTAL HEALTH

The present study aims to establish the validity of Forgiveness Scale and the relationship between forgiveness and mental health among college students of Islamic Azad University. The research sample consisted of validity evaluation phase sample (with 300 subjects: 150 females and 150 males) and hypothesis testing sample (with 300 subjects: 150 females and 150 males). All the subjects were selected via stratified random sampling from among the students studying in Ahwaz University. The data collecting tools were Forgiveness Scale (Forgiveness Scale; Rye and et al, 2001), Heartland Forgiveness Scale (HFS; to evaluate concurrent validity of Forgiveness Scale) and General Health Questionnaire (GHQ28). The Forgiveness Scale reliability coefficients were obtained by Cronbach coefficient Alpha method (0/92). It has also been found that Forgiveness Scale, significantly associated with Heartland Forgiveness Scale (at p-value<0/0001) with correlation coefficient of (0/84) as concurrent validity. The results proved acceptable high validity and reliability for Forgiveness Scale. Moreover, there was a significant correlation between forgiveness and mental health. Khadijeh Roshaniet.al (2007)

AN EXAMINATION OF THE PROCESS OF FORGIVENESS AND THE RELATIONSHIP AMONG STATE FORGIVENESS, SELF-COMPASSION, AND PSYCHOLOGICAL WELL-BEING EXPERIENCED BY BUDDHISTS IN THE UNITED STATES

The purpose of this study was to investigate the process of forgiveness and the relationship among state forgiveness, self-compassion, and psychological well-being experienced by Buddhists in the United States. An integral feminist framework was developed for this mixed-method study.

For the quantitative component of this study, a convenience sample of 112 adults completed an online survey. Multiple regression analysis was performed to examine: (a) the impact of gender, age, and the years spent in Buddhist practice on state forgiveness and self-compassion; (b) the outcome of psychological well-being in relation to state forgiveness and self-compassion; and (c) self-compassion as a mediator for the relationship between state forgiveness and psychological well-being. Quantitative results indicated: (a) state forgiveness positively predicted psychological well-being; (b) the years spent in Buddhist practice positively predicted self-compassion; (c) self- compassion positively predicted psychological well-being; and (d) self-compassion partially mediated the relationship between state forgiveness and psychological well- being. Age did not predict any of the three primary variables. Gender did not predict state forgiveness. being. Qualitative findings also suggested the following. First, two-way compassion toward self and the offender was a facilitating factor for forgiveness that may be unique to Buddhists. Second, one's actual experience of forgiveness may encompass not only cognitive, affective, and behavioral changes, but also transformation of self and perspective on meaning and purpose in life. Third, Enright and his colleagues' (1998) stage and process models of forgiveness were useful to understand Buddhists' experiences and processes of forgiveness. Lexington, Kentuckyet.al (2011)

PERSONALITY AND INDIVIDUAL DIFFERENCES

Conflict pervades social life. To forgive others, people must control their vengeful impulses. The efficiency by which the body uses glucose, an indicator of self-control, might have direct implications for interpersonal forgiveness. In four studies ($N = 693$), we tested the hypothesis that a physiological marker of deficient glucose use (i.e., type 2 diabetic symptoms) relates to less forgiveness. Higher type 2 diabetic symptoms correlated negatively with a dispositional tendency to forgive others (Study 1) and correlated positively with unforgiving motivations toward hypothetical transgressors (Study 2) and actual transgressors (Study 3). Diabetic symptoms correlated negatively with cooperative behavior in the Prisoner's Dilemma Game (Study 4). These findings provide the first evidence that forgiveness depends on how efficiently the body uses glucose. Daune macgregor et.al (2009).

FACT OF LIFE FOR SOCIAL ORGANISMS, AND NATURAL SELECTION

Exploitation is a fact of life for social organisms, and natural selection gives rise to revenge mechanisms that are designed to deter such exploitations. However, humans may also possess cognitive forgiveness mechanisms designed to promote the restoration of valuable social relationships following exploitation. In the current article, the authors test the hypothesis that decisions about forgiveness result from a computational system that combines information about relationship value and exploitation risk to produce decisions about whom to forgive following interpersonal offenses. The authors examined the independent and interactive effects of relationship value and exploitation risk across two studies. In Study 1, controlling for other constructs related to forgiveness, the authors assessed relationship value and exploitation risk. In Study 2, participants experienced experimental manipulations of relationship value and exploitation risk. Across studies, using hypothetical and actual offenses and varied forgiveness measures, the combination of low exploitation risk and high relationship value predicted the greatest forgiveness. Mastroeni S, et.al (2010).

FORGIVENESS RESULTS FROM INTEGRATING INFORMATION ABOUT RELATIONSHIP VALUE AND EXPLOITATION RISK

Forgiveness is proposed to be an important pathway through which the effects of religion on health are mediated. Three separate studies were conducted to examine this hypothesis. In Study 1, older adults (n = 605) completed measures of forgiveness, religiosity, and health. Feeling forgiven by God fully mediated associations between frequency of attendance, frequency of prayer, and belief in a watchful God with successful aging. Self-forgiveness and forgiveness of others partially mediated the religion–health relationships. In Study 2, 253 older adults completed measures of trait forgiveness, religiosity, and health. Trait forgiveness fully mediated associations between prayer and intrinsic religiosity with illness symptoms and 5 dimensions of successful aging. In Study 3, 80 middle-aged men and women completed state and trait forgiveness measures, as well as religiosity and health measures. State forgiveness fully mediated the relationships between existential well-being and both symptoms and medications, and trait forgiveness fully mediated the relationship between religious well-being and both intrinsic religiosity and quality of sleep. State forgiveness partially mediated the relationships between spirituality and both sleep and depression. Within adults, unselected with regard to religious affiliations or beliefs, a variety of religious variables, health outcomes, and forgiveness measures were interrelated. In the majority of cases, forgiveness either partially or fully mediated the religion–health relationships Jeni l. Burnette et.al (2012).

STUDIES IN RELATED WITH QUALITY OF LIFE QUALITY OF LIFE INDEX: DEVELOPMENT AND PSYCHOMETRIC PROPERTIES.

The purpose of the study on which this article is based was to assess the validity and reliability of an instrument designed to measure quality of life. Sixty-four items applicable to both healthy subjects and dialysis patients were tested with graduate students (n = 88); six items relative to dialysis were added, and the instrument was administered to dialysis patients (n = 37). Items were based on literature review, which supported content validity. Correlations between the instrument and an overall satisfaction with life question of 0.75 (graduate students) and 0.65 (dialysis patients) supported criterion-related validity. Support for reliability was provided by test-retest correlations of 0.87 (graduate students) and 0.81 (dialysis patients) and Cornbrash's alphas of 0.93 (graduate students) and 0.90 (dialysis patients). Marjorie j. R et.al (2014)

FACTORS AFFECTING STUDENTS' QUALITY OF LIFE: A CASE SECONDARY SCHOOL LEVEL

This study was conducted to examine different factors influencing the academic performance of secondary school students in a metropolitan city of Pakistan. The respondents for this study were 10th grade students (300 male & 300 female). A survey was conducted by using a questionnaire for information gathering about different factors relating to academic performance of students. The academic Performance was gauged by the result of their 9th grade annual examination. Standard t-test and ANOVA were applied to investigate the effect of different factors on students' achievement. The results of the study revealed that socio- economic status (SES) and parents' education have a significant effect on students' overall academic achievement as well as achievement in the subjects of Mathematics and English. The high and average socio-economic level affects the performance more than the lower level. It is very interesting that parents' education means more than their occupation in relation to their children's academic performance at school. It was found that girls perform better than the male students M.S. Farooq et.al (2011)

THE EFFECT OF QUALITY OF LIFE PROGRAMS ON QUALITY OF LIFE AMONG EMPLOYEES AT MULTINATIONAL COMPANIES IN MALAYSIA

In this study, the researchers examined the relationship between quality of work life programs and quality of life among employees at multinational companies in Banjul, Sarawak, Malaysia. In addition, the study examined the element s of quality of work life programs as a contributing factor to quality of life that can influence employee productivity. The participants consisted of 179 employees currently working at multinational companies in Bint lulu, Sarawak. The respondents were randomly selected and the data were gathered through the distribution of questionnaires.

Descriptive statistics showed that there were more female than male employees, mostly were fairly young, around 29 years old and below and majority of them hold position as general employee in the multinational companies. The study found that there was significant relationship between quality of work life programs and quality of life the most influence factor on quality of life were work environment followed by job facet s. The result also indicated that there was a positive and significant relationship bet weensy quality of work life programs and quality of life. The most influence factors were emotional wellbeing personal development, social inclusion and interpersonal relations. Therefore, the researcher highly recommend those multinational companies to plan an excellent quality of work life programs by focusing g on particular service element s that will further enhance the overall quality of life of employees.

As a conclusion, the researchers found that quality of work life programs influence quality of life of employees in organization. The researchers provided recommendations for future research to be implemented using different population, qualitative research, using other element s of programs and quality of life as well as in different sectors such as hotel industry. T. S. Nanjundeswaraswamy., et.al. (2012)

EFFECTS OF HIGH SCHOOL STUDENTS' PERCEPTIONS OF SCHOOL LIFE QUALITY ON THEIR ACADEMIC MOTIVATION LEVELS

This study aims to identify the effects of high school students' perceptions of school life quality on their academic motivation levels. The study was conducted on a sample of high school students (n=2371) in Amaya Province in the fall semester of 2013-2014 academic year. Study sample was selected with the help of cluster sampling method. Data were collected via personal information form developed by researchers, Academic Motivation Scale developed by Bozanoglu and Quality of School Life Scale developed by Sari. *Multiple Regression Analysis* was used in data analysis to determine high school students' perceptions regarding quality of school life on their academic motivation levels. According to research findings, all the variables of quality of school life predicted academic motivation and its subscales (exploration, self-actualization and using data). The most powerful quality of school life perception variables was found to be negative effects towards school and teachers and the least effective variable was social activity. Meltem akin kostereliogl u et.al. (2015).

CHARACTERISTICS OF PERSONAL NETWORKS ASSOCIATED WITH PHYSICAL AND PSYCHOLOGICAL QUALITY OF LIFE AMONG DEMOBILIZED INDIVIDUALS FROM THE COLOMBIAN ARMED CONFLICT

The study identifies relationships between the characteristics of personal networks of demobilized individuals and their quality of life, through the evaluation of a sample of 102 ex-combatants from a demilitarized zone in Colombia's Caribbean coast. The data was processed using centrality values calculation and statistical analysis through the Pearson correlation coefficient. Results showed moderate levels of modality, proximity and intermediation degrees regarding small, closed networks with an unsatisfied high demand for support resources. Quality of life showed medium performance levels, with inverse relationships between *mental health* ($p = .009 < .05$) and *vitality* ($p = .011 < .05$) and intermediation. *Positive feedback* related significantly to *general health* ($p = .041 < .05$), while negative interactions showed inverse relationships to *physical* functioning ($p = .012 < .05$), *physical role* ($p = .005$), *mental health* ($p = .001 < .05$), and *emotional role* ($p = .009 < .05$). In conclusion, among the highly cohesive personal networks, there were less observations of social support that fosters increased energy and psychological health, given that access to this support is limited to a small number of members of the personal network. Amar-Amar José Juan et.al (2013)

QUALITY OF LIFE, SELF-EFFICACY AND PSYCHOLOGICAL WELL-BEING IN BRAZILIAN ADULTS WITH CANCER: A LONGITUDINAL STUDY

Quality of life has been considered worthy of assessment in the treatment, prevention and rehabilitation of cancer patients. As it has a psychological dimension, is important to investigate the relationship between quality of life and psychological concepts like self-efficacy and psychological well-being. Objective of the present study is to examine the quality of life, self-efficacy and psychological well-being in adults with cancer. Methods: 50 patients completed self-report questionnaires: quality of life -bref, General Self- Efficacy Scale and GHQ-12 in two periods (T1 = timeline; T2 = follow up 1 year later). A paired t-test did not identify significant differences in the quality of life self-efficacy and psychological well-being between T1 and T2. However, men had a better overall quality of life and in the physical and social dimensions, and psycho- logical well-being in T1 compared with the women. In T2 there were significant differences between men and women only in the social and psychological dimensions of the quality of life. The self-efficacy in T2 was the only predictive variable of the quality of life in T2, explaining 71.9% of its variance. It is concluded that, in the period of one year, the quality of life, psychological well-being and self-efficacy were stable, but gender differences were identified. The variables measured in T1 were incapable of predicting the quality of life in T2. The gender differences found in quality of life and psychological well-being can be used to guide specific future interventions with these patients. Madariaga-Orozco Camilo et.al (2012)

CHILDHOOD CANCER SURVIVORS AND SIBLINGS REPORT POSITIVE PSYCHOLOGICAL HEALTH, GOOD HRQOL, AND LIFE SATISFACTION

Purpose: Psychological outcomes, health-related quality of life and life satisfaction are compared between 7,147 adult childhood cancer survivors and 388 siblings from the Childhood Cancer Survivor Study, examining demographic and diagnosis/treatment outcome predictors.

Methods: Psychological distress, quality of life, and life satisfaction were measured by the Brief Symptom Inventory-18, the Medical Outcomes Survey Short Form-36, and Cantril Ladder of Life, respectively. A self-report questionnaire provided demographic/health information and medical record abstraction provided cancer/treatment data. Siblings' and survivors' scores were compared using generalized linear mixed models, and predictor effects of demographic and cancer/treatment variables were analyzed by multivariate logistic regression.

Results: Although survivors report greater symptoms of global distress (mean, 49.17; SE, 0.12) than do siblings (mean, 46.64; SE, 0.51), scores remain below population norms, indicating that survivors and siblings remain psychologically healthy. Survivors scored worse than siblings on overall physical (51.30 ± 0.10 versus 54.98 ± 0.44; $P< 0.001$) but not emotional aspects of quality of life, but effect sizes were small, other than in vitality. Most survivors reported present (mean, 7.3; SD, 0.02) and predicted future (mean, 8.6; SD, 0.02) life satisfaction. Risk factors for psychological distress and poor quality of life were female gender, lower educational attainment, unmarried status, annual household income <$20,000, unemployment, lack of medical insurance, having a major medical condition, and treatment with cranial radiation.

Conclusion: Compared with population norms, childhood cancer survivors and siblings report positive psychological health, good HRQOL, and life satisfaction. The findings identify targeted subgroups of survivors for intervention. Los Angeles's Jonsson et.al (2007)

EFFECTS OF YOGA ON PSYCHOLOGICAL HEALTH, QUALITY OF LIFE, AND PHYSICAL HEALTH OF PATIENTS WITH CANCER: A META-ANALYSIS.

Yoga is one of the most widely used complementary and alternative medicine therapies to manage illness. This meta-analysis aimed to determine the effects of yoga on psychological health, quality of life, and physical health of patients with cancer. Studies were identified through a systematic search of seven electronic databases and were selected if they used a randomized controlled trial design to examine the effects of yoga in patients with cancer. The quality of each article was rated by two of the authors using the PEDro Scale. Ten articles were selected; their PEDro scores ranged from 4 to 7. The yoga groups compared to waitlist control groups or supportive therapy groups showed significantly greater improvements in psychological health: anxiety (P=.009), depression (P = .002), distress (P = .003), and stress (P = .006). However, due to the mixed and slow to fair quality and small number of studies conducted, the findings are preliminary and limited and should be confirmed through higher-quality, randomized controlled trials. Tsauo jy.et.al (2011)

SHORT-TERM EXERCISE APPROACHES ON MENOPAUSAL SYMPTOMS, PSYCHOLOGICAL HEALTH, AND QUALITY OF LIFE IN POSTMENOPAUSAL WOMEN

This study was designed to determine the effects of different short-term exercise programs on menopausal symptoms, psychological health, and quality of life in postmenopausal women. Material and Methods. Forty-two women were chosen from volunteering postmenopausal women presenting to the Department of Obstetrics and Genecology of Babyminder Hospital between March and December 2009. The women aged 45–60 years and experiencing menopause naturally were included in the study. They were randomly divided into aerobic and resistance exercise groups. The women exercised 3 days per week for 8 weeks under the supervision of a physiotherapist. Aerobic exercise training was performed through a bicycle ergometer. Before and after the training, lipid profiles were measured and menopausal symptoms, psychological health, depression, and the quality of life were assessed through questionnaires. In both exercise groups, no significant changes in lipid profiles were observed. In the resistance exercise group, excluding the urogenital complaints, there were significant improvements in all subscales of Menopausal Rating Scale (MRS). In the resistance exercise group, excluding the phobic anxiety, there were significant improvements in all subscales of The Symptom Checklist. Depression levels significantly decreased in both groups. Improvements were observed in all subscales of menopause-specific quality of life questionnaire in both groups except for sexual symptoms. Resistance exercise and aerobic exercise were found to have a positive impact on menopausal symptoms, psychological health, depression, and quality of life. Handan Tüzün et.al (2010)

LATE EMERGENCE OF COGNITIVE DEFICITS AFTER UNILATERAL NEONATAL STROKE

Using age-appropriate Wechsler scales of intellectual ability, this longitudinal study examined 26 children with a history of acutely diagnosed unilateral neonatal AIS as pre-schoolers (3 years 6 months to 5 years 11 months) and again as grade-school students (6 years 1 month to 12 years 5 months), and contrasted performance with the normative sample of the test.

As pre-schoolers, patients' performance did not differ from the normative sample for Full Scale IQ, Verbal IQ, or Performance IQ, and there were no significant differences associated with infarct laterality. As school-age children, performance was significantly lower than the normative sample for Full Scale IQ Working Memory and Processing Speed, but not for Verbal IQ or Performance IQ. Contrasts between Time 1 and Time 2 revealed a significant decline in Full Scale IQ, which reflected emerging deficits in nonverbal reasoning, working memory, and processing speed. Individual subject analyses revealed that 69% of the children showed significant declines in 1 or more IQ index measures. We found no significant differences in cognitive performance associated with lesion laterality, though males performed more poorly than females on several cognitive measures at Time 2.

These findings suggest that children with unilateral neonatal stroke, particularly males, are at increased risk for emerging deficits in higher-level cognitive skills during the school years. Continued follow-up of these children is needed, even those with no apparent deficits as toddlers or pre-schoolers. Rand Askalan, et.al (2007)

STRESS AND QUALITY OF LIFE OF SENIOR BRAZILIAN POLICE OFFICERS

This study examines levels of occupational stress, quality of life, work-related stressors, and coping strategies among senior police officers in Brazil. A quantitative questionnaire survey conducted among 418 senior members of the São Paulo Police Force reveals that high-ranking Brazilian police officers perceive their profession as being very stressful. A large proportion (43%) of police officers is found to have significant stress symptoms. A greater proportion of females (54%) than males (40%) are found to have stress. The most frequently reported stressor is interaction with other departments within the police force. Quality of life is found to be deficient in the 'professional' and 'health' areas. This study is the first to show a clear association between high levels of emotional stress and poor quality of life in Brazilian police officers. The large number of stress symptoms and poor quality of life identified in the present study indicates that there is a need for preventive actions inside the Brazilian police force to motivate lifestyle changes, improve stress-management skills, and promote a better quality of life among high-ranking police officers. Marilda.E et.al (2009)

PSYCHOSOCIAL FACTORS, QUALITY OF LIFE, AND PSYCHOLOGICAL DISTRESS: ETHNIC DIFFERENCES IN PATIENTS WITH HEART FAILURE

Advances in treatment have prolonged life in heart failure (HF) patients, leading to increased attention to quality of life quality of life and psychological functioning. It is not clear if ethnic differences exist in factors associated with psychological well-being. We examined psychosocial factors associated with depression and anxiety in 97 HF patients. Medical records were reviewed and patients (*M* age 53, 50% African American) completed surveys examining social support, coping, spirituality, and quality of life for their association with depression and anxiety. Multiple regressions suggested that psychosocial factors were associated with psychological health. Patients with lower social support, lower meaning/peace and more negative coping reported greater depression; positive coping, and lower meaning/peace were associated with higher anxiety. Ethnicity stratified models suggested that spiritual well-being was associated with depression only among African Americans and quality of life partially mediated this relationship. Findings suggest the importance of considering the unique psychosocial needs of diverse populations to appropriately target clinical interventions. Melanie k. Bean Ph.D. et.al (2010)

QUALITY OF LIFE IMPAIRMENT AND PSYCHOLOGICAL DISTRESS IN ELDERLY PATIENTS WITH PSORIASIS

The management of psoriasis, which has a major impact on quality of life, deserves a specific attention to elderly patients' problems and needs. Our aim was to describe the quality of life of elderly patients with psoriasis. This is a cross-sectional study on 305 psoriatic inpatients, aged > or = 65 years. Quality of life, measured by the Skindex-29, was compared in groups of patients based on clinical and socio demographic characteristics, and the possible determinants of psychological distress were investigated. The mean age of the patients was 71 years (range: 65-93). Clinical severity tended to increase with age. Psychological distress was higher in patients > 70 years of age, while quality of life showed an improvement for all the Skindex-29 scales in older age groups. Gender (women vs. men), and Skindex-29 emotions and functioning scales emerged as associated with psychological distress, after adjusting for age and clinical severity. These observations indicate that clinical severity of psoriasis increases among very elderly patients and is associated with different levels of skin-related quality of life and psychological distress. It is important for dermatologists to be aware of the specific impact of psoriasis in the different subgroups of the elderly population, to meet the peculiar needs of each group. S. Karger ag, basel et.al (2007)

PSYCHOLOGICAL PROFILES AND QUALITY OF LIFE DIFFER BETWEEN PATIENTS WITH DYSSYNERGIA AND THOSE WITH SLOW TRANSIT CONSTIPATION

Path physiological characteristics differ between slow transit constipation (STC) and dyssynergic defecation, but whether psychological profiles and quality of life are altered and whether they differ among these constipation subtypes are unknown. We prospectively evaluated psychological profiles and quality of life in 76 patients with dyssynergia, 38 patients with STC, and 44 control subjects using the revised 90-item Symptom Checklist and 36-item Short-Form Health Survey. In addition, we examined the correlations of psychological and quality of life domains with constipation symptoms and path physiological subtype Symptom scores for hostility and paranoid ideation were higher ($P<.001$) in patients with dyssynergic defecation than in patients with STC and control subjects. Scores for other psychological domains were higher ($P<.0001$) in patients with dyssynergic defecation and those with STC than in control subjects. Most quality of life subs cores were impaired ($P<.05$) in patients with dyssynergic defecation and some were impaired in patients with STC as compared with control subjects, but the two patient groups did not differ on these. The quality of life subs cores were strongly correlated ($rc \approx .9$) with the psychological subs cores in patients with dyssynergic defecation and those with STC, although more quality of life subs cores among patients with dyssynergic defecation and more psychological subs cores among patients with STC primarily contributed to the canonical correlations. A set of six commonly reported constipation symptoms showed significant correlations with quality of life and psychological subs cores, more so among patients with STC than among patients with dyssynergic defecation.

Patients with dyssynergic defecation had greater psychological distress and impaired health-related quality of life as compared with patients with STC and control subjects. Both patient groups were also more affected as compared with the control group. There was a strong correlation between psychological dysfunction and impaired quality of life, and both also correlated with constipation symptoms. Mastroeni S, et.al (2007)

PSYCHOLOGICAL QUALITY OF LIFE AND EMPLOYABILITY SKILLS AMONG NEWLY REGISTERED FIRST-YEAR STUDENTS: OPPORTUNITIES FOR FURTHER UNIVERSITY DEVELOPMENT

In accord with new European university reforms initiated by the Bologna Process, our objective was to evaluate influences on the relationship between psychological quality of life and the acquisition of academic employability skills among first-year students at the University in Luxembourg. At the beginning (2 months in) and the end (9 months) of the academic year, 973 newly registered students participated in this study involving two cross-university surveys. Students who redoubled or who had studied at other universities were excluded. Data were collected with an online questionnaire comprising the psychological Whoqol-bref subscale, AES scale, and questions about other related factors. The AES score decreased from 74.2 to65.6. At both time points, the psychological Whoqol-bref was positively correlated with environmental and social relations quality of life and perceived general health. Multiple regression models including interaction terms showed that a higher psychological quality of life was associated with better general health (difference satisfied-dissatisfied 9.44), AES (slope 0.099), social relationships quality of life (0.321), and environmental quality of life (0.298). No interaction with time effects was significant, which indicates that the effects remain stable with time. If the university could maintain the quality of life indicators at appropriate levels or manage decreases as they occur, it would have implications for health promotion and the creation of new student support systems. The SQA- LES project provides valuable information for universities aiming to develop a European Higher Educational Area. Kara Seaton et.al(2007)

OUR PURPOSE WAS TO DETERMINE THE FREQUENCY OF PSYCHIATRIC MORBIDITY AND TO ASSESS THE QUALITY OF LIFE OF WOMEN

Our purpose was to determine the frequency of psychiatric morbidity and to assess the quality of life of women with advanced breast cancer.

The 227 women in the sample were recruited in Melbourne, Australia, and were interviewed (prior to intervention) for a randomized controlled trial of supportive-expressive group therapy. The main outcome measures were DSM–IV psychiatric diagnoses plus quality of life data based on the EORTC quality of life-C30 (core) and quality of life -BR23 (breast module) instruments.

Forty-two present of the women (97/227) had a psychiatric disorder; 35.7% (81) of these had depression or anxiety or both. Specific diagnoses were minor depression in 58 women (25.6%), major depression in 16 (7%), anxiety disorder in 14 (6.2%), and phobic disorder in 9 (4%). Seventeen (7.5%) women had more than one disorder. In terms of quality of life, one-third felt less attractive, one-quarter were dissatisfied with their body image, and, in most, sexual interest had waned. Menopausal symptoms such as hot flashes affected less than one-third, whereas symptoms of lymphedema were experienced by 26 (11.5%).

*Significance:*Women with advanced breast cancer have high rates of psychiatric and psychological disturbance. Quality of life is substantially affected. Clinicians need to be vigilant in monitoring psychological adjustment as part of a comprehensive biopsychosocial approach. Senad Karavdic, et.al(2006)

CONCLUSION

Review of related literature consists of searching, identifying and evaluating report of relevant researchers. Its effort to get one self-familiarize with all that has been done in a particular area of researcher, which are valuable in formulating and studying the problem. Based on this review, a suitable methodology and well planned procedure for the present study is adopted and it will be explained in the next chapter.

❐

8

Research Design and Methodology

This chapter contains the detailed analysis of the proposed research procedure including the design of the study, description of the scoring, procedures and tools utilized for the study. The population sample for the study, collection of data, and the statistical treatment employed for data analysis.

DESIGN OF THE STUDY

Choosing a design for a study basically involves selecting the most appropriate techniques to solve the particular problem under investigation (Anderson, Durston and Poole (1970)).

Dehip between variables, the testing of hypothesis and the development of generalization principles or theories that have universal validity, it is concerned with functional relationship (Best, John, W., 1963).

OBJECTIVES OF THE STUDY

1. To know the levels of trait forgiveness and quality of life among the higher secondary students.
2. To find out the impact of gender on trait forgiveness and quality of life among the higher secondary students.

3. To find out the impact of father occupation on trait forgiveness and quality of life among the higher secondary students.
4. To find out the impact of mother occupation on trait forgiveness and quality of life among the higher secondary students.
5. To know the impact of type of family on trait forgiveness and quality of life among the higher secondary students.

HYPOTHESES OF THE STUDY

The following hypotheses are formulated for the present research.

1. There are no significant differences between trait forgiveness of boys and girls from the total sample
2. There are no significant differences between quality of life of boys and girls from the total sample.
3. There are no significant relationship between trait forgiveness and quality of life of boys and girls from the government school sample
4. There are no significance association between trait forgiveness and type of family from the total sample
5. There is no significant association between trait forgiveness and father occupation from the total sample
6. There is no significant association between trait forgiveness and mother occupation from the total sample
7. There are no significant association between quality of life and type of family the total sample
8. There are no significant Association between quality of life and father occupation from the total sample
9. There is no significant Association between quality of life and mother occupation from the total sample

METHODOLOGY

The investigator used the Survey Method in this research

VARIABLES OF THE STUDY

The present investigation includes the following variables.

(a) Research variables
- Trait Forgiveness-dependent Variable
- Quality of life-inDependent Variable

(b) Personal Variables
- Gender
- Type of Family
- Father's occupation

- Mother's occupation

(c) Institution Related Variables

- Type of School

POPULATION AND SELECTION OF THE SAMPLE

The Higher Secondary school Students constitute the population of the present study. In the study a sample of 300 Students were selected randomly from in and around the city of Thiruvannamalai District. The sample includes Government, Government Aided and Private Higher Secondary Schools. Stratified Random Sampling Technique was used for collecting of the Data.

The details of the sample from various schools are given in the following table.

TABLE. 8.1: Distribution of Sample in Terms of Educational Institutions

Type of Management	Name of the School	Boys	Girls	Total
Government	Government Higher Secondary School, Kunnagampoondi.	50	50	100
Government Aided	C.S.I Higher Secondary School, Arani.	50	50	100
Private	Vengateshwara Matriculation Higher Secondary School, Vandavasi.	50	50	100
Total		**150**	**150**	**300**

TOOLS IN THE STUDY

To test the hypotheses formulated, the following tools have been used in the present study Trait forgiveness: Berry, J. W., Worthington, E. L., O'Connor, L. E., Parrott, L., & Wade, N. G. (2005). It Consists of 5 Statements. It has only Positive Statements. And 5 negative Statements.Trait forgiveness. Trait forgiveness was measured with the Trait Forgiveness Scale (Berry et al., 2005). This scale is comprised of 10 items measuring an individual's general disposition for forgiveness. Items include, "I can usually forgive and forget an insult" and "I am a forgiving person," and were answered on a 7-point Liker-type scale ranging from 1 (strongly disagree) to 7 (strongly agree ; $\alpha = .80$). Higher scores reflect higher levels of trait forgiveness. Trait Forgiveness Scale (TFS). The Trait Forgiveness Scale (Berry, et al., 2005) measures an individual's overall tendency to forgive. It consists of ten 5-point Likert-scaled statements with answers ranging from strongly disagree to strongly agree. Statements which test takers are asked to rate include items such as, "I can forgive a friend for almost anything" and "I feel bitter about many of my relationships." The score is calculated by reverse coding five items and then adding the ratings together; a higher score means the test taker has higher levels of trait forgiveness

RELIABILITY TESTS RESULTED

In alpha coefficients of between .74 and .80. Convergent validity measures, obtained by correlating the TFS with another valid forgiveness measure (the Transgression Narrative Test of Forgiveness), resulted in a statistically significant correlation (Berry, et al., 2005).

To start with the following instructions have been given to the Higher Secondary school Students. The purpose of Trait forgiveness questionnaire is to measure the level of forgiveness.

SCORING

The scoring procedure for the tool for Trait Forgiveness is given in the table below:

TABLE. 8.2: Trait Forgiveness Inventory-Description and Scoring

Nature of Items	Score						
	TC	CLE	PC	U	PW	WLE	TW
Positive Statements 2,4,5,9,10	7	6	5	4	3	2	1
Negative 1,3,6,7,8	1	2	3	4	5	6	7

ADMINISTRATION

Name of Questionnaire

Quality of Life Scale by Burckhardt C.S& Anderson K.L(,2003)

Description

Self-administered questionnaire designed for use in patients with chronic illiness.

Cost & availability

None

Administration

Self-administered

Time to complete

5 minutes

Number of items

16

Scaling of items

7-point Likert-type scale ranging from "delighted" (7) to "terrible" (1)

Scoring

Total scale score (possible range: 16 - 112)

Reliability

test- retest reported5

internal consistency reported5

The Reliability Of Quality Of Life () Was Calculated Though Odd-Even Method And It Was Noted As (Normal Children- 0.837;For Slow Learners- 0.861) And The Validity's Calculated Through Square Root Of Reliability Method As (For Normal Children- 0.914;For Slow Learners- 0.28

VALIDITY

Flanagan's original 16-item scale was derived from 6500 critical incidents reported in interviews with 3200 American adults of all ages and health status 6. Burckhardt added one item (independence) after interviewing 204 people with chronic illnesses (diabetes, ostomy, osteoarthritis, rheumatoid arthritis) 5People with stogies (stable illness) score higher than those with diabetes (unstable illness); strong correlation between QOLS and another measure of quality of life (the Life Satisfaction Inventory); low to moderate correlations with measures of health status (subscales of the Duke-UNC Health Profile and the Arthritis Impact Measurement Scales). Higher correlations are between psychological and emotional subscales and the QOLS, and mood is known to influence quality of life perceptions.

SCORING

The scoring procedure for the tool for Quality of life is given in the table below:

TABLE. 8.3

Nature of Items	Score						
	T C	C L E	P C	U	P W	W L E	T W
Positive Statements 1,2,3,4,5,6,7,8,9,10,11,12, 13,14,15,16,	7	6	5	4	3	2	1

PILOT STUDY

A pilot study was conducted in the month of November 2014 to determine the suitability of the tools used in the present investigation. A random sample of 50 higher secondary students were selected to the study for establish the reliability and validity of the tools.

STATISTICAL TECHNIQUES USED

The suitable descriptive and inferential statistical techniques are used in the interpretation of the data to draw out a meaningful picture of results from the collected data. In the present study the following statistical measures are used.

I. Mean

$$\text{Mean } (\bar{X}) = A + \frac{\sum fd}{\sum d} \times i$$

Where, A = Assumed Mean

f = Frequency

d = Deviation from the assumed mean

i = Class interval

II. Standard Deviation

$$\text{Standard Deviation, } (\sigma) = \sqrt{\frac{\sum fd^2}{N} - \left[\frac{\sum fd^2}{N}\right]} \times i$$

Where, f = Frequency

d = Deviation from the assumed mean

i = Class interval

n = Total frequency.

III. Standard Error Deviation

$$\text{Standard Error Deviation, SED} = \sqrt{\frac{\sigma_1^2}{N_1} + \frac{\sigma_2^2}{N_2}}$$

Where, σ_1, σ_2 = Standard Deviations

N_1, N_2 = Total number of sample

IV. 't' Test

To compute the significance of difference between means of various measures,'t' test is used, 'f' ratio is calculated from the relation.

t. ratio = Equation

Where, M, M = Means of the groups.

SED = Standard error deviation

V. F-Test

F ratio = variance between the group / variance within the group

Correction term c = $\frac{\sum x_1 \sum x_2 + \sum x_3}{N}$

TSS = $x_2 - c$

BSS = $(\Sigma x_1)^2 / W_1 + (\Sigma x_2)^2 / W_2 + (\Sigma x^3)^2 / W_3$ - c

Where x_1, x_2, x_3 are score in different group

C = correction Terms

TSS = total sum of squares

BSS = sum of squares between groups

WSS = with in groups

VI. Co-efficient of Correlation (R)

Co-efficient of Correlation (R) = $\frac{N\sum x \sum y - \sum x \sum y}{\sqrt{\left(N\sum x^2 - \left(\sum x^2\right)\left(N\sum y^2 - \left(\sum y\right)^2\right)\right)}}$

XY - Variables,

N - Total strength

CONCLUSION

This chapter outlines the design of the present study, the procedure followed and the nature of the sample. It also describes hypotheses to be tested, the tools to be used and the methods of administration and scoring. Statistical techniques and delimitations have also been discussed. The analysis and interpretation of the data will be dealt with elaborately in the next chapter.

❒

9

Analysis and Interpretation of the Data

"Research data become meaningful in the process of being analyzed and interpreted regardless of how well the study is conducted an appropriate analysis can lead to inappropriate conclusions"- Mouly(1964).

Data analysis is a practice in which raw data is ordered and organized so that useful information can be extracted from it. The process of organizing and thinking about data is a key to understanding what the data does and does not contain. There are varieties of ways in which people can approach data analysis, and it is notoriously easy to manipulate data during the analysis phase to push certain conclusion.

Data Collection is the systematic recording of information, data analysis invoices working to uncover patterns and trends in data sets; data interpretation involves explaining these patterns and trends.

This chapter highlights the testing of the hypotheses already framed in this investigation, using appropriate statistical treatment and derivations of certain important results of this study.

HYPOTHESIS

Hypothesis-1

There is are significant differences between trait forgiveness of boys and girls from the total sample

TABLE. 9.1 Differentiation of Trait Forgiveness Scores of Boys and Girls from Government School

Variable	Gender	N	Mean	S.D	C.R	L.S
Trait Forgiveness	Boys	50	53.26	9.957	3.198	0.01
	Girls	50	47.08	9.361		

From the table 9.1 and from the figure A it clearly understood that the critical ratio values are significantly greater than that the table critical ratio values. Hence Hypothesis is rejected and proved that there are significant differences between trait forgiveness scale of boys and girls from the government secondary school.

TABL. 9.2: Differentiation of Trait Forgiveness Scores of Boys and Girls from Aided school

Variable	Gender	N	Mean	S.D	C.R	L.S
Trait Forgovemess	Boys	50	51.52	7.902	1.256	N.S
	Girls	50	49.28	9.818		

From the table 9.2 and from the figure B it is clearly understood that the calculated critical ratio values are not significantly less than that the table critical ratio values in the case of boys and girls from aided school sample. Hence hypothesis is accepted and proved that there are no significant differences between trait forgiveness of boys and girls from the aided secondary school.

From the table 9.3 and from the figure C it is clearly understood that the calculated critical ratio values are significantly less than that the table critical ratio values in the case of boys and girls from the private school sample. Hence the hypothesis is accepted and proved that there are no significant differences between trait forgiveness scale of boys and girls from the private secondary school.

HYPOTHESIS-2

There are no significant differences between quality of life of boys and girls from the total sample.

TABLE. 9.4: Differentiation of Quality of Life Scores of Boys and Girls from Government School

Variable	Gender	N	Mean	S.D	C.R	L.S
Quality of life	Boys	50	97.10	5.500	2.023	0.01
	Girls	50	93.48	7.684		

From the table 9.4 and from the figure D it is clearly understood that the calculated critical ratio values are significantly greater than that the table critical ratio values in the case of boys and girls from the government school sample. Hence hypothesis is rejected and proved there are significant difference between quality of life of boys and girls from the government secondary school

TABLE. 9.5: Differentiation of Quality of Life of Boys and Girls from Aided School.

Variable	Gender	N	MEAN	S.D	C.R	L.S
Quality of life	Boys	50	89.32	12.36		
	Girls	50	83.56	10.43	2.518	0.05

From the table 9.5 and from the figure E it is clearly understood that the calculated critical ratio values are significantly greater than that the table critical ratio values in the case of boys and girls from the aided school sample. Hence hypothesis is rejected and proved that there are significant differences between quality of life of boys and girls from the aided school.

TABLE. 9.6: Differentiation of Quality of Life Scores of Boys and Girls from Private School

Variable	Gender	N	Mean	S.D	C.R	L.S
Quality of life	Boys	50	97.96	10.52	3.783	0.01
	Girls	50	89.36	12.16		

From the table 9.6 and from the figure E it is clearly understood that the calculated critical ratio values are significantly greater than that the table critical ratio values in the case of boys and girls from the private school sample Hence hypothesis is rejected and proved that there are significant differences between quality of life of boys and girls from the private school

HYPOTHESIS-3

There are no significant relationship between trait forgiveness and quality of life of boys and girls from the government school sample

TABLE. 9.7: Relationship of Trait Forgiveness with Quality of Life of Boys and Girls from Government School

Variable	Gender	N	Coefficients	't' TEST	L.S
Trait Forgivenss with Quality of life	Boys	50	0.079	2.413	0.5
	Girls	50	0.025	1.733	N.S

Form the table 9.7 and from the figure F it is clearly understood that thecalculated correlation coefficient is more than the table values Hence hypothesis is rejected and proved that there are significant relationship between trait forgiveness and quality of life of boys in the cases of government school.

In the cases of girls of government school the calculated coefficient was less than that table of correlation coefficient values. Hence the hypothesis is accepted and proved there are no significant of relationship between trait forgiveness and quality of life of the sample.

TABLE. 9.8: Relationship of Trait Forgiveness with Quality of Life Scores of Boys and Girls form Aided School

Variable	Gender	N	Coefficients	't' TEST	L.S
Trait Forgivenss with Quality of life	Boys	50	0.187	1.319	N.S
	Girls	50	0.031	0.214	

From the table 9.8 and from the figure G it is clearly understood that thecalculated coefficients correlation values are not significantly laser than that the table values in the case of boys and girls from the aided school sample. Hence hypothesis is accepted and proved that there is no significant relationship between trait forgiveness and quality of life boys and girls from the aided secondary school.

TABLE. 9.9: Relationship of Trait Forgiveness with Quality of Life Scores of Boys and Girls form Private School

Variable	Gender	N	Coefficients	't' TEST	L.S
Trait Forgivenss with Quality of life	boys	50	0.833	10.435	0.01
	Girls	50	0.639	5.540	

From the table 9.9 and from the figure H it is clearly understood that the Correlation Coefficients values is more than Hence hypothesis is rejected and proved that there is significant relationship between trait forgiveness and quality of life in the cases of boys and girls the private higher secondary school.

HYPOTHESIS-4

There are no significance association between trait forgiveness and type of family from the total sample

TABLE. 9.10: Chi-Square between Trait Forgiveness and Type of Family of Boys and Girls form Secondary School.

Variable	Type of Management	Gender	N	D,F	X^2	L.S
Trait forgiveness and Type of Family	Government	Boys	50	2	1.11	N.S
		Girls	50	2	2	N.S
	Aided	Boys	50	2	7.026	N.S
		Girls	50	2	4.4003	N.S
	Private	Boys	50	2	4.255	N.S
		Girls	50	2	2	N.S

From the table 9.10 it is understood that the chi square values are not more than that of table values. Hence the hypothesis is accepted and proved that the are no significant association between type of family and trait forgiveness of boys and girls from the total sample.

HYPOTHESIS-5

TABLE. 9.11: Chi-Square Trait Forgiveness and Father Occupation of Boys and Girls from Secondary School;

Variable	Type of Management	Gender	N	D,F	X^2	L.S
Trait forgiveness and father occupation	Government	Boys	50	4	4.0604	N.S
		Girls	50	4	7.8919	N.S
	Aided	Boys	50	4	3.1478	N.S
		Girls	50	4	4.0192	N.S
	Private	Boys	50	4	3.582	N.S
		Girls	50	4	7.5976	N.S

There is no significant association between trait forgiveness and father occupation from the total sample

From the table 9.11 it is understood that the calculated chi square values are not more than that of table values. Hence the hypothesis is accepted and proved that there is no significant association between father occupation and trait forgiveness of boys and girls from the total sample.

HYPOTHESIS-6

There is no significant association between trait forgiveness and mother occupation from the total sample

TABLE. 9.12: Chi-Square Test between Trait Forgiveness and Mother Occupation Scores of Boys and Girls form Secondary School

Variable	Types of Management	Gender	N	D,F	X^2	L.S
Trait Forgiveness and Mother Occupation	Government	Boys	50	8	2.3042	N.S
		Girls	50	8	3.4096	N.S
	Aided	Boys	50	8	3.3103	N.S
		Girls	50	8	9.8411	0.5
	Private	Boys	50	8	3.4965	N.S
		Girls	50	8	15.6195	0.01

From the table 9.12 it is understood that calculated chi square values are not more than that of table values. Hence the hypothesis is accepted and proved that there are no significant association between mother occupation and trait forgiveness in boys and girls of government, aided and private school.

In the case of girls of aided school and private school the hypothesis is rejected and proved that there is significant association between trait forgiveness and mother occupation since calculated chi-square values are more than that of table chi-square values.

HYPOTHESIS-7

There are no significant association between quality of life and type of family the total sample

TABLE. 9.13: Chi-Square Quality of Life and Type of Family Scores of Boys and Girls form Secondary School

Variable	Type of Management	Gender	N	D,F	X^2	L.S
Quality of life and types of family	Government	Boys	50	2	4.539	N.S
		Girls	50	2	1.2697	N.S
	Aided	Boys	50	2	0.8903	N.S
		Girls	50	2	2.2181	N.S
	Private	Boys	50	2	0.644	N.S
		Girls	50	2	1.9921	N.S

From the table 9.13 it is understood that the chi square values are not more than that of table values. Hence the hypothesis is accepted and proved that there are no significant association between type of family and quality of life of boys and girls from the total sample.

HYPOTHESIS-8

There are no significant Association between quality of life and father occupation from the total sample

TABLE. 9.14: Chi-Square Test between Quality of Life and Father Occupation Scores of Boys and Girls form Secondary School

Variable	Type of Management	Gender	N	D,F	X^2	L.S
Quality of life and Father Occupation	Government	**Boys**	**50**	**4**	**2.3538**	N.S
		Girls	50	4	5.5401	N.S
	Aided	Boys	50	4	3.2909	N.S
		Girls	50	4	0.3484	N.S
	Private	Boys	50	4	3.3907	N.S
		Girls	50	4	4.6874	N.S

Hypothesis is accepted and proved that there are no significant relationship between father occupation and quality of life of boys and girls from the total sample.

HYPOTHESIS-9

There is no significant Association between quality of life and mother occupation from the total sample

TABLE. 9.15: Chi-Square Test between Quality of Life Mother Occupation Scores of Boys and Girls from Secondary School

Variable	Type of Management	Gender	N	D,F	X^2	L.S
Quality of life and mother Occupation	Government	Boys	50	8	8.0472	N.S
		Girls	50	8	7.3822	N.S
	Aided	Boys	50	8	8.2651	N.S
		Girls	50	8	1.9557	N.S
	Private	Boys	50	8	10.7065	0.05
		Girls	50	8	5.3924	N.S

From the table 9.15 it is understood that the calculated chi square values are not more than that of table values. Hence the hypothesis is accepted and proved that there is no significant association between mother occupation and quality of life in boys and girls of government aided and private school.

In the case of boys of private school the hypothesis is rejected and proved that there is significant association between quality of life and mother occupation. Hence calculated chi square values are more than of table chi square values.

CONCLUSION

This chapter summarizes the analysis of data, testing of hypotheses description and inference of the tables. A brief report of the research study together with the major findings and conclusion along with their educational implications has been presented in the succeeding chapter.

❒

10

Summary and Conclusion

According to Rummel J.Francis (2005), "Research is an endeavor to discover, develops and verifies knowledge. It is an intellectual process that has developed over hundreds of year sever-changing in purpose and form and always scarcity for truth. This chapter deals with major findings, educational implications, recommendations and conclusion. It has also become customary to conclude the research report with a very brief summary, restation in brief the research problem, the methodology, the major findings and the influences drawn from the results of research.

STATEMENT OF THE PROBLEM

The problem is stated as follows: "Trait Forgiveness on Quality of Life among Higher Secondary Students"

HYPOTHESES OF THE STUDY

1. **There is are significant differences between trait forgiveness of boys and girls from the total sample**
   - Hypothesis is rejected and proved that there are significant differences between trait forgiveness scale of boys and girls from the government secondary school.
   - Hypothesis is accepted and proved that there are no significant differences between trait forgiveness of boys and girls from the aided secondary school.

- Hypothesis is accepted and proved that there are no significant differences between trait forgiveness scale of boys and girls from the private secondary school.

2. **There are no significant differences between quality of life of boys and girls from the total sample.**
    - Hypothesis is rejected and proved there are significant differences between quality of life of boys and girls from the government secondary school.
    - Hypothesis is rejected and proved that there are significant differences between quality of life of boys and girls from the aided school.
    - Hypothesis is rejected and proved that there are significant differences between quality of life of boys and girls from the private school.
3. **There are no significant relationship between trait forgiveness and quality of life of boys and girls from the government school sample.**
    - Hypothesis is rejected and proved that there are significant relationship between trait forgiveness and quality of life of boys in the cases of government school.
    - Hypothesis is accepted and proved there are no significant of relationship between trait forgiveness and quality of life of the sample.
    - Hypothesis is accepted and proved that there is no significant relationship between trait forgiveness and quality of life boys and girls from the aided secondary school.
    - Hypothesis is rejected and proved that there is significant relationship between trait forgiveness and quality of life in the cases of boys and girls the private higher secondary school.
4. **There are no significance association between trait forgiveness and type of family from the total sample**
    - Hypothesis is accepted and proved that there are no significant association between type of family and trait forgiveness of boys and girls from the total sample.
5. **There is no significant association between trait forgiveness and father occupation from the total sample**
    - Hypothesis is accepted and proved that there is no significant association between father occupation and trait forgiveness of boys and girls from the total sample.
6. **There is no significant association between trait forgiveness and mother occupation from the total sample**

- Hypothesis is accepted and proved that there are no significant association between mother occupation and trait forgiveness in boys and girls of government, aided and private school.
- Hypothesis is rejected and proved that there is significant association between trait forgiveness and mother occupation since calculated chi-square values are more than that of table chi-square values.

7. **There are no significant association between quality of life and type of family the total sample**
   - Hypothesis is accepted and proved that there are no significant association between type of family and quality of life of boys and girls from the total sample.
8. **There are no significant Association between quality of life and father occupation from the total sample**
   - Hypothesis is accepted and proved that there are no significant relationship between father occupation and quality of life of boys and girls from the total sample.
9. **There is no significant Association between quality of life and mother occupation from the total sample**
   - Hypothesis is accepted and proved that there is no significant association between mother occupation and quality of life in boys and girls of government aided and private school.
   - Hypothesis is rejected and proved that there is significant association between quality of life and mother occupation. Hence calculated chi square values are more than of table chi square values.

EDUCATION IMPLICATIONS

Following an interpersonal wrongdoing, one possible option for the victim is to forgive the offender. Some scholars believe that the ability to forgive is natural and innate. That is, people are born with the capacity to forgive, which may vary depending on cultural and individual life experiences. Although forgiveness has long been part of human existence, there still remains some debate over the exact definition of forgiveness. Nonetheless, in the last 15 years there has been a surge of research which has examined predictors of situational and trait forgiveness. We have learned that victims' willingness to forgive depends, in part, on factors related to the offense, the relationship between the offender and the victim, as well as reactions and dispositions of the victim. Even though forgiveness is granted by the victim, the offender can also take meaningful steps to potentially foster forgiveness, such as by offering an apology. Forgiveness may have consequences beyond interpersonal processes, as indicated by its potential impact on physical and mental health. In general, forgiveness tends to have positive connotations, but evidence suggests that forgiveness may not always be associated with positive outcomes. Though forgiveness has mostly been studied in everyday interpersonal contexts, it is also relevant to criminal justice domains, as indicated by an emerging area of scholarship.

Forgiveness is relevant outside of everyday interpersonal contexts, and has spread to domains such as criminal justice. Following an injustice, such as a criminal offense, victims may seek retributive justice, which typically focuses on punishing the offender. Some victims, however, desire a restorative justice route, which has been found to foster forgiveness towards Offenders. Restorative justice is a victim-cantered approach, and aims to repair the emotional and material harms of the crime to the victim and the broader community. In restorative justice programs, victims can meet with offenders and mediators to engage in dialogue, negotiation, and problem solving. In many cases, offenders apologize and offer some form of restitution for their criminal acts. These programs often lead to more healing, more satisfaction with the process, and more victim forgiveness than traditional justice outcomes. Both victims and offenders may benefit from this alternative system. Although forgiveness is relevant to restorative justice, requiring or encouraging forgiveness in this setting may be problematic and perhaps inappropriate in some cases (e.g., if the offender did not apologize, or may re-offend), and promoting unconditional forgiveness may even lead to re-victimization. Considerable care needs to be taken to respect victims' feelings and restorative justice goals. Therefore, forgiveness is typically not an explicit goal of restorative justice; however, it is clear that the nature of restorative justice programs can indirectly lead to forgiveness. Research on forgiveness in restorative justice and other legal domains is still in its beginning stages, and determining the fit of forgiveness in various applied justice settings is a direction of future research.

Historically, education has been a means by which individuals improved their prospects for a more productive and personally satisfying life. Our society, investing in education, has reaped the benefits of meaning flu progress in all aspects of our nation's development. Led by the report of the National Commission on Excellence in Education, public debate about education took on a new urgency in 1983. Today, people are seeking new ways to improve the quality of education and thereby improve the quality of life. In this light there is growing public recognition that early childhood education programs can help students to be more successful throughout their school careers than would be possible without early education. The evidence generated by longitudinal research on the effectiveness of early childhood education programs of high quality strongly supports decisions by policymakers to use public funds to expand such programs. In particular, research concerning the key importance of early child- hood education to, learning and success in life for low-income children began a few years before the advent of the national Head Start program, in a series of specially designed and controlled research projects. Later, evil- nation studies were funded to study the impact of the national Head Start program. These two streams of work came to Fruition recently with re- mark able evidence of long-term effectiveness (Lazar, Darlington, Murray, Royce, & Snipper, 1982; Hubbell, 1983). The basic finding is that early childhood education of high quality can improve the lives of low-income children and their families; most important from the public viewpoint, it has payoffs for society as well in that it can enhance the quality of life for the community as a whole.

SUGGESTION FOR FURTHER RESEARCH

The suggestions for further research are:

1. This study was concentrated only on higher secondary students. Similar study could be extended to college level.
2. The present study was limited to few in Tiruvannamalai district could be extended to schools of other districts in Tamil Nadu state.
3. A comparative study on trait forgiveness on quality of life and of the Higher Secondary Students.
4. This type of study may be done by including more variables like trait forgiveness on quality of life etc.

CONCLUSION

This chapter gives an overall picture of the thesis work which consists of the exact Findings, Summaries, and Suggestions for Further research and Educational implications of study which is the goal and ultimate aim to be reached.

❒

11

The Problem and its Perspectives

Education is usually understood as a course of study to acquire a body of knowledge or skills undertaken to enhance one's ability to do a particular job and be able to earn more money. The more liberal definitions of education, where it is understood as development and refinement of one's personality, without necessarily an eye to economic advantage, have been out of use for long and one finds only scattered instance of the practice of education with such aims.

Education plays an important role in molding the personality of children Social adjustment is one of the important aims of education. In order to equip the child with necessary skills and information, concepts and attitudes and to enable him to adjust properly in his environment, our society has formulated a separate organization called school where he can develop all qualities and abilities, according to the social needs of the society.

Family Encouragement

Members of strong families feel they really belong in their family. Family members feel accepted for what they are and promote one another's self-esteem. They celebrate each other's successes and help each other learn from mistakes.

Strong families spend time together, but also give their members privacy. For example, family members encourage one another to become involved in individual hobbies, extracurricular activities, and relationships outside the family. Activities outside the family help foster the development of skills and maturity needed to be self-sufficient.

All family members are given the opportunity to develop their own identity as a unique and separate person. There are many ways to foster encouragement at home:

Discovering Talents Consider holding a family right to help family members discover their gifts or talents. Help them understand that a major purpose for talents is to benefit others, as well as for our own enjoyment. On a sheet of paper, have family members list things they feel they are good at children frequently list obvious talents such as music or athletics. Help them be aware that skills such as listening and being compassionate are also talents that should be celebrated and that can be developed. Look for these hidden talents in your children and point them out.

Encourage family members to develop their talents. Have them select a talent they would like to work on during a specified period of time. Provide opportunities for all to share their talents inside and outside the home.

Definition of Family Encouragement

"Strength Bombardment" During a family right, take turns sharing with each other the positive traits that make each family member special. Focusing on assets and strengths helps build feelings of self- and family worth.

Encouraging Words, Sometimes life gets rough and we need all the encouragement we can get. An encouraging word from a family member can really come in handy.

Types of Family

The diverse data coming from ethnography, history, law and social statistics, establish that the human family is an institution and not a biological fact found on the natural relationship of consanguinity. The different types of families occur in a wide variety of settings, and their specific functions and meanings depend largely on their relationship to other social institutions.

Although the concept of consanguinity originally referred to relations by "blood," cultural anthropologists have argued that one must understand the idea of «blood» metaphorically and that many societies understand family through other concepts rather than through genetic distance. Sociologists have a special interest in the function and status of these forms in stratified (especially capitalist) societies.

According to the work of scholars Max Weber, Alan Macfarlane, Steven Ozment, Jack Goody and Peter Laslett, the huge transformation that led to modern marriage in Western democracies was "fueled by the religion cultural value system provided by elements of Judaism, early Christianity, Roman Catholic canon law and the Protestant Reformation" Much sociological, historical and anthropological research dedicates itself to the understanding of this variation, and of changes in the family that form over time. «Times have changed; it is more acceptable and encouraged for mothers to work and fathers to spend more time at home with the children. The way roles are balanced between the parents will help children grow and learn valuable life lessons. There is great importance of communication and equality in families, in order to avoid role strain."

Conjugal (Nuclear) Family

The term "nuclear family" is commonly used especially in the United States, to refer to conjugal families. A "conjugal" family includes only the husband, the wife, and unmarried children who are not of age. Sociologists distinguish between conjugal families (relatively independent of the kindred of the parents and of other families in general) and nuclear families (which maintain relatively close ties with their kindred). However, in the 21st century, the "nuclear family", according to the 2010 Census, is "disappearing at a rapid rate are homes with "traditional" nuclear families Mom, Dad and two children."The nuclear family is being replaced by other family structures such as blended parents, single parents, and domestic partnerships.

Matrifocal Family

A "Matrifocal" family consists of a mother and her children. Generally, these children are her biological offspring, although adoption of children is a practice in nearly every society. This kind of family is common where women have the resources to rear their children by themselves, or where men are more mobile than women.

Extended Family

The term "extended family" is also common, especially in United States. This term has two distinct meanings. First, it serves as a synonym of "consanguine family" (consanguine means "of the same blood"). Second, in societies dominated by the conjugal family, it refers to "kindred" (an egocentric network of relatives that extends beyond the domestic group) who do not belong to the conjugal family. These types refer to ideal or normative structures found in particular societies. Any society will exhibit some underwear variation in the actual composition and conception of families.

Assertiveness

Assertiveness is a skill regularly referred to in social and communication skills training. Often wrongly confused with aggression, assertive individuals aim to be neither passive nor aggressive in their interactions with other people.

Although everyone acts in passive and aggressive ways from time to time, such ways of responding often result from a lack of

Self-confidence and, therefore, are inappropriate expressions of what such people really need to say.

Non-assertiveness may be seen as the use of inefficient communication skills, whereas assertiveness is considered a balanced response, being neither passive nor aggressive. This page examines the rights and responsibilities of assertive behavior and aims to show how assertiveness can benefit you.

Definition of Assertiveness

A disadvantage with this technique is that when resistance continues, your requests may lose power every time you have to repeat them. If the requests are repeated too often, it can backfire on the authority of your words. In these cases, it is necessary to have some sanctions on hand.

Fogging

Fogging consists of finding some limited truth to agree with in what an antagonist is saying. More specifically, one can agree in part or agree in principle.

Negative Inquiry

Negative inquiry consists of requesting further, more specific criticism.

Negative Assertion

Negative assertion is agreement with criticism without letting up demand.

Characteristics of Assertiveness

It is include expressing your feelings, needs, ideas, and rights in ways that don't violate the rights of others.

Assertive behavior is usually honest, direct, expressive, spontaneous, and self-enhancing.

- Use feeling-talk
- Talk about yourself
- Make greeting-talk.
- Accept compliments.
- Use appropriate facial talk
- Disagree mildly

- Ask for clarification.
- Ask why
- Express active disagreement

Benefits of Assertiveness

Some people are naturally more assertive than others. If your disposition tends more towards being either passive or aggressive, you need to work on the following skills to develop your assertiveness.

1. **Value Yourself and Your Rights**
    - Understand that your rights, thoughts, feelings, needs and desires are just as important as everyone else's.
    - But remember they are not more important than anyone else's, either.
    - Recognize your rights and protect them.
    - Believe you deserve to be treated with respect and dignity at all times.
    - Stop apologizing for everything.
2. **Identify your needs and wants, and ask for them to be satisfied**
    - Don't wait for someone to recognize what you need (you might wait forever!)
    - Understand that to perform to your full potential, your needs must be met.
    - Find ways to get your needs met without sacrificing others' needs in the process.
3. **Acknowledge that people are responsible for their own behavior**
    - Don't make the mistake of accepting responsibility for the how people react to your assertive statements (e.g. anger, resentment). You can only control yourself.
    - As long as you are not violating someone else's needs, then you have the right to say or do what you want.
4. **Express negative thoughts and feelings in a healthy and positive manner**
    - Allow yourself to be angry, but always be respectful.
    - Do say what's on your mind, but do it in a way that protects the other person's feelings.
    - Control your emotions.
    - Stand up for yourself and confront people who challenge your rights.

5. **Receive criticism and compliments positively**
    - Accept compliments graciously.
    - Allow yourself to make mistakes and ask for help.
    - Accept feedback positively be prepared to say you don't agree but do not get defensive or angry.
6. **Learn to say "No" when you need to. This is the granddaddy of assertiveness!**
    - Know your limits and what will cause you to feel taken advantage of.
    - Know that you can't do everything or please everyone and learn to be OK with that.
    - Go with what is right for you.
    - Suggest an alternative for a win-win solution.

Three types of Assertiveness

1. **Contextual Assertiveness**
   Many times it is important for you to let other people know what effects their behavior is having on your life. There are four parts to Contextual Assertiveness. While they may be expressed in any objective sequence, saying them in the order shown can help you remain objective while you're delivering your message.
2. **Empathic Assertiveness**
   This conveys your sensitivity and recognition of another person's feelings, wants and viewpoints, followed by a statement in which you state your requests, feelings andviewpoints. Assertion with empathy is often effective in caring relationships, because the listener is more likely to accept your assertion when he feels you have some understanding and respect for him. It is especially valuable in situations when you tend to overreact in an aggressive way. If you take a moment to try to understand the other person's viewpoint before you react, you are less likely to respond aggressively. On the other hand, your expression of empathy must be sincere in order to be effective. People can usually spot insincere expressions of empathy and resent such attempts to manipulate
3. **Escalating Assertiveness**
   Frequently a simple statement of assertion made in a friendly manner will be effective. On the other hand, you'll sometimes have to deal with people who persist in violating your rights or ignoring your stated preferences. In such cases, you can state your position with increasing

firmness without becoming aggressive. You may move from a request to a demand, from a preference to an outright refusal, or from a Empathic Assertion to a firm Basic Assertion.

Statement of the Problem

The present study entitled as "Family encouragement and assertiveness among the high school students in Erode district".

The Operational Definitions

Familyencouragement: According to "Aggarwal (1986) the family can increase children's academic success through involvement improves student moral, attitudes and academic achievement across all subject areas. According to shartarned, A.M (1997) U.S, Department of education research findings, children's success in reading comprehension is directly related to the availability of reading material in the home.

Assertiveness: In the study, assertiveness refers to the total score obtained by each subject based on the application of the simple assertiveness schedule.

Need for the study

Research has long documented a strong relationship between family background factors, such as income and parents educational levels, and student achievement. Studies have also shown that parents can play an important role in supporting their children's academic achievement. This paper examines findings from research about the impact of various family backgrounds and cultural factors on student motivation, as well as the role of parental beliefs, attitudes, and actions in fostering children's motivation. The paper does not attempt to be a comprehensive review of thc broad literature on family background and achievement, but rather is a sampling of some current findings from the field that appear to impinge on motivation.

Objectives of the Study

The following are the objectives of the present study.

1. To find out the level of family encouragement of high school students.
2. To find out the level of assertiveness of high school students.
3. To find out whether there is any significant difference between the mean scores of family encouragement of high school students with regard to:

Gender	:	(Male/Female)
Type of management	:	(Government/ Government Aided/Private)
Type of Family	:	(Joint/Nuclear)
Locality	:	(Rural/Urban)
Medium of instruction	:	(Tamil/English)

4. To find out whether there is any significant difference between the mean scores of assertiveness of high school students with regard to:
   Gender : (Male/Female)
   Type of management : (Government/ Government Aided/Private)
   Type of Family : (Joint/Nuclear)
   Locality : (Rural/Urban)
   Medium of instruction : (Tamil/English)
5. To find out whether there is any significant association between family encouragement and assertiveness of high school students.

Limitations of the Study

The present study has the following limitations.

1. The sample is restricted to 300 students.
2. Students from high schools alone considered for the study.
3. The study is conducted in limited schools of Erode District, Tamilnadu.
4. Only seven schools in Erode District have been selected for this study.

CONCLUSION

The first chapter highlights the introduction to the problem and its statement, the operational definitions of the terms, need for the study, objectives and limitations of the study, A review of related literature ,design if the study, analysis and interpretation of the data and summary of the results are dealt within the chapters that follow.

❐

12

Review of Related Literature

"The key to the vast store house of published literature may open door to sources at significant problem and explanatory hypothesis, and provide helpful orientation for definition of the problem background for selection of procedure and comparative data for interpretation of result. In order to be truly creative and original, one must read extensively and critically as a stimulus of thinking", ***Good (1989).***

Research takes advantage of the knowledge which has accumulated in the post as a result of constant human endeavour.It can never be undertaken in isolation of the work that has already been done on the problems which are defectively or interactively related to a study proposed by a researcher, a careful review of the research journals book, dissertations, theses and other sources of information's on the problem to be investigated is one of the important steps in the planning of any research study .A review of the related literature must precede any well planned research study.

The study of the related literature implies, locating, reading and evaluating reports of research as well as of casual observations and opinions that are related to the individuals planned research project.

Studies Related to Family Encouragement

Epstein (1992), Henderson (1987) and Liontos (1992) suggested some benefits of family encouragement for family and community.

- The National PTA (1972) describes the following type of family involvement:
- Family as the first educator in the home.
- Family as family with the school.
- Family as advocates for all children and youth in society.
- Head start (U.S Department of health and human services 1992) describes four primary avenues for family participation.
- Family can join in decision making about what kind of program to have to be operative.
- Family can be involved in classroom as paid employees, volunteers and observers.
- Family can participate in adult and family oriented activities which they have planned.
- The Arizona Department of education also distinguishes four categories of family involvement.
- Home school communication.
- Family as learners.
- Family as teachers.
- Family as advisors ***(Chris peels 1987).***

Hess R.D and Holloway S.D (2011) concluded that achievement for students depends upon the consensus between family and educators about the goals of education, the degree to which these goals are taken seriously and the ability of family and educators working together to counter knowledge. Values and goals that come from competing sources such as television and peer get diffuse and contradictory messages eroded the effectiveness of family or school efforts.

Hansen, D.A (1990) reported that achievement increases for elementary students of for who was not match between home and school. He examined the extent to which the interplay of family interactions, rules and classroom interaction and rules influence children's success in elementary schools. Basically he studies how things are and done in families compared to classrooms he found that children's grade 3-5 for those students for which there was continuity but declined for students experiencing discontinuity.

Fince M,Whelage G.G and RatterR.S (1999) have shown that school programme that have established a positive teacher student relationship particularly one that supports the students and helps the student feel connected have been successful in reducing the probability of dropping out.

Johnson D.W, Johnson R.T (2001), Maruyama G,Nelson D, and Sixon L (2000) have shown that students regardless of age ability subject areas leaving task have been found to achieve more in co-operative, rather than competitive or individualistic learning structures.

Additionally Slavin R.E (1987) has proved that students achieve more they help each other during independent seat work level of students socio status has an impact on what type of teacher student relationship and learning environment is best for the student, student of lower SES id better in school when there is more structure and control than do student of high this study was conducted by Connell, J.P.Halpern, Felsher BL, Clifford E, Usinger P (1988).

Henderson AT (1987) studied on successful family programme it showed us that effective family involvement programs are built on the following assumption. The primary educational environment comes from the family. Family involvement in a child's education is a major factor in improving school effectiveness the quality of education and a child's academic success. The benefits of family involvement are not confined to preschool or elementary school but extend on to high school. Low income and minority children have the most to again when schools involve family.

Eagle E (1989) found that higher achieving students came from home that emphasized family reading. According to Maccoby and Mortin (1984) children attend to respond to and follow the behavior of salient models more that they model verbal instruction or demands when the words and actions of themselves and making interest in their children's education have a greater impact on their teach that family who do not model such behaviors.

Comp bell, Liyod (1992) reported that family and school working for student success regional Clark conducted research on low income students identifies as well motivated high achievers, Clark's effective families shared a feeling of control over their lives, frequent communication of high expectations, dreams of future success, reliance on hard work and active engagement and emphasized on spiritual growth, tips for disseminating Clark's finding were provided.

Howell, S.C Brown, J.H.Eichenberger and Mas CA (1992) have found while studying children's post-divorce socio-emotional adjustment that families in which nurturance mutual support and some family rituals were maintained yielded the best performance behavior for children and problem solving were significant in promoting children social competence. In another study with over 400 fourth and sixth graders in china. Family acceptance and family resources such as education,occupation and personal psychological functioning have been shown to be strongly associated with children's social competence and use of little aggression.

Drum-Jean Ed (1993) reported on parenting the gifted child California Association for the gifted, in focuses on techniques foe effectively parenting gifted students in "Family the middle school gifted child". Shoran Freitas provides suggestions for communicating with adolescents and understanding their needs as they strive for increasing independence in search of the owner manual (Terrie Gray) documents the search for a child rearing formula. An adolescent already understanding their needs as they strive for increasing independence , and meeting the needs of your developing gifted child (Richard Swart) reviews the development of gifted children and describes how those developmental difference often account for school problems, difficulties in family relationships and emotional problems "Gifted kids do not come with a set of instructions" (Fran west book)discuss the gifted labels the need for permission to fail the need for a stimulating home environment teaching responsibility home under achievement and advocacy "Self-concept and the gifted child, Executive summary" (Robert D.Hoge and Joseph S.Renzuli) address difference between gifted and average children in their self-concepts effect on self-concepts of labeling child and impact on self-concept of placing the child in a separate enriched or accelerated classrooms ,other articles include "How to build achievers"(Laura Halthway), "A mother's joy a teachers reward"(Margert Gosfield), "Mousing on family modeling "(Martha Flournoy),"Advocacy notes"(Martha Flournoy) "Home school were present and future meet "(Isabelle indexer), "Resources for family, A gate reading list "(Jo Anne viserta Galinis) and "Mentoring it's not just for our children" (sue Beziinger)

Studies Related to Assertiveness

It is the ability to vindicate a claim or title, to affirm positively, to come forward and assume one's right, claims etc. A certain amount of assertiveness is desirable but too much or two little is undesirable (Taylor, 1997).

Assertiveness is an interpersonal behavior resultant of an intrapersonal cognitive state. In other words, it is a cognitive or behavioral phenomenon which was first identified and characterized by Lazarus in 1984.

Alberti and Emmons (1995) define assertiveness as behavior which promotes equality in human relationships, enabling an individual to act in his or her own best interest, to stand up for himself or herself without anxiety, to express honest feelings 76 comfortably and to exercise his or her own rights without denying the rights of others. Various levels of assertiveness have been categorized in the literature.

Higher assertiveness levels have been linked with self-esteem, adjustment, and success in college students and health care professionals. For example, higher levels of assertiveness and an increased sexual self-efficacy were reported in 195 college students regarding their abilities to refuse sexual advances (Akins lure, 1997).

Albayrak (1993) found that of 205 female college students, those with higher levels of assertiveness were regarded as more adjusted, as defined by peer popularity and scored higher on internal locus of control measures than those with lower levels of assertiveness. Studies of assertiveness levels conducted by Hebert (1992) and Curtis (1994) produced similar results.

Hebert (1992) found that those university students of both genders, 48 males and 192 females, who scored higher on a measure of assertiveness also held more internal control beliefs, while those who scored lower on the assertiveness measure held a belief in external control.

Curtis (1994) associated success, defined as the altering of therapeutic care to include specific physical therapies, with increased levels of assertiveness and effort in 86 physical therapists that had experienced inter professional conflicts with physicians.

(Akinsulure, 1997; Albayrak, 1993; Curtis, 1994; Hebert, 1992) suggest that higher levels of assertiveness may have some benefits in predicting psychological adjustment. Much like the positive correlation found between higher assertiveness levels and psychological adjustment, a definite correlation between lower assertiveness levels and psychological maladjustment has been found in the 77 literature. Lower assertiveness levels specifically have been linked to anxiety, stress, and depression.

Lee and Ellis (2003) found that although coping strategies of nursing personnel depended on experience and seniority, a group of 56 graduate nurses generally lacked assertiveness and expressed high anxiety. In a study examining the relationship between problem-solving coping and adjustment in 48 college men and 54 college women, Mundt (2005) found that the women consistently reported more problems with assertiveness and exploitation, whereas the men in the study reported more extreme problems with domination and emotional coldness.

Chan (2007) analysis of responses given by 183 Chinese university undergraduate students also indicated that nonassertive behaviors correlated with depressed mood.

(Chan, 2003; Lee & Ellis, 2003; Mundt, 2002) provide empirical data upon which to suggest a possible relationship between lower assertiveness levels and psychological maladjustment, much like that found between higher assertiveness levels and psychological adjustment. Ways of Coping and Assertiveness Coping is defined as the constantly changing cognitive and behavioral effort an individual uses to manage specific external and/or internal demands appraised as taxing to or exceeding his or her resources (Lazarus &Folk man, 1994).

Lazarus and Folkman (1999), there are two forms of coping: problem focused coping or behavioral and emotion-focused coping or cognitive. Problem focused coping is used predominantly in situations appraised as changeable, 78 whereas; emotion-focused coping is used predominantly in situations appraised as not amenable to change. Although the two forms of coping, emotion-focused and problem-focused, are beneficial in clarifying distinctions between cognition and behavior, they do not reflect the richness and complexity of human coping processes.

Lazarus and Folkman (1999) identified ways of coping in order to describe those strategies that may serve both an emotion-focused and a problem-focused function. Their efforts eventually led to the identification of eight coping scales: confronted coping, distancing, self-controlling, seeking social support, accepting responsibility, and escape-avoidance, problem-solving and positive reappraisal. The original two scales, emotion-focused and problem-focused coping, provided the foundation upon which the eight coping subscales were built.

Lazarus and Folkman (2005) contend these eight subscales better reflect the complex human coping process. Furthermore, recent research has divided these eight coping subscales into positive and negative forms (Aldwin, 2005). Of these, the self-controlling ways of coping subscale and the escape-avoidance subscale have been highly correlated with distress. Because coping is a complex changing process, attempts to better describe coping have led to the examination of variables thought to impact it.

Ways of coping have been found to be largely the product of a stressful situation where their use is specific only to that particular moment and demand (Folkman & Lazarus, 2000; Folkman, Lazarus, Dunkel; Mccrae, 2004; Mccrae & Costa, 2001). If the situational context to which coping is directed is thought to be one determinant of coping methods, further analysis of other variables, such as individual differences, has been conducted for their effects on the coping process.79 A comprehensive review of the coping literature over the past several decades was conducted, in which coping was found to be sensitive to situational and individual factors. The review specifically focused on research that reported coping strategies as a result of both factors, which create a unique cognitive / behavioral process in order to manage particular stressors. Several of these studies have examined specific situational and individual characteristics which produce differences in ways of coping. Assertiveness Training Assertiveness training means people how to be appropriately assertive in social situations, often included as part of health behavior modification programs in the assumption that some poor health habits such as excessive alcohol consumption or smoking, develop in part to control difficulties in being appropriately assertive, is highly important.

Then only he can be a success in life, in the school or the work place (Chenevert, 2006). Assertiveness training is one of a group of cognitive or behavioral therapies. It is a learning-based technique designed to reduce anxiety that occurs in interpersonal situations. Assertiveness training involves cognitive restructuring to affect some action-oriented event in order to facilitate assertive communication skills which aid in overcoming personal barriers to self-expression (Alberti & Eammons, 1990a, 1990b; Alberti & Emmons, 1995; Wolpe, 1990; Wolpe & Lazarus, 1966). This strategy is particularly useful in people who are inhibited or fearful of doing and saying things which are reasonable and well within the rights of the person to say or do (Chenevert, 1994). The person, as a desired result of 80 assertiveness training, becomes unafraid to assert himself or her and is comfortable in developing the skills required to satisfy his or her needs (Alberti & Emmons, 1995; Kahn, 1981). Assertive behavior is now considered healthy behavior for all people that, when present, mitigates against personal powerlessness and results in personal empowerment (Kipper, 1992).

Assertiveness training, as a form of cognitive/behavioral therapy, emphasizes cognitive processes to influence behavior for the purposes of resolving personal and social problems, thus enhancing human functioning (Kazdin, 1978; Kwekkeboom, 2009; Kwekkeboom, Huseby, & Ward, 2008).

Cognitive or behavioral therapy has evolved to view human behavior as amenable to systematic and structured counseling or cognitive restructuring. Behavior modification aims to increase a person's skills so that the number of his or her response options is increased. By overcoming debilitating behaviors that restrict choices, one is freer to select possibilities that were not available earlier (Corey, 1996). Because cognitive or behavioral therapists believe that behavioral procedures are more powerful than strictly verbal ones in affecting cognitive processes (Bandura, 1977, 1986, 1991), they maintain the importance of altering a person's beliefs in order to effect an enduring change in behavior and emotion.

Cognition and behavior are thought to continuously and reciprocally influence each other new behavior can alter thinking, and that a new mode of thinking can, in turn, facilitate the new behavior. The general goal of cognitive/behavioral therapy is to create new conditions for learning which foster self-help. A variety of these therapeutic procedures exist; one is assertiveness training. Assertiveness training offers an 81 treatment of choice for many clients with interpersonal difficulties. Focus on a client's negative self-statements, self-defeating beliefs, and faulty thinking are paramount. The challenge of those beliefs that accompany a lack of assertiveness will teach the client how to make constructive self-statements and how to adopt a new set of beliefs that will result in assertive behavior. The role of assertiveness training in health care situations is basically nonexistent. The history of health care delivery may provide an explanation of this deficiency. Early studies and anecdotal writings demonstrate the demoralization of patients that has occurred in medical institutions. Traditionally, members of the medical profession have assumed complete control of health care issues and treatments, negating client desires, requests, or wishes and thereby, fostering powerlessness. As decisions regarding health care became more and more authoritarian in nature, the consumer, or client, fell at the mercy of the system one that assumed the client does not think. Programme in assertiveness training, though, have shown the ability to affect significant cognitive and behavioral changes in populations of students and professional workers.

Blood (2005) examined techniques on assertive communication, as a part of a cognitive/behavioral treatment package in a group of 72 adolescents who stutter. Program results indicated fewer incidences of non-fluent communication, positive changes in attitude, and feelings of control in all participants after 12 months of treatment.

CONCLUSION

The study of related literature has helped the investigator to have a clear perspective of the problem chosen for the present investigations. Designing the method of research, description of the variable, sample selection, selection of suitable tools, administration and scoring methods of responses have been undertaken based on the review which is discussed in the succeeding chapter.

❐

13

Design of the Study and Method of Investigation

This chapter reflects the thinking that has been at the background of the hypotheses framed in relation to the determination of family encouragement and assertiveness instrument further it shown light on designing tools to test and select the appropriate sample, besides explaining the research procedure followed in the investigation.

Hypotheses of the Study

The following hypotheses have been framed in the present study:

1. The level of family encouragement of high school students is average.
2. The level of assertiveness of high school students is average.
3. There is no significant difference between the mean scores of family encouragement of high school students with regard to

   Gender : (Male/Female)
   Type of management : (Government/ Government Aided/Private)
   Type of Family : (Joint/Nuclear)
   Locality : (Rural/Urban)
   Medium of instruction: (Tamil/English)

4. **There is no significant difference between the mean scores of assertiveness of high school students with regard to**

   Gender : (Male/Female)
   Type of management : (Government/ Government Aided/Private)
   Type of Family : (Joint/Nuclear)
   Locality : (Rural/Urban)
   Medium of instruction : (Tamil/English)

5. **There is no significant correlation between Family encouragement and assertiveness among the high school students.**

Tools used in the Present Study

The following tools were used for the present study

1. The Family Encouragement scale developed by Mohana Sekhar.
2. The Assertiveness Questionnaire developed by Martha Davis and associates.

Family Encouragement

This is a ticker type rating scale consisting of 18 statements to access the level of family encouragement given by the family.Mohanasekar,Department of education, University of Bombay constructed this total. There were 18 statements of which 8 statements are negative declarative form and 10 0f them are in positive form, four point scale Always,Frequently,and Rarely and Never had been provided for each item. The subject responded to each item by a tick mark (√) in one of the three columns provided after each statement there was no time limit but to complete 18 items, the subject had taken approximately 20 minutes.

TABLE. 13.1: Nature of the School Family Encouragement Questionnaire

S. No	Nature of Items	Item Numbers	Number of items	Total
1	Positive	1,2,4,5,7,9,10,12,13,14,18	11	18
2	Negative	3,6,8,11,15,16,17	7	

Administration

The questionnaire is self-administering and there was no time limits allotted and the directions for filling the personal information and for answering the questionnaire were printed in test forms. The students were asked to read the instructions carefully and make their responses by putting tick (√) marks against the choices provided. They were assured that there was no right or wrong responses, also that their responses were to be used for research purpose and would be kept highly confidential.

Scoring Procedure

Family encouragement questionnaire consist of 18 items out of which 10 are positive item (3 to 0) and the remaining are negative item and reversed (0 to 3).

TABLE.13.2: Showing the Detail of the Scoring of Family Encouragement Scale

S.No	Nature of items	Always	Frequently	Rarely	Never
1	Positive	3	2	1	0
2	Negative	0	1	2	3

The scores of all the 18 items when added up formed the total score, maximum score that could be obtained was 48 and minimum was 0.

ASSERTIVENESS

Description

Simple Rathus Assertiveness schedule modified by the investigator to measure the assertiveness of the students. Out of the 30 questions 17 statements are related negatively while 13 statements positively.

TABLE. 13.3: Showing the Nature of Items of the Assertiveness Questionnaire

Nature of statements	Item Numbers
Positive	3,6,7,8,10,18,20,21,22,25,28,29
Negative	1,2,4,5,9,11,12,13,14,15,16,17,19,23,24,26,30

Administration

In administering this questionnaire 40 minutes were taken by the students. They were encouraged to respond all the items. The examiner read the directions aloud while the students read them silently. If questions arose during the session, the examiner responds were supportive but non-committal.

Scoring Procedure

The scale consists of 30 statements with 5 alternative responsesviz "strongly agree", "agree", "undecided", "disagree", "strongly disagree"anchored from 0 to 5. The minimum score is 0 and the maximum score is 120.

TABLE. 13.4: Showing the Detail of the Scoring of Assertiveness Questionnaire

Type of Question	Response	Score
Positive	Strongly Agree	4
	Agree	3
	Undecided	2
	Disagree	1
	Strongly Disagree	0
Negative	Strongly Agree	0
	Agree	1
	Undecided	2
	Disagree	3
	Strongly Disagree	4

Sample of the Study

A sample of 300 high school students was selected randomly from schools such as State Government Schools, Government Aided Schools, and Private Schools.

TABLE. 13.5: The Distribution of the Sample among Different Types of Schools

Type of school	Name of school	Number of Students Selected		
		Boys	**Girls**	**Total**
Government	Government High school, Kuppichipalayam, Erode.	50	50	100
Government Aided	Punitha Ingyasiriyar Higher secondary school, Boothapadi, Erode.	50	50	100
Private	Sri Vasavi Matriculation High School, Chittode, Erode.	Nil	50	50
	St.Marys Higher secondary School, Bhavani, Erode.	50	Nil	50
Total		**150**	**150**	**300**

Pilot Study

A pilot study was conducted in order to determine whether the research is feasible among students, whether there would be adequate response from the students and to access the reliability and adaptability of the test materials to the groups selected. It was conducted for a sample of 50 students on October 2014.

Establishing Reliability of the Tools Used

The reliability of a test may be defined as the degree of consistency with which the test measure what it does measures. A test score is called reliable, when we have reasons to believe it to be stable and trustworthy...

RELIABILITY

Family Encouragement

To compute the reliability of family encouragement for the sample shown, odd even method was used. The reliability was computed and it was found to be 0.76

Assertiveness Questionnaire

The reliability of this tool is assessed by split-half technique and it is measured to be 0.92, indicating high reliability of the tool.

Establishing Validity of the Tools Used

Validity means the ability to produce findings that are in agreement with conceptual (or) theoretical values. It refers to the success of the scale in measuring what it meant to measure. A test is valid, when it measure, truly and accurately the ability (or) quality one wants to measure. Thus, validity means truthfulness of the test.

Validity

Family Encouragement

The validity of index of family encouragement was found by computing the square root of the reliability co-efficient which worked out to be 0.88

Assertiveness Questionnaire

The validity of index assertiveness was found by computing the square root of the reliability co-efficient which worked out to be 0.96

Main Study

- The Tools are described below
- Family Encouragement.

Assertiveness was used to collect the data for the main study.

Following the procedures mentioned for the tests, the tests were administrated sample of 300 9th standard students in the month of October2014, the time schedules of the tests are given below.

TABLE. 13.6: Showing the timeSchedule of Administration of the Tools Used

S.No	Name of the tool	Time Taken
1	Family Encouragement	20 minutes
2	Assertiveness	40 minutes

Statistical Techniques Used

a) MEAN

Mean ($\bar{x}$) = $A + \frac{\sum fd}{\sum f} \times i$

Where,

A = Assumed mean

f = frequency

d = deviation from the assumed mean

i = Class interval

b) STANDARD DEVIATION

Standard Deviation, $SD(\sigma) = \sqrt{\frac{\sum fd^2}{N} - \left[\frac{\sum fd}{N}\right]^2} \times i$

Where,

f = Frequency

d = Deviation from the assumed mean

I = Class interval

N = Total frequency

c) 't' TEST

To continue the significance of difference between means of various measures test is used't' ratio is calculated from the relation.

T-ratio $= \frac{M_1 \sim M_2}{\sqrt{\frac{\sigma_1^2}{N_1} + \frac{\sigma_1^2}{N_2}}} = \frac{M_1 \sim M_2}{S \in D}$

Where,

= Means of the groups

SED = Standard Error Deviation

d) 'F'-TEST

F- Ratio = Variance between the group/Variance within the group Correction term 'C'

$$C = \frac{\sum x_1 + \sum x_2 + \sum x_3}{N}$$

$$BSS = \left(\sum x_1\right)^2 / W_1 + \left(\sum x_2\right)^2 / W_2 + \left(\sum x_3\right)^2 / W_3 - C$$

$$TSS = \sum x_1^2 + \sum x_2^2 + \sum x_3^2 - C$$

WSS = TSS - BSS

Where, x_1, x_2, x_3 are score in different group

C = correction Terms

TSS= Total Sum of Squares

BSS= Between Sum of Squares

WSS= Within Sum of Squares

e) CO-EFFICIENT OF CORRELATION (r)

$$r = \frac{N\sum x \sum y - \sum x \sum y}{\sqrt{\left(N\sum x^2 - \left(\sum x^2\right)\right)\left(N \sum y^2 - \left(\sum y\right)^2\right.}}$$

X, y – Variables,

N- Total strength.

CONCLUSION

This chapter outlines the design of the present study, the procedure followed and the nature of the sample. It describes the hypotheses to be tested the tools used and scoring , the collected data were analyzed using appropriate statistical techniques described above to study the effect of Family encouragement and assertiveness the result of which are discussed in the light of hypotheses formulated and the next chapter presents analysis and discussion part of the study.

14

Analysis and Interpretation of the Data

Research consists of systematic observation and description of the characteristic of properties for the purpose of discovering relationships starts with the description of the measures of the variables and goes on to the higher levels of statistical analysis. The data collected will be carefully edited, systematically classified and tabulated, scientifically analyzed and interpreted and rationally concluded.

In the present study the data collected with regard to the family encouragement and assertiveness among high school students in Erode city were analyzed with reference to the objectives and hypotheses of the study. The data have been subjected to the statistical analysis and the results have been summarized and tabulated in this chapter.

CLASSIFICATION OF THE SAMPLE BASED ON THE

Variables of the Study

Family Encouragement

Based on the information obtained from the IX standard students regarding their family encouragement, the students are divided into three groups namely low, moderate and high level of family encouragement, the details of which are presented below.

TABLE. 14.1: Showing the Level of Family Encouragement among High School Students

Level	Range	Number of Student	Percentage (%)
Low	Below 27	85	28.3
Average	Between 28 to 34	132	44.0
High	Above 35	83	27.7
TOTAL	300		100.0

From the table, it is clear that the level of family encouragement among High School students is average in nature.

Hence the hypothesis 1 stating that "The level of Family encouragement among High School students is average in nature" is accepted.

ASSERTIVENESS

Based on the information obtained from the IX standard students regarding their Assertiveness, the students are divided into three groups namely low, moderate and high level of Study Involvement, the details of which are presented below.

TABLE. 14.2: Showing the Level of Assertiveness among High School Students

Level	Range	Number of Students	Percentage (%)
Low	Below 53	76	25.3
Average	Between 54 to 62	132	44.0
High	Above 63	92	30.7
Total		300	100.0

From the table, it is clear that the level of assertiveness among high school students is moderate in nature.

Hence the hypothesis 2 stating that "The level of assertiveness among High School students is average in nature" is accepted.

INFLUENCE OF GENDER ON FAMILY ENCOURAGEMENT

The scores of family encouragement of high school students based on gender (Boys / Girls) have been analyzed and the obtained results are presented below

TABLE. 14.3: Showing the Significant Difference between the mean Scores of Family Encouragement of Boys and Girls

Group comparison	N	Mean	SD	't' Value	Level of Significance
Boys	152	30.80	5.407	0.523	NS
Girls	148	31.14	5.819		

From the table, it is noted that girls have significantly higher Family encouragement than the boys.

Hence the hypothesis 3 stating that"There is no significant difference in theFamily encouragement of high school students based on gender" is accepted.

INFLUENCE OF TYPE OF FAMILY ON FAMILY ENCOURAGEMENT

The scores of Family encouragement of high school students based on type of family (Nuclear/Urban) have been analyzed and the obtained results are presented below.

TABLE. 14.4: Showing the Significant Difference between the mean Scores of Family Encouragement of Nuclear and Joint Family Students

Groups comparison	N	Mean	SD	't' value	Level of Significance
Joint	67	30.94	5.521	0.038	NS
Nuclear	233	30.97	5.643		

The above table reveals that nuclear family students have high Family encouragement than joint family students.

Hence the hypothesis 4 stating that "There is no significant difference between the mean score of Family Encouragement of High School students with respect to Type of family" is accepted.

INFLUENCE OF THE TYPE OF MANAGEMENT ON FAMILY ENCOURAGEMENT

The scores of Family encouragement of high school students based on type of management (Government / Government Aided / private) have been analyzed and the obtained result is presented below.

TABLE. 14.5: ANOVA Showing the Significant Difference between the mean Scores of Family Encouragement Government, Government Aided and Private High School Students

Source	Sum of Squares	DF	Mean Squares	'F' Value	Level of Significance
Between groups	1179.311	2	589.655	21.302	0.01
Within groups	8221.286	297	27.681		
Total	**9400.597**	**299**			

Type of management	Number of cases	Mean	SD	Critical Ratio	Level of Significance
Government Vs	102	29.54	4.806	0.381	NS
Government aided	109	29.81	5.384		
Government Vs private	102	29.54	4.806	5.941	0.01
	89	34.01	5.597		
Government aided Vs	109	29.81	5.384	5.369	0.01
Private	89	34.01	5.597		

The above table clearly indicates that there is significant difference between in the mean scores of Family encouragement of students influenced by type of management.

Analysis has to be done to find out the significant difference between the type of management on family encourage

Table 14.6 Showing the significant difference between the family encouragement among high school students based on the type of management

In the first case, the calculated value (0.381) is less than the table value (1.96). Therefore there is no significant difference between the mean scores of family encouragement of high school students based on government and government aided schools.

In the second case, the calculated value (5.94) is greater than the table value (1.96) at 0.01 level. Therefore there is significant difference between the mean scores of family encouragement of high school students based on government and private schools.

In the third case, the calculated value (5.369) is greater than the table value (1.96) at 0.01 level. Therefore there is significant difference between the mean scores of family encouragement of high school students based on government aided and private schools.

Hence private school students have significant difference in the family encouragement compared to that of government and government aided school students.

Therefore the framed null hypothesis is partially verified.

INFLUENCE OF THE TYPE OF LOCALITY ON FAMILY

Encouragement

The scores of Family encouragement of high school students based on locality (Rural /Urban) have been analyzed and the obtained results are presented below.

TABLE. 14.7: Showing the Significant Difference between the mean Scores of Family Encouragement with Regard to Rural and Urban High School Students.

Group Comparison	N	Mean	SD	't' value	Level of significance
Rural	203	29.93	5.338	4.778	NS
Urban	97	33.12	5.568		

The above table, it is clear that urban students are having more Family encouragement than rural students.

Hence the hypothesis 6 "There is no significant difference between the mean score of Family encouragement of High School students with respect to Locality" is accepted.

INFLUENCE OF THE TYPE OF MEDIUM OF INSTRUCTION ON FAMILY ENCOURAGEMENT

The scores of Family encouragement of high school students based on medium of instruction (Tamil /English) have been analyzed and the obtained results are presented below.

TABLE. 14.8: Showing the Significant Difference between the mean Scores of Family Encouragement with Regard to Tamil and English Medium High School Students

Medium of instruction	N	Mean	SD	't' value	Level of significance
Tamil Medium	199	29.81	5.177	5.220	0.01
English Medium	101	33.24	5.750		

The above table, it is clear that English Medium students got more Family encouragement than Tamil Medium students.

Hence the hypothesis 7 "There is no significant difference between the mean score of Family encouragement of High School students with respect to Medium of instruction" is rejected.

INFLUENCE OF GENDER ON ASSERTIVENESS

The scores of Assertiveness of high school students based on gender (Boys / Girls) have been analyzed and the obtained results are presented below.

TABLE. 4.9: Showing the Significant Difference between the mean Scores of Assertiveness of Boys and Girls

Gender	N	Mean	SD	Critical Ratio	Level of Significance
Boys	152	56.51	8.156	4.023	0.01
Girls	148	60.29	8.132		

From the table, it is noted that girls have significantly high Assertiveness than boys.

Hence the hypothesis 8 stating that "There is no significant difference between the mean score of Assertiveness of High School students with respect to Gender" is rejected.

INFLUENCE OF TYPE OF FAMILY ON ASSERTIVENESS

The scores of Assertiveness high school students based on type of family (Nuclear/Urban) have been analyzed and the obtained results are presented below.

TABLE. 4.10: Showing the Significant Difference between the mean Scores of Assertiveness of Nuclear and Joint Family Students

Type of family	N	Mean	SD	Critical Ratio	L.S
Joint	67	57.63	8.979	0.830	NS
Nuclear	233	58.59	8.165		

The above table reveals that Nuclear family students have high Assertiveness than the Joint family students.

Hence the hypothesis 9 stating that "There is no significant difference between the mean score of Assertiveness of the High School students with respect to Type of family" is accepted.

INFLUENCE OF TYPEOF MANAGEMENT ON

Assertiveness

The scores of Assertiveness of high school students based on type of management (Government/Government-Aided / Private) have been analyzed and the obtained result is presented below.

TABLE. 14.11: ANOVA Showing the Significant Difference between the mean Scores of Assertiveness of Government, Government-Aided and Private High School Students

Source	Sum of squares	DF	Mean Squares	'F' Value	Level of Significance
Between groups	255.393	2	127.697	1.843	NS
Within groups	20582.793	297	69.302		
Total	**20838.187**	**299**			

The above table clearly that indicates that Assertiveness of students are not influenced by type of management.

Hence the hypothesis 10 stating that "There is no significant difference between the mean score of Assertiveness of High School students with respect to Type of management" is accepted.

INFLUENCE OF LOCALITY ON ASSERTIVENESS

The scores of Assertiveness of high school students based on locality (Rural/ Urban) have been analyzed and the obtained results are presented below.

TABLE. 14.12: Showing the Significant Difference between the Mean Scores of Study Involvement with Regard to Rural and Urban High School Students

Group comparison	N	Mean	SD	't' value	Level of Significant
Rural	203	57.94	8.522	1.299	NS
Urban	97	59.28	7.940		

From the above table, it is clear that urban students having significant influence of Assertiveness than rural students.

Hence the hypothesis 11 stating that "There is no significant difference between the mean score of Assertiveness of High School students with respect to Locality" is accepted.

INFLUENCE OF THE TYPE OF MEDIUM OF INSTRUCTION ON ASSERTIVENESS

The scores of Assertiveness of high school students based on medium of instruction (Tamil /English) have been analyzed and the obtained results are presented below.

TABLE.14.13: Showing the Significant Difference between the mean Scores of Family Encouragement with Regard to Tamil and English High School Students

Medium of instruction	N	Mean	SD	't' value	Level of significance
Tamil Medium	199	57.83	8.512	1.574	NS
English Medium	101	59.44	7.950		

The above table, it is clear that English medium students having more Assertiveness than Tamil medium students.

Hence the hypothesis 12 "There is no significant difference between the mean score of Family encouragement of High School students with respect to Medium of instruction" is accepted.

CORRELATION BETWEEN FAMILY ENCOURAGEMENT ANDASSERTIVENESSOF HIGHER SECONDARY SCHOOL STUDENTS

Correlation between Family Encouragement and Assertiveness of high school students has been computed and present in the following table.

TABLE. 14.14: Showing the Correlation between Family Encouragement and Assertiveness of High School Students

Comparison of Variables	Sample size	Correlation coefficient 'r'	Level of Significance
Family Encouragement VsAssertiveness	300	0.161	0.05

The above table reveals clearly that there is significant positive correlation between Family Encouragement and Assertiveness.

Hence the hypothesis 13 stating that "There is no significant correlation between the mean score of Family encouragement and assertiveness of High School students" is rejected.

CONCLUSION

This chapter summarizes the analysis of data, testing of hypotheses description and inference of the tables. A brief report of the research study together with the major findings and conclusion along with their educational implications has been presented in the succeeding chapter. ❐

15
Summary and Conclusion

The present chapter, apart from providing a brief summary of the entire study presents the findings and the educational implication of the present study. Suggestions for replicating the study in other settings are also listed.

Statement of the Problem

The problemsare titled as follows: "Family Encouragement and Assertiveness among High School Students in Erode District".

Objectives of the Study

The following objectives have been set in the present study:

1. To find out the level of family encouragement of high school students.
2. To find out the level of assertiveness of high school students.
3. To find out whether there is any significant difference between the mean scores of family encouragement of high school students with regard to

   Gender : (Male/Female)
   Type of management : (Government/ Government Aided/Private)
   Type of Family : (Joint/Nuclear)
   Locality : (Rural/Urban)
   Medium of instruction : (Tamil/English)

4. To find out whether there is any significant difference between the mean scores of assertiveness of high school students with regard to

Gender	:	(Male/Female)
Type of management	:	(Government/ Government Aided/ Private)
Type of Family	:	(Joint/Nuclear)
Locality	:	(Rural/Urban)
Medium of instruction	:	(Tamil/English)

5. To find out whether there is any significant association between Family encouragement and assertiveness of high school students.

Hypotheses of the study

The following hypotheses have been framed to conduct the present study:

1. The level of family encouragement of high school students is average.
2. The level of assertiveness of high school students is average.
3. There is no significant difference between the mean scores of family encouragement of high school students with regard to

Gender	:	(Male/Female)
Type of management	:	(Government/ Government Aided/Private)
Type of Family	:	(Joint/Nuclear)
Locality	:	(Rural/Urban)
Medium of instruction	:	(Tamil/English)

4. There is no significant difference between the mean scores of assertiveness of high school students with regard to

Gender	:	(Male/Female)
Type of management	:	(Government/ Government Aided/Private)
Type of Family	:	(Joint/Nuclear)
Locality	:	(Rural/Urban)
Medium of instruction	:	(Tamil/English)

5. There is no significant correlation between Family encouragement and assertiveness among the high school students.

Population and Sample of the Study

To cover the entire population is an impossible task for any survey or research. What is feasible and generally practiced is to study a sample representative of the population. Therefore a sample of 300 students had been drawn by stratified random sampling method for the present study. The sample consists of both boys and girls of high school students from Government, Government Aided and private schools in Erode district in Tamil Nadu.

Tools Used for the Study

The following tools have been selected by the investigator to carry out this study.

1. The family encouragement scale developed by MohanaSekhar.
2. The assertiveness questionnaire developed by Martha Davis and associates.

Major Findings

The following are the major findings of the present study.

- The level of family encouragement among High School students is average in nature.
- The level of assertiveness among high school students is moderate in nature.
- Girls have significantly higher Family encouragement than the boys.
- Nuclear family students have high Family encouragement than joint family students.
- Private high school students level higher than government and government aided students.
- Urban students are having more Family encouragement than rural students.
- English Medium students got more Family encouragement than Tamil Medium students.
- Girls have significantly high Assertiveness than boys.
- Nuclear family students have high Assertiveness than the Joint family students.
- Assertiveness of students are not influenced by type of management.
- Urban students are more Assertiveness than rural students.
- English medium students having more Assertiveness than Tamil medium students.
- There is significant positive correlation between Family Encouragement and Assertiveness among high school students.

Educational Implications

Any educational research is worthwhile if the results produce fruitful educational implications. As so far the present investigation is concerned, it can be claimed that useful information obtained could be useful in enhancing the educational success of the college students.

The results of the present study reflect that male college students lag behind female counterparts in academic performance. It may due to autonomous nature of the boys or may be due to nurturing style and liberty provided by the parents and society. So it is recommended that self-discipline among male college students so that they could perform well in their academics.

Urban students are found to be better in the academic achievement than the rural students through the results of the study. This might be due to their past educational experiences, environment and family attitude toward the educational aspirations. So it is highly recommended that there should be good schools in rural areas also. Awareness should be provided to parents and families through awareness camps, seminars or workshops to provide encouragement to their children for better results in academics.

The present study points out that the students who receive high parental encouragement are better at academic performance than the students who receive less parental encouragement. Hence it is recommended that parents should take interests in the educational activities of their children. By implicating this, the educational achievement of the students could be enhanced.

The results of the present study have indicated that students who possess high level of intelligence are better at academic performance than the students who are less intelligent. Although intelligence is considered to be hereditary but the impact of environment and nurturing cannot be refuted. So it is recommended and healthy food and salubrious environment should be provided to the students. So that they could develop to their maximum and show good results in the academics.

The findings of the present investigation are important to bring the improvement in the standard of education. Since the fear of failure is essentially a personality disposition, hence it is to be tackled during the formative period of the children. During this period, the parents and teachers have a greater responsibility in shaping the attitude of students about themselves and towards events and goals. The teachers should identify those students who have high fear of assertiveness and help them to develop assertiveness.

One of the important rewards of developing assertiveness is that it tends to neutralize the anxieties that many people experience in various social situations. There will be some anxiety before individuals assert themselves, as they contemplate what they will say or do, but this is largely the same anxiety that is experienced when they try any new behavior that they have avoided heretofore. However, once they try an assertive response, and practice it, there is usually a marked reduction in social anxieties. Indeed, learning appropriate assertive behavior is one of the main ways by which social anxiety is now being treated.

Limitation

The present study has the following limitations.

1. The sample is restricted to 300 students.
2. Students from high schools alone considered for the study.
3. The study is conducted in limited schools of Erode District, Tamil Nadu.
4. Only seven schools in Erode District have been selected for this Study.

Suggestions for Further Study

The following areas have been suggested by the investigator for further study.

1. In the present study, the sample is taken from high school level. The study can be conducted upon the students from primary, secondary and higher level.
2. The present study has been done only in some schools of Erode districts. Similar study comprising different district can be attempted.
3. The sample size is restricted to 300 students in the present study. Further study can be done by including more number of students.
4. The impact of parental involvements and teachers involvement on achievement can also be studied.

CONCLUSION

The purpose of the present investigation was to study family encouragement and assertiveness status in relation to achievement of high school students. This study is sure to find the usefulness in the field of education and findings of this study can serve as a database for further research.

❒

16

The Problem and its Perspectives

Education is a process of development from birth to death. It is widely accepted that the process of education begins at birth and continues throughout life. Some believe that education begins even earlier than this, as evidenced by some parents playing music or reading to the baby in the womb in the hope it will influence the child's development.

The word `Education' is often used to refer solely to formal education. However, it covers a range of experiences, from formal learning to the building of understanding through day today experiences. Ultimately, all that we experience serves as a form of education.

The main aim of education is to develop harmonious personality of the learner. Education is considered to be the most significant agent of basic change in the status of a human being besides occupation and economic status.

Education will give to the individual a strong and healthy body, helps him in building up one's character and attains self mastery and supply him with good opportunities of discovering and developing harmoniously his natural abilities.

Finally the education commission (1964-1966) observes that education must serve as a powerful instrument of social, economic and cultural transformation necessary for the realization of the national goals.

THE CONCEPT OF PROCRASTINATION

Academic procrastination can be understood as knowing that one is supposed to, and perhaps even wanting to, complete a task but failing to perform the activity within the expected or desired time frame. Every person has task to perform, but for one reason or another, completion of these task is often postponed. The general propensity to engage in such dilatory behavior is called procrastination.

Procrastination appears to be a significant problem especially among high school students. Although there suggested that fear of failure and task evasiveness are two district reasons for procrastination. Fear of failure incorporates concerns about meeting other people's expectation, about meetings perfectionist standards, and about lack of self-confidence.

WHAT IS PROCRASTINATION?

Basically, procrastination is the act of putting off essential task until a later time, most of the time non essential tasks are done in lieu of the more critical ones. Although this procrastination definition seems pretty simple the effects of procrastination are not. Procrastination may be one of the biggest challenges we will have to overcome.

When begin to think about today's society, there is less and less time in the day, so it is very important that to manage the time efficiently and limit procrastination as much as possible. For some reason, having an emotional reaction when doing something which doesn't want to do, don't enjoy doing, or are convinced that it cannot be done. Learning to acknowledge this reaction will not only make to realize that it is procrastination, but will also help on our quest to stop procrastination.

Procrastination is something that most people have at least a little experience with. No matter how well-organized and committed the person is, chances are that the person may have found self frittering away hours on trivial pursuits (watching TV, updating the Facebook status, shopping online) person should have been spending that time on work or school-related projects. Whether he is putting off finishing a project for work, avoiding homework assignments, or ignoring household chores, procrastination can have a major impact on our job, our grades, and our life.

MEANING OF PROCRASTINATION

The meanings of procrastination are

- To put off doing something, especially out of habitual carelessness or laziness.
- To postpone or delay needlessly.

For example,When it comes to school, that means putting off doing the schoolwork, which can lead to losing the edge on studies and getting lower-than-expected marks.

DEFINITION OF PROCRASTINATION

According to Clarry Lay, a prominent writer on procrastination occurs when there's "a temporal gap between intended behavior and enacted behavior". That is, procrastination is occurring when there's a significant time period between when people intend to do a job, and when actually do it.

CHARACTERISTICS OFPROCRASTINATION

1. Disappointment is a way of life. Procrastination makes constantly disappoint other people and the afflicted person by not keeping promises that are made.
2. Constantly seek excitement and attention through the negative attention generated by passive aggressive behavior. The excitement comes from not knowing how the person we have "wronged" will react when we see him/her again.
3. Constantly place people in a position of power over by default.
4. Have taken on the role of nice but ineffectual people.
5. Do not like to be depended upon.
6. Regularly late for appointments.
7. Regularly procrastinate greatly over the things needed to be done. In school this results in incomplete grades, at work in projects that get delayed or dropped, at home in a disheveled place that make embarrassed to bring people to.
8. Tend to put off making decisions. Many of our decisions are made for us by the process of indecision, life's inevitable way of making the decisions for whether it is liked or not.
9. Tend to stay single to a late age or not to get married at all, tend to greatly delay breaking off inappropriate relationships, and/or tend to avoid committed relationships.
10. Tend to avoid concentrating on projects at hand, engaging in daydreaming or switching to other less important tasks.

CAUSES OF PROCRASTINATION

Fear of the Outcome

Sometimes there will be a fear of failure. Sometimes there will be a fear subconsciously and then it is a need to have to be deal with all the disruption (growth) and change that follows success. And other times it's the fear of rejection or simply our fear of looking like a fool. The best way found to defeat fear is to stare it down. Connect to fear, feel it in body, realize it and steadily address it. Greet it by name "Welcome, fear."If conscious of it, soon it becomes shy, hangs its head, and mooches off, scraping one shoe on the ground.

Helplessness in the Face of Complexity

Looking at a task in hand and feeling intensely un-resourceful. It may remind of something had to be done. Having the skills to conquer it (even though that's no longer the case) or it may actually be a daunting task at our current skill level, either way, the task seems far too complex, so gives the thought to avoid it. This time the solution is to break it down. Take that complex task and break it down to its bare essential components and then tackle each one of those components one at a time. Sometimes it's also helpful to recall one of the previous successes with conquering a complex task just to get a positive mindset.

Rebellion and laziness

Rebellion is about control. Assert control by choosing when (or whether) to do the task. There was a home-schooled son who is very rebellious. The mother came up with a clever hack. She said, "We're going to do what kids who are in school do. We're going to sit and do school work for 8 hours a day." The son rebelled, naturally. When the rebellion was in full effect, the mother offered an alternative. That the home school style. If the boy finish early, could go somewhere fun." And her son worked more productively than ever. So when it is noticed of feeling rebellious and lazy about a task, think of a way to reward for getting it done now. Also, remind of the consequences of not doing it.

Lack of Focus and Fatigue

Distractions are everywhere. It must be learnt to ignore them. Minimize distractions by secluding. Find a quiet space where can concentrate on the task at hand. And only take breaks as a reward for accomplishing smaller sub-tasks. Also, it's hard to focus when fatigued. So get enough sleep, eat healthy and exercise regularly.

THE CONCEPT OF MINDFULNESS ATTENTION AWARENESS

The term "mindfulness attention awareness" has been used to refer to a psychological state of awareness, the practices that promote this awareness, a mode of processing information and a character trait. This brief document provides a working definition of mindfulness attention awareness, an overview of the scientific rationale for offering mindfulness attention awareness to children and adolescents, a review of the professional and personal benefits of practicing mindfulness attention awareness, specific suggestions for developing own mindfulness attention awareness practice and two examples of practices can be used in classroom.

While there are many definitions of mindfulness attention awareness, the definition here it is used with children and adolescents Mindfulness attention awareness is paying attention to life, here and now, with kindness and curiosity. One of the primary ironies of modern education is that asking students to "pay attention" dozens of times a day, yet it is never taught them *how*. The practice of mindfulness attention awareness teaches students how to pay attention, and this way of paying attention enhances both academic and social-emotional learning.

As human beings have the unique capacity to pay attention to/be aware of internal and external worlds and the interactions between the two, can attend to the breath, the body, thoughts, emotions, tastes, smells, sights, sounds, and our impulses and actions and their effects on others and environment. This ability to pay attention is a natural, innate human capacity.

What is Mindfulness Attention Awareness?

Mindfulness attention awareness means maintaining a moment-by-moment awareness of our thoughts, feelings, bodily sensations, and surrounding environment. Mindfulness attention awareness also involves acceptance, meaning that we pay attention to our thoughts and feelings without judging them—without believing, for instance, that there's a "right" or "wrong" way to think or feel in a given moment. When practicing mindfulness attention awareness, the thoughts tune into what are being sensed in the present moment rather than rehashing the past or imagining the future.

Mindfulness attention awareness is "the intentional, accepting and non-judgemental focus of one's attention on the emotions, thoughts and sensations occurring in the present moment", which can be trained by meditational practices.

Benefits of Mindfulness Attention Awareness

The term "mindfulness attention awareness" has been used to refer to a psychological state of awareness, the practices that promote this awareness, a mode of processing information and a character trait. To be consistent with most of the research reviewed in this article, it can be defined mindfulness attention awareness as a moment-to-moment awareness of one's experience without judgment. In this sense, mindfulness attention awareness is a state and not a trait. While it might be promoted by certain practices or activities, such as meditation, it is not equivalent to or synonymous with them.

Several disciplines and practices can cultivate mindfulness attention awareness, such as yogabut most of the literature has focused on mindfulness attention awareness is developed through mindfulness attention awareness meditation (i.e) those self-regulation practices that focus on training attention and awareness in order to bring mental processes under greater voluntary control and thereby foster general mental well-being and development and/ or specific capacities such as calmness, clarity and concentration (Walsh & Shapiro, 2006).

Researchers theorize that mindfulness attention awareness meditation promotes meta-cognitive awareness, decreases rumination via disengagement from preservative cognitive activities and enhances attention capacities through gains in working memory. These cognitive gains, in turn, contribute to effective emotion-regulation strategies.

Importance of Mindfulness Attention Awareness

Students are being diagnosed with depression, anxiety, eating disorders, cutting, addictions and other self-destructive behaviors at epidemic rates. Cruelty, bullying and violence are on the rise. Most, if not all, children could benefit from learning to focus their attention, to become less reactive, and to be more compassionate with themselves and others.

Fortunately, science is now documenting the negative impact that stress is having on learning every day, in classrooms across the country. The neurological processes that explain this interaction are collectively called *executive function*, which includes—

- goal-directed behavior
- planning
- organized search
- impulse control

Not surprisingly the research proves executive function correlates with working memory, emotional regulation, and resilience.

Personal and Professional Benefits of Developing a Mindfulness attention awareness Practice

Before exploring steps for developing practice, let's examine the personal and professional benefits of doing so. As an educator, it is known teaching is often extremely stressful. The profession requires that to teach specific academic content. Mindfulness attention awareness training decreases burnout and compassion fatigue and increases empathy and effective communication.

The SMART in Education (**S**tress **M**anagement and **R**elaxation **T**echniques in **E**ducation) program is an 8-week, 36 contact hour accredited teacher renewal program designed for educators and administrators. The program cultivates the skills necessary for educators to become aware of and regulate their thoughts, emotions and behavior so as to more effectively manage stress and improve health and well-being; to reclaim a sense of wholeness and happiness in one's personal life and relationships, and to rekindle one's motivation to teach and improve classroom instructional quality.

Teaching mindfulness attention awareness is like teaching anything else: to teach with excellence must know and be passionate about the subject. Since mindfulness attention awareness is an experiential discipline, to offer it with integrity, the teaching must come out of r own practice.

How to Teach Mindfulness Attention Awareness in the Classroom?

Mindfulness attention awareness is a concept many young children, adolescents and adults may have a hard time grasping. However, with guidance, most youth can experience their natural inner stillness and quietness, what can be called the Still Quiet Place. Please be aware the written practices below are *not* intended to be used as scripts to be read the students. While offering experience, language and suggestions, ultimately teaching *must* come from the depths of own practice; must be able to deal skilfully with *whatever* comes up. In any given classroom there will be at least a few children who have lived through one or more of the following: neglect, divorce, illness, death of a family member, emotional, physical, and/or sexual abuse, violence in their homes or communities, being uprooted from their homes, and war. Unfortunately, in some classrooms these experiences are the norm. These circumstances require that to stretch the capacity to *respond* to suffering with clarity and compassion. Even with the best intentions there are possibilities to do if expose a wound that with absence or without the skill to attend to.

THE CONCEPT OFSTUDY HABITS

Some people believe that really successful students are just born that way. True, some students are able to breeze through school with little or no effort. However, the vast majority of successful students achieve their success by developing and applying effective study habits. So if there is need to become a successful student, not to get discouraged, not to give up, just work to develop the study habits.

WHAT IS STUDY SKILLS?

Study skills or study strategies are approaches applied to learning. It is generally critical to success in school, considered essential for acquiring good grades, and useful for learning throughout one's life. RespiciusRwehumbiza in his book "Understanding Examination Techniques and Effective study Strategies" in 2013 asserted that, most students fail in examinations simply because they lack study skills and/or examination taking techniques.

Study skills are an array of study skills, which may tackle the process of organizing and taking in new information, retaining information, or dealing with assessments. They include mnemonics, which aid the retention of lists of information, effective reading, and concentration techniques, as well as efficient note taking.

More broadly, any skill which boosts a person's ability to study and pass exams can be termed a study skill, and this could include time management and motivational techniques. Study skills are discrete techniques that can be learned, usually in a short time, and applied to all or most fields of study.

DEFINITION OF STUDY HABITS

The definition of study habits is the behaviors used when preparing for tests or learning academic material.

Example: A person who waits until the very last night before an exam and then stays up all night trying to cram the information into his head is an example of someone with bad study habits. Study habits act as another variable connected with distance learners' performances. Study habits reflect students' usual act of studying and also call forth and serve to direct the learner's cognitive processes during learning. Study habits includes a variety of activities: time management, setting appropriate goals, choosing an appropriate study environment, using appropriate note-taking strategies, choosing main ideas, and organization

Ten Study Habits of High Effective Students

Some people believe that really successful students are just born that way. True, some students are able to breeze through school with little or no effort. However, the vast majority of successful students achieve their success by developing and applying effective study habits. The following are the top 10 study habits employed by highly successful students. So if student want to become a successful student, just work to develop each of the study habits below and you're see your grades go up, the knowledge increase and your ability to learn and assimilate information improve.

Don't try Cram all studying into one Session.

Successful students typically space their work out over shorter periods of time and rarely try to cram all of their studying into just one or two sessions. If student want to become a successful student then need to learn to be consistent in studies and to have regular, yet shorter, study periods.

Plan when going to study

Successful students schedule specific times throughout the week when student is going to complete their studying -- and then stick with the schedule. Students who study sporadically and whimsically typically do not perform as well as students who have a set study schedule.

Study at the Same Time

Not only is it important that plan when the student is going to study but that also create a consistent, daily study routine. When student study at the same time each day and each week student are studying will become a regular part of their life. Student will be mentally and emotionally more prepared for each study session and each study session will become more productive.

Each study Time should have a Specific Goal

Simply the studying without direction is not effective. Student need to know exactly what need to accomplish during each study session. Before student start studying set a study session goal that supports overall academic goal.

Never Procrastinate Planned Study Session

It is very easy, and common, to put off study session because of lack of interest in the subject, because student have other things need to get done first or just because the assignment is hard. Successful students do not procrastinate studying. If student procrastinate the study session, their studying will become much less effective and may get everything accomplished that need to. Procrastination also leads to rushing, and rushing is the number one cause of errors.

Start with the Most Difficult Subject First

The most difficult assignment or subject will require the most effort and mental energy should start with it first. Once completed the most difficult work it will be much easy to complete the rest of the work. Believe it or not, starting with the most difficult work will greatly improve the effectiveness of their study sessions and your academic performance.

Always Review Student Notes before Starting an Assignment

Obviously, before student can review the notes their must first have notes. Always make sure to take good notes in class. Before start each study session and before start a particular assignment review notes thoroughly to make sure student know how to complete the assignment correctly.

Make Sure Students are not Disturbed while Studying

When students are disturbed and distracted while studying it will lead to very ineffective studying. Before start studying find a place where student won't be disturbed.

Use Study Groups Effectively

Working in groups enables to get help from other students when struggling to understand a concept, to complete assignments more quickly, and to teach others whereby helping both the other student and teachers to internalize the subject matter. However, study groups can become very ineffective if student not structured and if groups members come unprepared. Effective students use study groups effectively.

Review Notes, Schoolwork and other Class Materials over the Weekend

Successful students review what learned during the week over the weekend. These way students are well prepared to continue learning new concepts at the beginning of each week that build upon previous coursework and knowledge acquired the previous week.

HOW TO IMPROVE THE STUDY HABITS

Study with a Partner or in Groups, and Peer Teach

Group studying helps the students engage and process the information more deeply. Student can also divide the class topics and take turns teaching them as creatively as they like. Sometimes the best way to learn something is to teach it, even if you haven't mastered it yet. Actively engaging the information with someone else not only helps you to learn, but makes studying more enjoyable. Just avoid turning the sessions into social hour.

Paint Bigger Pictures

The students have to find ways to connect what student are learning to real life or to other related concepts. It's harder to remember each piece of a puzzle individually than it is to recall the completed picture. Find ways to relate pieces of information to each other and cluster them. Creating context gives information meaning and also turns learning into an experience rather than simple absorption.

Feed the Brain

A hungry brain is an ineffective one. The brain needs the proper nutrients to keep it going. Healthy foods provide nutrients to the brain cells to keep them energized. Hydration is also equally important. Student brain cells need water to function properly and increase their efficiency. Staying hydrated is known to combat anxiety and increase short-term and long-term memory function.

Take Breaks

The brain is like a muscle. It needs exercise to make it stronger, but it can also tire if overwork it. Imagine that each minute of studying is a push-up and student has to complete 100. If try to do all at once, person will fatigue to the point where person can't continue. Essentially burn out and, despite how hard person tries to push, person can't get your chest off the ground. The brain is no different. Person can try to pound the information in after studying non-stop for an hour, but learn little. If divide studying into 15-30 minute blocks with quick breaks in between, the brain will feel refreshed, grateful and ready for the next challenge the person throw at it.

STATEMENT OF THE PROBLEM

The present study is entitled as "The effects of Procrastination, Awareness of Mindfulness attention on the Study habit among higher secondary school students"

The Operational Definition

Procrastination

Klingsieck suggests that following definition based on existing research: *Procrastination is the voluntary delay of an intended and necessary and/or [personally] important activity, despite expecting potential negative consequences that outweigh the positive consequences of the delay.*

In this investigation Procrastination scale is prepared by Clarrylay and validated by investigator.

Mindfulness Attention Awareness

Mindfulness is basically just a particular way of paying attention. It is a way of looking deeply into oneself in the spirit of self-inquiry and self-understanding. (Kabat-Zinn, 1990)

In the study, Mindfulness Attention Awareness scale is standardized by *Brown*, K.W. & *Ryan*, R.M. (*2003*) and validated by investigator

Study Habit

Young (1952) says that study habits play a significant part in scholarship which effect students interest and motivation. Improvements of study habits, not only help in promoting better work, but also influence student's morale and sense of satisfaction.

In the study, it is measured by study habit inventory standardized by DR.B.V.PATEL.

Higher Secondary Students

In the present study, XI standard students studying under Tamil Nadu State board higher secondary education have been considered.

OBJECTIVES OF THE STUDY

The objectives framed in the present study are listed below:

1. To find out the level of Procrastination of higher secondary students.
2. To find out the level of Mindfulness attention awareness of higher secondary students.
3. To find out the level of Study habit of higher secondary students.
4. To find out whether there is any significant association between the categories of Procrastination of higher secondary students and the categories of following with regard.

Gender	:	Male / Female
Type of management	:	govt /govt aided/ private
Medium of instruction	:	Tamil/English
Fathers Education	:	Illiterate/School level College level
Mothers Education	:	Illiterate/School level College level

5. To find out whether there is any significant difference between the associations of Mindfulness attention awareness of higher secondary students based on the following with regard to.
   - Gender
   - Type of management
   - Medium of instruction
   - Fathers Education
   - Mothers Education
6. To find out whether there is any significant difference between the mean scores of Study habit of higher secondary students based on the following presage variables.

- Gender
- Type of management
- Medium of instruction
- Fathers Education
- Mothers Education

7. To find out whether there is any significant association between the categories of Procrastination and Mindfulness attention awareness of higher secondary students
8. To find out whether there is any significant association between the categories of Procrastination and Study habit of higher secondary students.
9. To find out whether there is any significant association between the categories of Mindfulness attention awareness and study habit of higher secondary students.

NEED FOR THE STUDY

Procrastination, the act of needlessly delaying tasks to the point of experiencing subjective discomfort, Procrastination can be understood as knowing that one is supposed to and perhaps even wanting to, complete a task but failing to perform the activity within the expected or desired time frame. When person know what to do nut that don't do it. Delaying or putting off activities that one intends to complete.

Assessment of procrastination has focused almost entirely on the measurement of study habits, such as minutes spent studying and attitude towards studying. Yet procrastination involves for more than deficient time management and study skills. Some of the possible reasons for procrastination are evaluation anxiety, difficulty in making decisions, lack of assertion, fear of consequences of success, task evasiveness and overly perfectionist standards about competency.

The study habits mean setting of subject to be learned or investigated and the tendency of the learners to study when the opportunity is provided. The learners who have academic procrastination delay their action; they fail to use the opportunity effectively. Study habits are the adopted way and manner, when a student plans their private readings, after class room learning. The student with the nature of procrastination eventually fails to plan their private reading and even if they plan delay to put into action. Hence procrastination affects the study habits of the students in its extremity.

Awareness of mindfulness is the intentional and focus of one's attention on the emotions, thoughts and sensations occurring in the present moment. The persons of increased awareness of mindfulness would posses increased attention, executive function that is working memory planning, organization and impulse control, increased emotional regulation, decreased depression, decreased negative effect over all increased self esteem. Awareness of mindfulness attention provides the optimal conditions for learning and teaching and also supports all pedagogical approaches.

Lack of mindfulness attention primarily affects the study habits of the students. Study habits are defined as those techniques such as summarizing, note taking, outlining or locating material which students employ to axis themselves in the efficient learning of the material at hand. The lack of mindfulness attention leads to unsystematic and inefficient study habits of the students.

Hence the present research is undertaken to find out whether there is any significant effect of Procrastination and Awareness of Mindfulness Attention on the study habits among higher secondary school students.

LIMITATIONS OF THE STUDY

The following are the limitations of this study.

- The sample size is restricted only to 300 students drawn randomly, due to paucity of time and energy.
- The investigation is restricted to class higher secondary students.
- The study has been restricted only to Chennai District.
- Only three schools in Chennai district have been selected for this study.

CONCLUSION

The first chapter highlights the introduction to the problem and its statement, the operational definitions of the terms, need for the study, objectives and limitations of the study. A review of related literature, design of the study, analysis and interpretation of the data and summary of the results are dealt within the chapter that follows.

❒

17

Review of Related Literature

In the context of identification of a problem for research, the purpose of systematic reading is beneficial to discover the major issues and research methodologies related to the chosen area, opinion articles, theoretical discussions and reviews of research give a theoretical grounding to a research study. Comprehensive sources such as the Encyclopedia of Educational Research Dissertations, Abstracts International, The Handbook of Research, Survey of Educational Research and similar publications are gold mines which could assist the investigator to develop insight into the problem, formulate hypotheses for the study, develop a proper research design for the study and facilitate to interpret the research findings in the right of what has already been reported and recorded.

NEED FOR SURVEY OF LITERATURE

Extensive critical readings in a field make the investigator familiar with the accumulated facts in this field. Study of related literature sensitizes the individual to familiarize the new avenues of research. It furnishes the research with indispensable suggestions about comparative data, good procedure, likely methods and tried techniques. She/he will be inspired to be alert to research possibilities that have been overlooked and research approaches that have proved to be sterile, findings in many studies provide evidence suggesting need for change in the existing facts. But, such changes can be implemented only after being thoroughly validated in a variety of context. Therefore, replication or extension of completed studies serves resource to research problems.

STUDIES RELATED TO PROCRASTINATION

Piers Steel (2007), a Canadian industrial psychologist, found that procrastination is on the rise and that increased procrastination makes us poorer, fatter, and unhappier on the whole. During his 10-year study, Steel discovered that while in 1978 only 5% of Americans thought of themselves as chronic procrastinators, today the figure is a whopping 26%. Why the change? It could be because there are so many ways to easily distract ourselves these days, from video games to iPads, Steel theorized. While procrastination may not seem like a big deal when you're doing it, Steel found that it actually takes a big toll on corporate profits (to the tune of billions of dollars in lost profits), as well as the mental, physical, and financial health of those who procrastinate chronically.

Bruce Tuckman, Ohio State University compared the grades of severe, moderate, and low procrastinators in a study skills class. The worst procrastinators got an average grade of 2.9 (on a 4.0 scale) while those who procrastinated very little earned an average of 3.6 — a substantial difference. This studies show that many procrastinators justify their habits by saying that they work better under pressure, but his findings demonstrate that this likely isn't true at all and is in reality just wishful thinking.

One reason many people procrastinate is because they believe they can easily complete something in a short amount of time later, when it's closer to the deadline. Unfortunately, a study by the U.S. Department of Labor has shown that people are generally pretty bad at estimating how long a task will take to complete, at least consciously. The authors of the study refer to this as the "planning fallacy" and it could be why so many people end up stressed out or unable to complete projects when they're down to the wire. Strangely, the researchers believe that people really do know how long it will take them to work on something, and that's precisely why they put it off; it's easier to believe the lie and relax now than to face the reality and have to work.

A recent study in the Journal of Clinical and Experimental

Neuropsychology suggests that those who procrastinate, essentially a failure in self-regulation, also had many other characteristics in common including: reduced agency, disorganization, poor impulse and emotional control, poor planning and goal-setting, reduced use of meta-cognitive skills, distractibility, poor task persistence, and time- and task- management deficiencies. Additionally, they believe the deficiencies in these characteristics could have to do with differences in brain structure and function, specifically in the pre-frontal cortex, even though those studied appeared on the surface to be neurologically healthy.

Cumhuriyet University in Turkey (2001), researchers set out to determine who was more likely to procrastinate: high school students, undergraduates, or graduate students. Undergrads were found to be more likely to procrastinate overall, though all grade levels admitted to procrastination to some degree. High school students and undergraduates were found to procrastinate more when it came to exams and grad students when it came to writing papers.

A German study found that getting people to think about concrete problems, even something as simple as opening a new bank account, can actually improve their performance in their other work, even if it's entirely unrelated. Researchers think it has to do with getting the brain to focus on what is concrete, absolute, and present, perhaps giving new perspective to tasks that might have otherwise seemed too abstract to tackle. It echoes something that productivity experts have been touting for ages: if you want to get something done, you have to break it down into more concrete parts. Otherwise, you'll be much more apt to procrastinate..

A study conducted at Stanford in the 1960s and 1970s offered children a treat (a marshmallow, pretzel, or cookie) with some strings attached. They could eat the treat right away if they couldn't resist it or if they could wait a few minutes they would be able to get two treats. At the end of the study, a third of the children couldn't resist the temptation. Researchers continued to follow these children into adulthood as they went to college, got jobs, and started families of their own. Those who were unable to resist temptation at a young age were found to have more behavioral problems, trouble maintaining friendships, difficulty paying attention, and scored a whopping 210 points lower on average on the SAT than their more-patient peers. This inability to self-regulate was found to have lasting effects on health, happiness, and success in the participants.

A study conducted at MIT (2007) compared three different classes using different deadline-setting techniques for a series of paper due for the class. In the first class, students were allowed to set their own deadlines. In the second, all the papers were due on the final day of class. In the third, students had to turn in papers on set dates throughout the semester. Which performed the worst? Despite having the longest amount of time to work, students who turned papers in on the last day got the worst overall grades, as most admitted to putting off the bulk of the work until the end of the semester. The class with the highest grades was that which required papers turned in at set intervals throughout the semester, perhaps because it helped to spread out procrastination and forced students to do at least some amount of work each week.

Career and IQ assessment service Queendom.com studied procrastination through a recent online survey. Along with reaffirming many long-held beliefs about procrastination, the study also revealed some gender differences in procrastination. Women are more likely to procrastinate on issues related to health, because of perfectionism, or because of a low tolerance for frustration. Overall, however, men may procrastinate more than women. Interestingly, procrastination seems to differ by age as well, with more people 25 and over procrastinating than those in younger age groups.

Researchers at DePaul University in Chicago believe that procrastination and levels of self-esteem may be tied to one another. Their study found that those who had lower self-esteem, participated in self-defeating behavior, and exercised interpersonal dependency were much more likely to be procrastinators. Low self-esteem most often led participants in the study to put off completing tasks and to choose situations that were counterproductive to meeting their long-term goals. This study, among others, demonstrates that procrastination may be much more complicated and deeply rooted in our personalities than many of us realize.

Madhan Bet al., found that Trait procrastination is believed to be highly prevalent among college students and detrimental to their educational performance. As the scenario among dental students is virtually unknown, this study was conducted to evaluate the prevalence of trait procrastination among dental students and to analyze its influence on their academic performance. A total of 174 fourth-year dental students from three dental colleges in India voluntarily completed the Lay's Procrastination Scale-student version (LPS). The mean percentage marks scored in the subsequent final university examinations were used as a measure of academic performance. The descriptive statistics were computed to evaluate the prevalence of significant procrastination (LPS score ≥60). Mann-Whitney U test and multiple linear regressions were used to assess the influence of age and gender on procrastination severity, and the latter was again used to analyze the association between procrastination severity and academic performance. The results indicated that 27 percent (n=47) of the students exhibited a significant extent of trait procrastination; neither age nor gender affected its severity ($p<0.05$). Procrastination had a significant and negative impact on the academic performance of the student (beta=-0.150, $p=0.039$). These findings highlight the need for active measures to reduce the causes and consequences of procrastination in dental education.

STUDIES RELATED TO MINDFULNESS ATTENTION AWARENESS

Miles Thompson, Jeremy Gauntlett-Gilbert, Mindfulness interventions within adult populations are becoming increasingly popular. Research suggests that mindfulness can deliver lasting improvements in self-awareness and emotional stability to adults with severe and chronic conditions. As yet, research within child and adolescent populations is in its initial stages, although mindfulness shows great clinical promise for young people. This article aims to provide an overview of mindfulness to professionals who are working in child or adolescent settings. Initially, it will provide the reader with some orientation to and definitions from the field, before summarizing the current evidence for the utility of the approach. The article recommends specific clinical modifications for mindfulness with children and adolescents, as well as reviewing how to monitor and enhance the development of this skill. Finally, it highlights important differences among mindfulness, relaxation and other meditative techniques.

Christine A. Burke Interest in applications of mindfulness-based approaches with adults has grown rapidly in recent times, and there is an expanding research base that suggests these are efficacious approaches to promoting psychological health and well-being. Interest has spread to applications of mindfulness-based approaches with children and adolescents, yet the research is still in its infancy. I aim to provide a preliminary review of the current research base of mindfulness-based approaches with children and adolescents, focusing on MBSR/MBCT models, which place the regular practice of mindfulness meditation at the core of the intervention. Overall, the current research base provides support for the feasibility of mindfulness-based interventions with children and adolescents; however there is no generalized empirical evidence of the efficacy of these interventions. For the field to advance, I suggest that research needs to shift away from feasibility studies towards large, well-designed studies with robust methodologies, and adopt standardized formats for interventions, allowing for replication and comparison studies, to develop a firm research evidence base. Keywords Mindfulness meditation-Children-Adolescents-Families-Schools

Kirk Warren Brown, Richard M Ryan Mindfulness is an attribute of consciousness long believed to promote well-being. This research provides a theoretical and empirical examination of the role of mindfulness in psychological well-being. The development and psychometric properties of the dispositional Mindful Attention Awareness Scale (MAAS) are described. Correlational, quasi-experimental, and laboratory studies then show that the MAAS measures a unique quality of consciousness that is related to a variety of well-being constructs, that differentiates mindfulness practitioners from others, and that is associated with enhanced self-awareness. An experience-sampling study shows that both dispositional and state mindfulness predict self-regulated behavior and positive emotional states. Finally, a clinical intervention study with cancer patients demonstrates that increases in mindfulness over time relate to declines in mood disturbance and stress.

Ruth A Baer, Gregory T Smith, Kristin B Allen A self-report inventory for the assessment of mindfulness skills was developed, and its psychometric characteristics and relationships with other constructs were examined. Participants included three samples of undergraduate students and a sample of outpatients with borderline personality disorder Based on discussions of mindfulness in the current literature, four mindfulness skills were specified: observing, describing, acting with awareness, and accepting without judgment. Scales designed to measure each skill were developed and evaluated. Results showed good internal consistency and test-retest reliability and a clear factor structure. Most expected relationships with other constructs were significant. Findings suggest that mindfulness skills are differentially related to aspects of personality and mental health, including neuroticism, psychological symptoms, emotional intelligence, alexithymia, experiential avoidance, dissociation and absorption.

STUDIES RELATED TO STUDY HABITS

Mayer and George (1936) in order to investigate methods of study and efficiency of learning found that those who have learned most efficiently were those who prepared the lessons in the systematic way.

Cuff (1949) made an attempt to find out the general rules of study habits that are essential for effective learning. He concluded that some of them who were successful had a definite time for the study of specific lessons, took notes on lecturers, ignored distractions, skimmed over material before detailed reading, sought favorable environment for study, reviewed previous work including silent recitation, etc.

Jamuar (1961) found a significant relationship between study habits and personality patterns, besides study habits has been found to be significantly correlated with such factors as father's occupation and family relationship.

An investigation was carried out by Barry et al (1974) on study habits and locus of control as factors of academic achievement. They administered Rotter's internal-external control scale and question on study habits of 150 girls and 150 boys high school students. They observed that internally oriented males used their study time more efficiently than external oriented boys.

Michael, D (1979) conducted an experimental study on 9th grade pupils. Two experimental groups each having 150 students were matched for mental age, chronological age, sex, school, year, curriculum and teacher. The experimental group was given instruction on how to study for two 45 minutes, periods each week. But the control group was not given any instructions. They transfer effects of the course were measured again by a testing History, Latin, Algebra courses taken by all members of both the groups. This study indicated that the students of very poor ability and students of very high intelligence did not profit from such a course.

Nelson Geoffrey (1984) found that families with high degree of parent, child interaction and climate providing support and structure, were generally associated with high level of self-concept, subjects with the highest level of scholastic self-concept had both classroom and family environment high in support and structure. It is concluded that environment is important for effective and intellectual growth in students.

Patel and **Yashomati (1985)** studied the impact of study habits and academic achievement among backward students in the STD VIII at rural and urban schools in India. Study Habits Inventory by Dr. P.V. Patel (1974) and terminal examination grades reveal that study habits are important determinant of school achievements for both boys and girls in rural as well as urban setting.

In a study by **Cade Eldon Hurburt (1986),** it was found that subject especially boys have poor attitude about their schools and teachers and those subjects also have inferior study habits and skills.

Nagalinkam (1988) made an attempt to find out the attitude of the students towards mathematics and study habits and their relationship with achievement in mathematics. A simple of 300 students of STD IX four high schools were randomly selected for the study in Shillong. The tools used were Likert type attitude scale meant to measure the attitude of student's towards mathematics an achievement test and Rao's Study Habits Inventory. Descriptive statistics and analysis of variance were used to treat the data. No significant difference was found in the attitude towards mathematics. No significant difference was found in t, male and female students belonging to high average and low scores on mathematics achievement did not show significant difference in their attitude as well as study habits score.

Smitra L. Patel (1988) made an investigation to find out the extent of relationship between academic achievement and intelligence, attitude towards study, teacher and school. For the purpose of the study an intelligent test and attitude scale measuring attitude towards study, towards teacher and school were administered and 200 students studying in different Gujarati medium school and the data were analyzed, using the statistical technique of coefficient correlation and partial correlation. It was found that intelligence and attitude towards study has significant influence on academic achievement.

Nagappa (1995) examined the study habits among STD IX high school students in Mysore City. A Study Habit Scale was constructed by the investigator. Selected by following multistage random sampling techniques. The study records that there was significant inter-correlation among the seven different area of the study habits scale. Good study habits group was the smallest in size compared to other two categories. There was significant relationship between the level of study habits and the sex of the students. The girls percentage was more than the boys in the good study habits group. Their percentage was less than boys in the average study habits group but their percentage was higher than boys in the poor study habits group. Pupils studying in private school were better than pupil studying in government school in their study habits. Both boys and girls in private school possessed better study habits than the boys and girls in government schools.

CONCLUSION

The study of related literature has helped the investigator to have a clear perspective of the problem chosen for the present investigation. Designing the method of research, description of the variable, sample selection, selection of suitable tools, administration and scoring methods of responses have been undertaken based on the review which is discussed in the succeeding chapter.

❐

18

Design of the Study and Method of Investigation

This chapter focuses on the design of the study, research tools used in the study, nature and selection of the sample and a brief description of the procedure adapted for the collection of data. This chapter also includes the view of reliability and validity of the variables used for the study.

HYPOTHESES OF THE STUDY

The hypotheses framed in the present study are listed below:

1. The level of procrastination of higher secondary students is average in nature.
2. The level of mindfulness attention awareness of higher secondary student is average in nature.
3. The level of study habit of higher secondary students is average in nature.
4. There is no significant association between the categories of Procrastination of higher secondary students with regard to

Gender	:	Male / Female
Type of management	:	Govt/Govtaided/ Private
Medium of instruction	:	Tamil/English
Fathers Education	:	Illiterate/School level/College level
Mothers Education	:	Illiterate/School level/College level

5. There is no significant association between the Mindfulness attention awareness of higher secondary students with regard to
   - Gender
   - Type of management
   - Medium of instruction
   - Fathers Education
   - Mothers Education
6. There is no significant difference between the mean scores of Study habit of higher secondary students with regard to.
   - Gender
   - Type of management
   - Medium of instruction
   - Fathers Education
   - Mothers Education
7. There is no significant association between the categories of Procrastination and Mindfulness attention awareness of higher secondary students.
8. There is no significant association between the categories of Procrastination and Study habit of higher secondary students.
9. There is no significant association between Mindfulness attention awareness and study habit of higher secondary students.

TOOLS AND TECHNIQUES USED

The following tools have been used in the present study.

1. Procrastination scale prepared by Clarry lay
2. Mindfulness attention awareness scale prepared by *Brown*, K.W. & *Ryan*, R.M. (*2003*).
3. Study habit inventory prepared by DR.B.V.Patel.

PROCRASTINATION SCALE

Description

Procrastination scale has been used in order to find the level of procrastination of students. **(Appendix-I)** The inventory consists of 20 items. It is measured by a 6 point scale.

Administration

To get the comprehensive Procrastination score, a copy of the Procrastination scale was distributed to each student, after explaining the purpose of it. Students were encouraged to present a real character about their procrastination. They took 10 minutes to complete the scale.

Scoring

The scores of procrastination scale were added from questions 1, 2, 5, 7, 9, 10, 12, 16, 17, and 19. If the total comes to between 40 and 50 points, procrastination may be limiting the success and happiness.

MINDFULNESS ATTENTIION AWARNESS INVENTORY

Description

Mindfulness Attention Awareness scale has been used in order to find the level of Mindfulness attention awareness of students. The inventory consists of 15 items. It is measured by a 6 point scale.

Administration

Proper seating arrangement was made for the students and assurance was given that the response obtained from them would be kept confidential. After the instructions, administrator explained a few questions.

Scoring

The scores were added and then the total was divided by 15. This gives the average score for the fifteen statements. The higher the score, the higher the mindfulness. Typically the average score is around 3.86. The highest score is 6 and the lowest score is 1.

STUDY HABIT INVENTORY

Description

Study Habits Inventory has been used in the study to find out the study habits of the XI standard students. This tool consists of 45 statements covering different areas of student behavior such as home environment and planning, reading and note taking, planning of subject, habits of concentration, preparation for examination, general habits and attitudes and school environment.

TABLE. 18.1: Nature of Statements of the Study Habits Inventory

S.No	Nature of Statements	Item numbers
1	Positive statements	1,2,3,4,8,9,10,11,12,13,16,17,18,19,22,25,26,32,33, 36,37,38,39,40,41,42,43,44 (Total= 28)
2	Negative statements	5,6,7,14,15,20,22,23,24,27,28,29,30,31,34,35,45 (Total= 17)

Administration

Before administering the test, the following instructions and directions were given to the students.

The aim of the questionnaire that has been given to you is to know the study habits. There are totally 45 statements in the inventory. Among them, each statement is based on five points scale. The five points are always, often, something, seldom, and never. For each statement, you put a tick on any one of the five categories. Be frank and record your responses accordingly for all the items, without omitting any and 30 minutes were set for the completion of this inventory.

Scoring Procedure

In case of positive statements of study habits, the student is to be given 'always' – 5; 'often' – 4; 'sometimes' – 3; 'seldom' – 2; 'never' – 1, if he puts a tick mark in the columns respectively.

In the case of negative statements of study habits, the score is to be awarded in reverse order to the former (i.e) 'always' – 1, 'often' – 2 , 'sometimes' – 3; 'seldom' – 4; 'never' – 5, if he puts a tick mark in the column respectively.

A total score on the inventory for each student was obtained by summing up the scores.

Sample

The present study was concerned with higher secondary schools. Hence, the students of standard XI from various government schools, government aided schools and private schools were taken to constitute the population for the present study. Stratified random sampling technique was adopted in the present study. The size of the sample was 300.

TABLE. 18.2: Showing the Details of the Domposition of the Sample

Type of schools	Name of School	Number of students selected		
		Boys	Girls	Total
Government	Model Government Higher Secondary School, Triplicane	48	39	87
Government Aided	Wesely Higher Secondary School, Chennai	82	-	82
Private	Rex Matriculation Higher Secondary School, Triplicane	69	62	131
	Total	**199**	**101**	**300**

PILOT STUDY

Before finalizing the final form of the tools and collecting data for main study, a pilot study was attempted in November 2014. It was conducted on 50 eleventh standard students drawing from each school selected randomly from the whole sample to establish reliability and validity of the various tools used in the study.

ESTABLISHING RELIABILITY AND VALIDITY

The reliability of a test may be defined as the degree of consistency with which the test measures, what it does measure. A test score is called reliable, when we have reasons to believe it to be stable and trustworthy.

Reliability

Procrastination Scale

The reliability co-efficient for the inventory computed by test-retest method yielded a high reliability coefficient of 0.69 This value reveals that the tool used is highly reliable.

Mindfulness attention awareness Scale

The reliability of **Mindfulness attention awareness** inventory is obtained by test-retest method and it is equal to 0.86 indicating that the tool is highly reliable.

Study Habit Inventory

The reliability of this tool is assessed by split-half technique and it is measured to be 0.71 indicating high reliability of the tool.

Validity

Validity is one of the most important considerations of good measuring device. It relates to the question what the test measures, validity of a test refers to the test quality to measure what it s intended to measure. This means a test is valid, when it can measure the achievement of objectives for which it is designed. A test is valid, when it measures truly and accurately the ability or quality one wants to measure. Thus, validity means truthfulness of test.

Procrastination Scale

The validity of this tool was found out by computing the square root of the reliability co efficient which worked out to be 0.83. Hence this tool is considered to be highly valid.

Mindfulness Attention Awareness Scale

The index of validity is considered to be the square root of reliability which is equal to its 0.92 indicating that this tool is highly valid.

Study habit Inventory

The validity of this tool is calculated to be the square root of reliability i.e. $\sqrt{0.71} = 0.84$ It clearly shows that this tool is highly valid.

MAIN STUDY

The validated tools were made use for the main study to collect the necessary data in November 2014.

The time schedule for each of these tests finalized on the basis of the pilot study.

TABLE. 18.3: Showing the Time Schedule of Administered Tools

S.No.	Name of test	Time Taken (Minutes)
1.	Procrastination Scale	10
2.	Mindfulness attention awareness Scale	10
3.	Study habit Inventory	20
	Total	**40**

STATISTICAL TECHNIQUES USED

Suitable descriptive and inferential statistical techniques were used in the interpretation of the data to draw out a more meaningful picture of results from the collected data. In the present study, the following statistical measures were used.

1. Mean

$$\bar{X} = A + \frac{\sum fd}{\sum f} \times i$$

Where

A = Assumed mean

f = frequency

d = deviation from the assumed mean

i = class interval

2. Standard Deviation

$$\sigma = \sqrt{\frac{\sum fd^2}{N} - \left(\frac{\sum fd}{N}\right)^2} xi$$

where

f = frequency

i = class interval

N = Total frequency

d = Deviation from arithmetic mean

3. Standard Error Deviation

$$SED = \sqrt{\frac{\sigma_1^2}{N_1} + \frac{\sigma_2^2}{N_2}}$$

Where

= Standard deviation

N_1 N_2 = Total number of sample

4. t-Test

To compute the significance of difference between mean of various measures, t-test was used. 't' ratio was calculated from the relation.

$$\text{t-value} = \frac{M_1 - M_2}{\sqrt{\frac{\sigma_1^2}{N_1} + \frac{\sigma_2^2}{N_2}}}$$

Where

$M_1 M_2$ = Mean of the groups

$\sigma_1 \sigma_2$ = Standard Deviations

$N_1 N_2$ = Total number of sample

5. Correlation Co-efficient

$$r = \frac{N\sum XY - \sum X \sum Y}{\sqrt{\left[N\sum x^2 - (\sum X)^2\right]} - \left[\sqrt{\left[N\sum Y^2 - (\sum Y^2)\right]}\right]}$$

where

X, Y = Variables

N = Total strength

6. Chi-Square Distribution

$$x^2 = \sum \frac{(fo - fe)^2}{fe}$$

Where fo = Observed frequency

fe = Expected frequency

7. F-Test

$$C = \frac{(\sum x_1 + \sum x_2 + \sum x_3)^2}{N}$$

$$TSS = \sum x_1^2 + \sum x_2^2 + \sum x_3^2 - C$$

$$BSS = \frac{(\sum x1)^2}{n_1} + \frac{(\sum x2)^2}{n_2} + \frac{(\sum x3)^2}{n_3} - C$$

$$WSS = TSS - BSS$$

$$t_1 = \frac{BSS}{dfB}; t_2 = \frac{WSS}{dfW}$$

$$F = \frac{t_1}{t_2}$$

Where

C = Correction term

$\sum X_1, \sum X_2, \sum X_3,$ = Sum of the scores of each groups.

N = Total number of Sample

n_1, n_2, n_3 = Number of sample of each groups

TSS = Total Number of Squares

BSS = Sum of squares between the group means

WSS = Sum of squares within the group

dfB = Degrees of freedom for the between group means.

dfw = Degrees of freedom for within group means

t_1 = Mean sum of squares between the group

t_2 = Mean sum of squares within the group.

CONCLUSION

This chapter outlines the design of the present study, the procedure followed and the nature of the sample. It describes the hypotheses to be tested, the tools used and methods of administration and scoring. Adopting the methods and procedures discussed earlier in this chapter, tests were administered and marked. The obtained data were then analysed, using appropriate statistical techniques described above to study the effect of Procrastination, Mindfulness attention awareness and Study habit, the results of which are discussed in the light of hypotheses formulated and the next chapter presents this analysis and discussion part of the study.

❐

19

Analysis and Interpretation of the Data

This chapter highlights the analysis of the data obtained regarding the influence of the variables of the study using appropriate techniques verifying hypotheses, framed for the present study. The findings were interpreted and discussed.

CLASSIFICATION OF THE SAMPLE BASED ON THE VARIABLES OF THE STUDY

Procrastination

Based on the information obtained from the XI standard students regarding their Procrastination, the students are divided into three groups namely low, moderate and high level of Procrastination, the details of which are presented below.

TABLE. 19.1: Showing the Categorization of Students Based on Procrastination

Groups	Procrastination Range	Number of students	Percentage (%)
Low	26 and below	79	26.3
Moderate	27 to 33	136	45.3
High	34 and above	85	28.3
		Total	**100**

The above table reveals that the level of procrastination of higher secondary students is average in nature. Hence hypothesis I stating that, "The level of procrastination of higher secondary students is moderate in nature" is accepted

Mindfulness Attention Awareness

Based on the information obtained from the XI standard students regarding their Mindfulness Attention Awareness, the students are divided into three groups namely low, moderate and high level of Mindfulness Attention Awareness, the details of which are presented below.

TABLE. 19.2: Showing the Criteria of Classifying the Sample into three Groups of Mindfulness Attention Awareness

Groups	Mindfulness Attention Awareness range	Number of students	Percentage
Low	2.01 and below	75	25.0
Moderate	2.02 to 3.92	149	49.7
High	3.93 and above	76	25.3
		Total	**100**

From the table, it is seen that the level of Mindfulness attention awareness of XI standard students is average in nature.

Hence hypothesis-II stating that, "The level of Mindfulness Attention Awareness of higher secondary students is average in nature" is accepted.

Study Habit

Based on the information obtained from the XI standard students regarding their Study habit, the students are divided into three groups namely low, moderate and high level of study habit, the details of which are presented below.

TABLE. 19.3: Showing the Criteria of Classifying the Sample into three Groups of Study Habit

Groups	Study Habit	Number of students	Percentage (%)
Low	122 and below	77	25.7
Moderate	123 to 140	146	48.7
High	Above and 141	77	25.7
		Total	**100**

From the table, it is seen that the level of Study habit of XI standard students is moderate in nature.

Hence hypothesis-III stating that, "The level of Study Habit of higher secondary students is average in nature" is accepted.

ASSOCIATION BETWEEN PROCRASTINATIONAND GENDER

Association between Procrastination and gender of higher secondary students has been computed and presented in the following table.

TABLE. 19.4: Showing Chi-Square Test Revealing the Extent of Association between the Procrastination and Gender

Procrastination	Gender		Total
	Male	Female	
Low	52 (52.40)	27 (26.59)	79
Moderate	90 (90.21)	46 (45.78)	136
High 57 (56.38)		28 (28.61)	85
Total	**199**	**101**	**300**

Df= 2

Value

As the calculated value (0.031) is lesser than table value (5.991) at 0.05 level, it is clear that procrastination and gender are not significantly associated.

Hence hypothesis vi (a) stating that, "there is no significant association between the level of procrastination of higher secondary students with regard to gender" is accepted.

ASSOCIATION BETWEEN PROCRASTINATION AND TYPE OF MANAGEMENT

Association between procrastination and type of management of higher secondary students has been computed and presented in the following table.

TABLE. 19.5: Showing Chi-Square Test Revealing the Extent of Association between the Procrastination and Type of Management

Procrastination	Type of management			Total
	Govt	Govt aided	Private	
Low	16 (22.91)	29 (21.59)	34 (34.49)	79
Moderate	49 (39.44)	39 (37.17)	48 (53.38)	136
High	22 (24.65)	14 (23.23)	49 (37.11)	85
Total	**87**	**82**	**131**	**300**

Df = 4 Value = 16.981

As the calculated value (16.981) is greater than table value (13.277) at 0.01 level, it is clear that procrastination and type of management are significantly associated.

Hence hypothesis vi (b) stating that, "there is no significant association between the categories of procrastination of higher secondary students with regard to type of management" is rejected.

ASSOCIATION BETWEEN PROCRASTINATION AND MEDIUM OF INSTRUCTION

Association between procrastination and medium of instruction of higher secondary students has been computed and presented in the following table.

TABLE. 19.6: Showing Chi-Square Test Revealing the Extent of Association between the Procrastination and Medium of Instruction

Procrastination	Medium of instruction		Total
	Tamil	English	
Low	25 (30.54)	54 (48.45)	79
Moderate	65 (52.58)	71 (83.86)	136
High	26 (32.86)	59 (52.13)	85
Total	**116**	**184**	**300**

Df = 2 Value = 8.759

As the calculated value (8.759) is greater than table value (5.991) at 0.05 level, it is clear that procrastination and medium of instruction are significantly associated.

Hence hypothesis vi (c) stating that, "there is no significant association between the categories of procrastination of higher secondary students with regard to medium of instruction" is rejected.

ASSOCIATION BETWEEN PROCRASTINATION AND MOTHER'S EDUCATION

Association between procrastination and mother's education of higher secondary students has been computed and presented in the following table.

TABLE. 19.7: Showing Chi-Square Test Revealing the Extent of Association between the Procrastination and Mother's Education

Procrastination	Mother's Education			Total
	Illiterate	School	College	
Low	12 (15.27)	57 (54.77)	10 (8.95)	79
Moderate	26 (26.29)	95 (94.29)	15 (15.41)	136

High	20 (16.43)	56 (58.93)	9 (9.63)	85
Total	**58**	**208**	**34**	**300**

Df = 4 Value = 1.896

As the calculated value (1.896) lesser than table value (9.488) at 0.05 level, it is clearly stated that procrastination and mothers education are not significantly associated.

Hence hypothesis vi (d) stating that, "there is no significant association between the categories of procrastination of higher secondary students with regard to mothers education" is accepted.

ASSOCIATION BETWEEN PROCRASTINATION AND FATHER'S EDUCATION

Association between procrastination and father's education of higher secondary students has been computed and presented in the following table.

TABLE. 19.8: Showing Chi-Square Test Revealing the Extent of Association between the Procrastination and Father's Education

Procrastination	**Father's Education**			**Total**
	Illiterate	**School**	**College**	
Low	15 (19.48)	53 (49.24)	11 (10.27)	79
Moderate	36 (33.54)	81 (84.77)	19 (17.68)	136
High	23 (20.96)	53 (52.98)	9 (11.05)	85
Total	**74**	**187**	**39**	**300**

Df = 4 Value = 2.395

As the calculated value (2.395) is lesser than the table value (9.488) at 0.05 level, it is clear that procrastination and father's education are not significantly associated.

Hence hypothesis vi (d) stating that, "there is no significant association between the categories of procrastination of higher secondary students with regard to fathers education" is accepted.

ASSOCIATION BETWEEN MINDFULNESS ATTENTION AWARENESS AND GENDER

Association between Mindfulness attention awareness and gender of higher secondary students has been computed and presented in the following table.

TABLE.19.9: Showing Chi-Square Test Revealing the Extent of Association between the Mindfulness Attention Awareness and Gender

Mindfulness attention awareness	Gender		Total
	Male	Female	
Low	61 (49.75)	14 (25.25)	75
Moderate	99 (98.83)	50 (50.16)	149
High	39 (50.41)	37 (25.58)	76
Total	**199**	**101**	**300**

Df=2 Value = 15.232

As the calculated value (15.232) greater than table value (9.210) at 0.01 level, it is clearly stated that Mindfulness attention awareness and gender are significantly associated.

Hence hypothesis vi (a) stating that, "there is no significant association between the categories of Mindfulness attention awareness of higher secondary students with regard to gender" is rejected.

ASSOCIATION BETWEEN MINDFULNESS ATTENTION AWARENESS AND TYPE OF ANAGEMENT

Association between Mindfulness attention awareness and type of management of higher secondary students has been computed and presented in the following table.

TABLE. 19.10: Showing Chi-Square Test Revealing the Extent of Association between the Mindfulness Attention Awareness and Type of Management

Mindfulness attention awareness	Type of management			Total
	Govt	Govt aided	Private	
Low	3 (2.75)	31 (20.5)	41 (32.75)	75
Moderate	60 (43.21)	34 (40.72)	55 (65.06)	149

High	24 (22.04)	17 (20.77)	35 (33.18)	76
Total	87	82	131	300

Df = 4 Value = 33.770

As the calculated value (33.770) is greater than table value (13.277) at 0.01 level, it is clearly stated that Mindfulness attention awareness and Type of management are significantly associated.

Hence hypothesis vi (b) stating that, "there is no significant association between the categories of Mindfulness attention awareness of higher secondary students with regard to type of management" is rejected.

ASSOCIATION BETWEEN MINDFULNESS ATTENTION AWARENESS AND MEDIUM OF INSTRUCTION

Association between Mindfulness attention awareness and type of management of higher secondary students has been computed and presented in the following table.

TABLE. 19.11: Showing Chi-Square Test Revealing the Extent of Association between the Mindfulness Attention Awareness and Medium of Instruction

Mindfulness attention awareness	**Medium of instruction**		**Total**
	Tamil	English	
Low	15 (29)	60 (46)	75
Moderate	72 (57.61)	77 (91.38)	149
High	29 (29.38)	47 (46.61)	76
Total	**116**	**184**	**300**

Df = 2 Value = 16.885

As the calculated value (16.885) is greater than table value (9.210) at 0.01 level, it is clearly stated that Mindfulness attention awareness and Medium of instruction are significantly associated.

Hence hypothesis vi (c) stating that, "there is no significant association between the categories of Mindfulness attention awareness of higher secondary students with regard to medium of instruction" is rejected.

ASSOCIATION BETWEEN MINDFULNESS ATTENTION AWARENESS AND FATHER'S EDUCATION

Association between Mindfulness attention awareness and father's education of higher secondary students has been computed and presented in the following table.

TABLE. 19.12: Showing Chi-Square Test Revealing the Extent of Association between the Mindfulness Attention Awareness and Father's Education

Mindfulness attention awareness	Father's Education			Total
	Illiterate	School	College	
Low	11 (18.5)	52 (46.75)	12 (9.75)	75
Moderate	44 (36.75)	84 (92.87)	21 (19.36)	149
High	19 (18.74)	51 (47.37)	6 (9.88)	76
Total	74	187	39	300

Df = 4 Value = 8.369

As the calculated value (8.369) is lesser than the table value (9.488) at 0.05 level, it is clear that Mindfulness attention awareness and fathers education are not significantly associated.

Hence hypothesis vi (d) stating that, "there is no significant association between the categories of Mindfulness attention awareness of higher secondary students with regard to fathers education" is accepted.

ASSOCIATION BETWEEN MINFULNESS ATTENTION AWARENESS AND MOTHER'S EDUCATION

Association between Mindfulness attention awareness and mother's education of higher secondary students has been computed and presented in the following table.

TABLE. 19.13: Showing Chi-Square Test Revealing the Extent of Association between the Mindfulness Attention Awareness and Mother's Education

Mindfulness attention awareness	Mother's Education			Total
	Illiterate	School	College	
Low	12 (14.5)	52 (52)	11 (8.5)	75
Moderate	34 (28.80)	97 (9.70)	18 (16.88)	149
High	12 (14.69)	59 (52.69)	5 (8.61)	76
Total	**58**	**208**	**34**	**300**

Df = 4 Value = 5.325

As the calculated value (5.325) is lesser than the table value (9.488) at 0.05 level, it is clearly that Mindfulness attention awareness and Mother's education status are not significantly associated.

Hence hypothesis vi (d) stating that, "there is no significant association between the categories of Mindfulness attention awareness of higher secondary students with regard to mothers education" is accepted.

INFLUENCE OF GENDER ON STUDY HABIT

The scores of school discipline of higher secondary students of boys and girls have been analyzed as shown below.

TABLE. 19.14: Showing the Significant Difference between the mean Scores of Study Habit of Higher Secondary Students of Boys and Girls

Group comparison	N	Mean	S.D.	`t' value	Level of significance
Boys	199	132.38	16.769	2.252	0.05
Girls	101	127.91	15.164		

From the above table, it is inferred that boys are significantly higher than their counter part with regard to study habit.

Hence the hypothesis viii(a) stating that, "There is no significant difference between the mean scores of Study habit of higher secondary students with regard to gender" is rejected.

INFLUENCE OF TYPE OF MANAGEMENT OF THE STUDENTS ON STUDY HABIT

The scores of school discipline of higher secondary students based on their Type of management (Govt/Govt aided / Private) have been analyzed and the obtained result is presented below.

TABLE. 19.15: ANOVA Showing the Significant Difference between the mean Scores of Study Habit of Govt, Govt aided and Private Students

Source	Sum of squares	df	Mean squares	`f' Ratio	Level of significance
Between groups	125.560	2	628.280	2.369	NS
Within groups	78751.877	297	265.158		
Total	**80008.437**	**299**			

As the obtained 'f' value 2.369 is lesser than the table value (3.02) at 0.05 level. Therefore there is no significant difference between the mean scores of study habit of Govt, Govt aided and private students

Hence the hypothesis viii(c) stating that, "There is no significant difference between the mean scores of study habit of higher secondary students with regard to the type of management of the students" is accepted.

INFLUENCE OF MEDIUM OF INSTRUCTION OF THE STUDENTS ON STUDY HABIT

The scores of school discipline of higher secondary students based on their medium of instruction of the students (Tamil/English) have been analysed and the obtained result is presented below.

TABLE. 19.16: Showing the Significant Difference between the mean Scores of Study Habit of Tamil and English students

Group comparison	N	Mean	S.D.	`t' value	Level of significance
Tamil	116	133.59	16.845	2.294	0.05
English	184	129.17	15.853		

From the above table, it is clear that tamil medium students have high significant study habit than English medium students.

Hence the hypothesis viii (b) stating that, "There is no significant difference between the mean scores of study habit of higher secondary students with regard to the medium of instruction" is rejected.

INFLUENCE OF FATHER'S EDUCATIONAL STATUS OF THE STUDENTS ON STUDY HABIT

The influence of father's educational status (Illiterate / School level / College level) of higher secondary students on study habit has been investigated and obtained results have been tabulated in the following table.

TABLE. 19.17: ANOVA Showing the Significance of the Difference between the mean Scores of Study Habit of Higher Secondary Students Based on their father Educational Status

Source	Sum of squares	DF	Mean squares	`F' Ratio	Level of significance
Between groups	1162.360	2	581.180	2.189	NS
Within groups	78846.077	297	265.475		
Total	**80008.437**	**299**			

As the obtained F-value (2.189) is lesser than the table value 3.02 at 0.05 level, Therefore there is no significant influence of the father educational status on the study habit of higher secondary students

Hence hypothesis viii (d) stating that, "There is no significant difference between the mean scores of study habit of higher secondary students with regard to the father educational status" is accepted.

NFLUENCE OF MOTHER'S EDUCATIONAL STATUS OF THE STUDENTS ON STUDY HABIT

The influence of mother's educational status (Illiterate/School level/College level) of higher secondary students on study habit has been investigated and obtained results have been tabulated in the following table.

TABLE. 19.18: ANOVA Showing the Significance of the Difference between the mean Scores of Study Habit of Higher Secondary Students based on their Mother Educational Status

Source	Sum of squares	DF	Mean squares	`F' Ratio	Level of significance
Between groups	891.168	2	445.587	1.673	NS
Within groups	79117.286	297	266.388		
Total	**80008.437**	**299**			

As the obtained F-value 1.673 is lesser than the table value 3.02 at 0.05 level, there is no significant influence of the mother educational status on the study habit of higher secondary students.

Hence hypothesis viii (d) stating that, "There is no significant difference between the mean scores of study habit of higher secondary students with regard to the mother educational status" is accepted.

ASSOCIATION BETWEEN PROCRASTINATION AND MINDFULNESS ATTENTION AWARENESS

Association between procrastination and mindfulness attention awareness of higher secondary students has been computed and presented in the following table.

TABLE. 19.19: Showing the Chi-Square Test Revealing the Extent of Association between the Procrastination and Mindfulness Attention Awareness

Procrastination	Mindfulness attention awareness			Total
	Low	Moderate	High	
Low	16 (19.75)	38 (39.23)	25 (20.01)	79
Moderate	28 (34)	82 (67.54)	26 (4.05)	136
High	31 (21.25)	29 (42.21)	25 (21.53)	85
Total	**75**	**149**	**76**	**300**

DF = 4 Value = 17.388

As the calculated value (17.388) is greater than the table value (13.277) at 0.01 levels, the procrastination and Mindfulness attention awareness are significantly associated.

Hence hypothesis VII stating that, "There is no significant association between the categories of Procrastination and Mindfulness attention awareness status of higher secondary students" is rejected.

ASSOCIATION BETWEEN PROCRASTINATION AND STUDY HABIT

Association between procrastination and study habit of higher secondary students has been computed and presented in the following table.

TABLE. 19.20: Showing the Chi-Square Test Revealing the Extent of Association between the Procrastination and Study Habit

Procrastination	Study Habit			Total
	122 and below	**123 to 140**	**Above and 141**	
Low	21 (20.27)	41 (38.44)	17 (20.27)	79
Moderate	36 (34.90)	67 (67.64)	33 (34.90)	136
High	20 (21.81)	38 (41.36)	27 (21.81)	85
Total	**77**	**146**	**77**	**300**

DF = 4 Value = 2.530

As the calculated value (2.530) is lesser than table value (9.488) at 0.05 level, it is clearly that Procrastination and Study habit are not significantly associated.

Hence hypothesis VII stating that, "There is no significant association between the categories of Procrastination and Study habit status of higher secondary students" is accepted.

ASSOCIATION BETWEEN MINDFULNESS ATTENTION AWARENESS AND STUDY HABIT

Association between Mindfulness attention awareness and study habit of higher secondary students has been computed and presented in the following table.

TABLE. 19.21: Showing the Chi-Square Test Revealing the Extent of Association between the Mindfulness Attention Awareness and Study Habit

Mindfulness Attention Awareness	Study Habit			Total
	122 and Below	**123 to 140**	**Above and 141**	
Low	24 (19.25)	35 (36.5)	16 (19.25)	75

Moderate	35 (38.24)	72 (72.51)	42 (38.24)	149
High	18 (19.50)	39 (36.98)	19 (19.50)	76
Total	**77**	**146**	**77**	**300**

DF = 4 Value = 2.669

Comparing the obtained value (2.669) less than table value (9.48) at 0.05 level. We find that Mindfulness attention awareness and study habit are not significantly associated.

Hence hypothesis IX stating that, "There is no significant association between the categories of Mindfulness attention awareness and Study habit of higher secondary students" is accepted.

CONCLUSION

The findings and conclusion thus obtained from the analysis of this chapter have been summarized and presented along with a brief report of statement of the problem, objectives, design of the study and implications of the study in the chapter to follow.

❐

20

Summary, Findings and Conclusion

This chapter deals with the consolidation of the various findings presented in the previous chapter. Findings are statement of factual information based upon the data analysis. Conclusion is answers to the question raised or the statements of acceptance or rejection of the hypotheses proposed. In this chapter the researcher deals with the aspects pertaining to the tools used for the investigation, objectives and hypotheses of study, based on analysis the major findings arrived at, all finally the educational implication together with suggestion for further study. The aim of the present investigations is to study the Procrastination, Mindfulness awareness attention and Study habit of higher secondary students.

STATEMENT OF THE PROBLEM

The present study is entitled as, "The effects of Procrastination, Awareness of Mindfulness Attention on the Study Habits among higher secondary school students".

OBJECTIVES OF THE STUDY

The objectives framed in the present study are listed below:

1. To find out the level of Procrastination of higher secondary students.
2. To find out the level of Mindfulness attention awareness of higher secondary students.
3. To find out the level of Study habit of higher secondary students.
4. To find out whether there is any significant association between the categories of Procrastination of higher secondary students with regard to.

a. Gender	:	Male / Female
b. Type of management	:	govt /govt aided/ private
c. Medium of instruction	:	Tamil/English
d. Fathers Education	:	Illiterate/School level/College level
Mothers Education	:	Illiterate/School level /College level

4. To find out whether there is any significant association between the Mindfulness attention awareness of higher secondary students with regard to.
   - Gender
   - Type of management
   - Medium of instruction
   - Fathers Education
   - Mothers Education
5. To find out whether there is any significant difference between the mean scores of Study habit of higher secondary students with regard to.
   - Gender
   - Type of management
   - Medium of instruction
   - Fathers Education
   - Mothers Education
6. To find out whether there is any significant association between the categories of Procrastination and Mindfulness attention awareness of higher secondary students.
7. To find out whether there is any significant association between Procrastination and Study habit of higher secondary students.
8. To find out whether there is any significant association between the Mindfulness attention awareness and Study habit of higher secondary students.

HYPOTHESES OF THE STUDY

The hypotheses framed in this present study are listed below:

1. The level of procrastination of higher secondary students is average in nature.
2. The level of mindfulness attention awareness of higher secondary students is average in nature.
3. The level of study habit of higher secondary students is average in nature.
4. There is no significant association between the categories of Procrastination of higher secondary students with regard to.

a. Gender	:	Male / Female
b. Type of management	:	Govt /Govt aided/ Private
c. Medium of instruction	:	Tamil/English
d. Fathers Education	:	Illiterate/School level/ College level
e. Mothers Education	:	Illiterate/School level/College level

5. There is no significant association between Mindfulness attention awareness of higher secondary students with regard to
   a. Gender
   b. Type of management
   c. Medium of instruction
   d. Fathers Education
   e. Mothers Education
6. There is no significant difference between the mean scores of study habit of higher secondary students with regard to
   a. Gender
   b. Type of management
   c. Medium of instruction
   d. Fathers Education
   e. Mothers Education
7. There is no significant association between the categories of Procrastination and Mindfulness attention awareness of higher secondary students.
8. There is no significant association between the categories of Procrastination and Study habit of higher secondary students.
   There is no significant association between the Mindfulness attention awareness and study habit of higher secondary students.

Sample of the Study

A stratified random sampling technique was adapted for the selection of sample. The schools selected for this study are divided into different strata: Government, Government Aided and Private schools. The random sampling technique was adopted to select the sample. Data were collected from 300 students, 87 students were drawn from government school, 82 from government aided school and 131from private school. The students studying in standard XI in the schools of Chennai city were chosen as sample.

TOOLS AND TECHNIQUES USED

The following tools have been used in the present study.

1. Procrastination Scale prepared by Clarry lay
2. Mindfulness Attention Awareness Scale prepared by*Brown*, K.W. & *Ryan*, R.M. (*2003*).
3. Study HabitInventory prepared by Dr.B.V.Patel.

DATA COLLECTION

A pilot study was conducted to establish the reliability and validity of the different tools/Inventory/Tests used, to stream line the instructions to be given to students and to find the optimum time duration for each tool.

The main study was conducted during the month of November 2014. All the tests were scored and each student was assigned scores for the different variables dealt in the study.

MAJOR FINDINGS

A careful analysis of the data had resulted in the following findings.

1. The level of procrastination of higher secondary students is average in nature.
2. The level of Mindfulness attention awareness of higher secondary students is average in nature.
3. The level of Study habit of higher secondary students is moderate in nature.
4. Procrastination and gender are not significantly associated.
5. Procrastination and type of management are significantly associated.
6. Procrastination and medium of instruction are significantly associated.
7. Procrastination and mother's education are not significantly associated.
8. Procrastination and father's education are not significantly associated.
9. Mindfulness attention awareness and gender are significantly associated.

10. Mindfulness attention awareness and Type of management are significantly associated.
11. The Mindfulness attention awareness and Medium of instruction are significantly associated.
12. The Mindfulness attention awareness and father's education are not significantly associated.
13. The Mindfulness attention awareness and Mother's education status are not significantly associated.
14. Boys are significantly higher than their counter part with regard to study habit.
15. There is no significant difference between the mean scores of study habit of govt, govt aided and private students
16. Tamil medium students have high significant study habit than English medium students.
17. There is no significant influence of the father educational status on the study habit of higher secondary students
18. There is no significant influence of the mother educational status on the study habit of higher secondary students.
19. The procrastination and Mindfulness attention awareness are significantly associated.
20. Procrastination and Study habit are not significantly associated.
21. Mindfulness attention awareness and study habit are not significantly associated.

LIMITATIONS OF THE STUDY

The following are the limitations of this study.

1. The sample size is restricted only to 300 students drawn randomly, due to paucity of time and energy.
2. The investigation is restricted to higher secondary students.
3. The study has been restricted only to Chennai District.
4. Only three schools in Chennai district have been selected for this study.

EDUCATIONAL IMPLICATIONS

The students can be relived from procrastination. The solution for this is to understand what could be the reason preventing from doing what is ought to be done. Some of the major causes are listed and the solutions are suggested.

1. Fear

When overwhelmed with too many things to do such as a particularly complex task or an act that requires a lot of detail, in such case the students may feel, “This will require more time”. Because the persons are afraid of not being able to do the task correctly, or having no confidence to do it. The best way to get rid of this is to divide the task into several portions.

2. Lack of Self-Regulation

Faced with a daunting task, the students tend to panic and do first the most important and urgent matter. Masked by this project, the students have been granted a license to delay all other important tasks. They shun our will-power and get carried away by the emotions. Establishing fixed daily routines could be the remedy. If a schedule is fixed to do small stuff, it works like small lamp posts that guide during the day. It gives own internal criteria what ought to be done and must be done by end of the day. There is time to stop and do something important. Faced with two important tasks- a big and a small one- the person can easily tell himself or his team mates for the big task- give five minutes to do this. The person does two things in a matter of time. If a schedule is fixed for some bullet time for small tasks, the students will be able to exercise a little more self-control and not be carried away by emotions.

3. Short Span Attention

In the middle of a very detailed job, the students may gasp for breath and think students will not be able to take another minute on what they are doing. They want to take coffee, want to check their email, and want to check their Face book and whatsapp. Some attention deficit disorder has infected many of the students due to the growing technology of ‘distractions.’ The best way to avoid this is to cut off distractions. Just simply shut off the social networks while working. Find a way to focus on what are the things to be done. Stick the pants on the chair while finishing a proposal. Set a time to finish what are being done and do not stand up until it is finished. Carrying on another 10 or 15 minutes to finish something is better than carrying the thought of a pending task over the sleep.

4. Lack of Purpose or Motivation

This happens when working on some extra sideline or spending quality time with the family. By the time the students get work, they could be so tired; they do not want to do anything. The only thing that will keep them from physical breakdown is the motivation to keep going. Being there physically is one thing, being there whole-heartedly is another thing. It is valid to say the mind is tired, the body is weak. And although these symptoms are more often the creation of the minds, it is brought about by the lack of purpose or motivation. Practicing implementation intention helps to get rid of the lack of purpose or motivation.

5. Lack of Accountability

When there is no one chasing on this task and the students are totally responsible for their own, the students lose grip of their project. It is so easy to think, "This can be delayed for next week since having more pressing needs." No matter how important a matter is, without any pressure, there is no taking responsibility. To avoid this peer or partner motivation can be encouraged. Be thankful if someone is nagging about a task undone. It may be a teacher, parent or friends. They are the instruments to be responsible. Take this into the positive light and make it work. How the Teacher can Show positive attention to the Student. The teacher can put a list of ways to deliver positive attention that can be done quickly, without disrupting classroom instruction, and the student actually finds rewarding.

A few ideas for giving positive attention to make the students to have highly mindfulness attention awareness are:

- Pat the student on the shoulder
- Check in with the student about how he or she is progressing with an assignment
- Make eye contact and smile at the student
- Pass the student a note with a cheerful comment, specific praise, or compliment
- Give brief, specific praise about the student's work or behavior
- Give the student a few words of encouragement
- Invite the student to summarize for the group the main points of a classroom discussion
- Converse briefly with the student
- Select the student to carry out a classroom task

Mindfulness Attention Awareness can be cultivated through mindfulness meditation, a systematic method of focusing the attention. It can be learnt to meditate on own, following like repeating a phrase or focusing on the sensation of breathing, allowing the parade of thoughts that inevitably arise to come and go. Mindfulness meditation builds upon concentration practices. This helps the mindfulness attention awareness to build up.

- Pay attention. The person also notice external sensations such as sounds, sights, and touch that make up the moment-to-moment experience. The challenge is not to latch onto a particular idea, emotion, or sensation, or to get caught in thinking about the past or the future. Instead he watches what comes and goes in the mind, and discover which mental habits produce a feeling of well-being or suffering.

- Stay with it. At times, this process may not seem relaxing at all, but over time it provides a key to greater happiness and self-awareness as you become comfortable with a wider and wider range of your experiences.

Cultivate mindfulness informally by focusing the attention on the moment-to-moment sensations during everyday activities. This is done by single-tasking—doing one thing at a time and giving it your full attention. Mindfulness training leads to reduced activation of the default network, a collection of brain regions that typically show greater activation at rest than during externally directed cognitive tasks. Students can do 'brain training' exercises to get better at those specific brain training exercises. But here a mindfulness intervention was having a broad effect on memory, verbal skills and concentration. The reason it works is because it dampens down mind wandering, the natural tendency to daydream, time-travel and generally goof off. Successful students have good study habits. Here are some tips for improving the study habits

1. **Use 30-Day Trials:** Trial periods work under the principle that by committing to a change for a month, it will become a habit. Since it is study technique the students want to reinforce, pick one or two habits and work on them for an entire month.
2. **The Learn-It-Once Approach:** Spend the time learning things as they come up in the courses. Attend classes with the perspective that it could be tested at any moment. It should only be material that they were just presented that they might not have had time to fully learn. Waiting before tests, assignments or finals is taking things too far.
3. **Morning Review:** Wake up a half hour earlier and spend that time reading from the textbook. If already the chapters are read, spend the time rewriting the key concepts into a notebook. A half-hour out of the day in the morning probably won't create a huge impact on the schedule, yet over the entire term it can be invaluable in boosting the understanding.
4. **Link Courses to Daily Life:** Spend some time each week looking for practical ways to use the information which is being learnt. If able to find situations from the daily life that are similar to the subjects, they can go from abstract theories to concrete tools.
5. **Background Reading:** Invest some of the precious time each week in reading the background of the ideas surrounding the subjects. Pick out interesting topics in the news or books that make use of ideas from the field of study. Background reading can reinforce the ideas by connecting them with reality.
6. **Set Daily Study Times:** Set periods of time that can be spent studying each day. Once the students spend a month reinforcing these learning

periods, it will become automatic. Regular studying times prevent the need for cramming and can give them consistency in the schedule.

7. **Read Papers Upside Down:** A good editing habit when checking over the essays and assignments is to read them upside down. This prevents the persons from speed reading the page and missing grammatical or sentence structure errors. This also gives a better feeling of how an essay might be read through fresh eyes, letting improve the style.
8. **Schedule a Balance:** Compress the work and studying into the weekdays and mornings so there is no need to work all of the time. Good habits also involve taking time for rest as well.

SUGGESTIONS FOR FURTHER RESEARCH

Based on the above work, the researcher suggests the following research work could be undertaken and extended to different areas.

1. This study was concentrated only on XI standard students. Similar study could be extended to college level.
2. The present study is limited to schools in Chennai District. It could be extended to other schools of other districts at Tamil Nadu State.
3. A comparative study can be undertaken among high school students.

GENERAL FINDINGS AND DISCUSSION

SECTION A: Procrastination and type of management are significantly associated.

As the calculated chi square values (16.981) is greater than the table value (13.277) at 0.01 level.

In Government Schools mostly, Students are not aware about the education because of their family circumstance students are deviated due to the unwanted activities. In private Schools even though the teachers are paying good attention and tender care towards the students, their concentration is lacking due to diversion. The students' circumstances will be purely contrasting than that of the Government students'. In Government Aided Schools, the student's level will be moderate and their diversion is the same as the other students. The teacher's attention will also be moderate towards the students. The student's behavior is also due to their surroundings.

Section B: Procrastination and medium of instruction are significantly associated.

As the calculated chi square value (8.759) is greater than the table value (5.991) at 0.05 level,

The Procrastination of the English Medium students' are due to the parental support, over confidence of the students, lavish life and also the unawareness of the educational system. The procrastination is mainly due to the present communication gadgets like I phone, I pod etc. The parents don't want their children to be punished by the teachers even for the sake of their good education. The Procrastination of the Tamil medium students are due to the unawareness of good education of their family situation. The parents won't show much care on their as they have to be work hard to enable their family. Students won't be mostly parental or completing their works on time due to the over work load of their tasks based on daily wages as to save their family.

Section C: Awareness of mindfulness attention of gender are significantly associated

As the calculated value (15.223) greater than the table value (9.210) at 0.01 level, it is clearly stated that awareness of mindfulness attention of gender are significantly associated.

The boys are generally lacking in justifying the positive and negative aspects. The boys will be easily attracted by the pleasures and won't have the ability of selecting the good one. The girls in some way have the ability to analyze the positive and negative aspects because of their awareness. The problems will be tackled by them as their inner mind is purely conscious of the unwanted problems.

Section D: Awareness of Mindfulness attention and type of management are significantly associated.

As the calculated value (33.770) is greater than table value (13.277) at 0.001 level. Mindfulness attention awareness is related with government, government aided, and private schools. In Government schools students are not aware about the education. Because of their family circumstances students are deviated due to the unwanted activities. In private schools even though the teachers are paying good attention and tender care towards the students their concentration is lacking due to diversion. The students' circumstances will be purely contrasting than the of the Government school students. In the Government aided schools, the students' level will be moderate and their diversions are the same as the other students' .The teachers' attention will also be moderate towards the students. The students' behavior is also due to their surroundings.

Section E: Awareness of mindfulness attention and medium of instruction are significantly associated.

As the calculated value (16.885) is greater than table value (9.210) at 0.01 level. The mindfulness attention awareness of the English medium students is due to the parental support, over confidence of the students. The lack of mindfulness attention awareness among English medium students is because of the luxuriousness. There are more diversions among the students of English medium students than that of the Tamil medium students with their modern life style and technological diversions like whatsapp, face book and other social network. The mindfulness attention awareness of the Tamil medium students is due to the unawareness of the good education and the family background makes the students emotionally imbalanced.

Section F: Boys are significantly higher than their counter part with regard to study habit.

As the calculated t value 2.252 is greater than the table value 1.96 at 0.05 level. Here there is significant influence beteen study habit and gender. Many researchers have shown that there is the gender difference has independent effects on study habits. The boys have the intellectual power more when compared to girls as they are exposed to the life situations more than the girls. Most of the girls are engaged in house hold activities where the boys don't have many disturbances. The boys have diversions but they are stress free while compared to girls.

Section G: Tamil medium students have high significant study habits than English medium.

As the calculated value 2.294 is greater than the table value 't' 1.96 at 0.05 level. Hence there is significance influence between study habit percentage medium of instructions.

As the Tamil medium students as they study in their mother tongue understand the subjects more easily than the students of English medium students. The sustainable fear is more seen in the Tamil medium students when compared to English medium students. Tamil medium students no need to spend special time to understand the subjects as it is in their mother tongue. So they can inculcate more study habits than that of the English medium students.

Section H: Procrastination and Mindfulness attention awareness are significantly associated.

There is a significant positive association between procrastination and awareness of mindfulness attention is more related to students as that is more important as the student stage forms the basis for the human life. The character of a person is much more molded during the student stage. The mindfulness attention awareness which is developed through education helps them to live a sustained life. The procrastination is the general characteristic feature seen among all stages of the human beings. But it is more related to students as it is stage where the students are emotional and lack of self control.

CONCLUSION

The purpose of the present investigation to investigate the relationships among the variables of Procrastination, Mindfulness Attention Awareness and Study Habit. The investigation is sure to find some usefulness in the field of education and findings of the investigation can serve as a database for further research.

❒

Bibliography

1. Abu - Sunhee (1997) DAI-A 58/11, Utah State University p.4181
2. A vramides Busila (1986), *the effect of counseling style on abstracts"* New York University. International Vol-47. No. 12.
3. Aggarwal, J.C (1991), Essential of Educational psychology, Vikas Publishing House, New Delhi.
4. Al-Rihani, Sulaiman (1985) "The effect of the family socialization patterns on children's feelings of security". Jordon University, Amman. Benjamin Woman, B. Dictionary of Behavioural Science, New York von Noestrend Reindhold Co. 1973.
5. Best, John W. (1997) Research Methodology, New Jersey: Englewood Cliffs.
6. Alexander Bay (1990), *"Indian Educational Review"* Fifth Survey P.1235, Vol.24(1) 84-89.
7. Arora Reela. (1998), Fifth Survey Vol,2, p. 1860.
8. Anaheim et al, (1995), *"Academic achievements of High Ability Students in Egalitarian Education"* The Scandinavian Journal of Educational Research. Vol.39/2, Pp. 157-167.
9. Baker, B.L. (1981), Clark .D.B and Yasu Ja P.M, *"Predictors of Success in Parent training"*
10. Berkman .L.F, and Syma .S.L. 1979), *"Social Networks, host resistance and morality"*, Pp.186-204.
11. Barbarasch, Barry Stuart (1997) DAI-A5R/03, Temple University p.74R Chaube S.P. and Chaube .A. (1999) *"Foundation of education"*. Vikas publishing House Pvt.Ltd, New Delhi. p.2SI

12. Bjorck C, Bjorck J, Clinton D, Sohlberg S, Norring CS, Submitted Self image and treatment dropouts in eating disorders.
13. Biggs, Mary (1995), Librarians as Educators: Assessing our self image, Public and Access Services Quarterly. Vol VI pp 41.50
14. Blair *et al,* refereed to certain classical studies on teacher adjustment. Educational psychology Macmillan company, New York 1962.
15. Bullock, Janis, R., (1993), Children's Loneliness and Their Relationships with Family and Peers, Family Relation, V.42, No.l, p.46-49.
16. Bigelow, B.J., (1992), The Social Rules that Children Use International Journal of Behavioural Development, V.15, No.3, p.315-36.
17. Carlson, Elizabeth (1992), How Successful Deaf Teenagers Experience and Cope with Isolation American, Annals of the Deaf, V.137, No.3, p.261-70.
18. Chandhur B.K. 'A survey into a survey of the Adjustment in Teachers (Probing into probable carries of adjustment difficulties if any) unpublished M.Ed., Dissertation, C.I.E. Delhi - 1957.
19. Cooper, Joanne, E (1994), Metaphorical "J" Journal keeping and self image in administrative women, relatives, Vol. 56, pp 11-22.
20. Crow L.D. Psychology of human adjustment, New York - 1969.
21. Crow and Crow. Adolescent Development and adjustment, New York: Wodrw
22. Crow and Crow, Adolescent development and adjustment, New York.
23. Chandy Sumi (1991), Fifth Survey of Research in Education, p.1865.. Deb Madhu Grewal, Hidraipal (1990), Fifth Survey of Research in Education, p.1868.
24. Dube .A.R. (1989), "Academic Attainment and Moral of Students taught by teachers using direct and Indirect Influence". Fifth Survey of Research in Education, p. 1878.
25. Doctor Z.N (1984), *"Classroom climate and the psyche of pupils and their Achievement"*. Further survey of their Research in Edu7cation, Vol. 1, p.821.
26. Derbush, Sanford .M et al, (1991), American Journal of Education Vol.99, 114p.543 Gnanaraj .J.
27. Dandapani, S. (2004), A Text book of Advanced Educational Psychology, New Delhi: Anmol Publications.
28. Dish ion Thomas, J., (1996) preventive parenting with love, Encouragement, and Limit Castalia Publishing Company, P.O. Box 1587.
29. Dwindle, Michael (1992), A Longitudinal Study of Stress Buffering for Adolescent Problem Behaviours Developmental Psychology, V.28, No.3, p.522-30.

30. Ester men, Kimberly (1995), Comparing Rural Adolescents from Farm and Non-farm Families. Journal of Research in Rural Education (VllNo.2, p.84-91.

31. Frecknaii, Peter (1992), An Evaluation of Parental Assessment of the Big Brothers/ Big Sisters Programme in New York City, Adolescence, V.27, N.107, p.715-18.

32. Gnanadayam (1968) "*Educational Sociology*" 52.

33. Gomati Mani (1991) "Education in the International context. " Garrisons (1992) "An evaluation of the academic achievement of gifted students from high and low achieving schools 1991". Boston University. Dissertation Abstracts International V 01.82.

34. Gamely, Malabika (1989), "*Indian Educational Review*" Fifth Survey, P, 1860, V 0124 (!) p, 84-89.

35. Georgia Jain Shikha (1991) Fifth Survey, p 1879.

36. Giordrano, Reggie (1993), The Family and Peer Relation of Block Adolescents, Journal of Marriage and the Family, V.55, N.2, p.277- 87.

37. Heath and Jamela (1992) prediting the Educational Aspiration and Graduate plans of Black and White college and university students. When Do Dreams Become realities? ASHE Annual Meeting paper.

38. Hunag Shwu Yung (1995), Effects of Flome and School learning environment on the academic achievement of eight grade Asian American Students."Jain Shikha (1991), Fifth Survey of Research in Education..P.1879.

39. Hugh Bell. M. Bell Adjustment Inventory, Manual, and Palo Alto Consulting psychological Pren 1962.

40. Ingénues R.S. Patterns of adjustments, Tokyo; McGraw Hill Inc. 1976. P. 6- 8.

41. Hoffmann, John P. (1994) Investigation the Age Effects of Family Structure Adolescent Marijuana Use, Journal of Youth and Adolescence, V.23, No.2, p, 215-35.

42. Janie .E. William (1990),. "*Modeling tests anxiety, Self concept and high school students. Academic Achievement 1990*", Journal of Research and development in Educational Vo 125, 1991 Athens,

43. Jaffe, Alan's. (1981) "Comparison of state legislators with a control group on Maslow's security - Insecurity measure", North western memorial Hospital Inst, of Psychiatry', Chicago.

44. Jack Nobbs, Robert Hine, Margaret E. Fleming (1975) "*Sociology*", *MacMillan Education, London;p.* 44.

45. Joshi, D.D. (1985) "Role of security - Insecurity feeling in academic achievement", Govt. Post gradual college, pithogarh, India

46. Kamala Bhata and Balder Bhatia (1974), *"The Philosophical and Sociological foundations of education"*. Doaba House, Delhi .P.l 02-115.
47. Kimball Young, Raymond .W. Mack (1959). *"Sociology and Social life."* American, book company, Newyork United States of America. P.348.
48. Marion, S.Mirochink, D, Maccaul, and others (1991) The Educational and more experience of rural youth. A contentual and regional analysis orono. ME center for research and evaluation university of maine.
49. Max Weiner and Walter Murray (1963) Analyzer look at the culturally derived and their level of aspiration, Journal of Educational Sociology, March, pp 319-321.
50. Meaffee, Mary Elizabeth (1997) DAI-A58/ off from their voices, American Indian in higher education and the phenomenon stepping at (Dropout Persistence) p.2039.
51. Meccarthey, Florence (1997) DAI-A 58/08, Women Instructions in higher education. Newyork United States of America. P.348.
52. Milstein, Lindo (1997), AAI-A, 57/12, Family relationship when women and men return to college Adult Students.p.5020.
53. Niebrzydowski Leon, (1995), Adolescents Family Situation and Their Self- Disclosure in Interpersonal Relationship
54. Levit, Mary, J, (1995), the Social Convoys of Children and Adolescents.
55. Pansu, Pascal: Gillibert, Daniel; Applied Psychology. 51(4)! 505-526, Oct 2002.
56. Part, Diana (1993) Fostering Seen by the Careerism Children, Adoption Fostering, V.17, p.26-31.
57. Pinel, J. P.(2000), Biopsychology (4thed). Boston: Allyn and Bacon.
58. Rai, B. C(2001), Social Psychology, Prakashan – Kendra, Lucknow.
59. *Radhi. J* (1989) "Home environment Parent child relationship and children's competence during adolescence, *p.* 1018
60. Richard T. Schaefer (1989) *"Sociology"*. Third Edition, M.C. Graw Hill, Inc. Newyork. p.319.
61. R.M Macires and Charles H.Perge (1971), *"Society: An Introductions Analysis"* Mac Millan. London Press.s Rahela S.P., Vyas K.C, Dhanpat Rai and Son. "Sociological Foundations of Education in contemporary India "p. 145.
62. Smith, Delores, E. (1995), Gender and Age variation in the self image of Jasmaican Adolesents. Adolescents, Col.30,pp.643-54.
63. Smith MuClialle'J (1995): Dissertation Abstract International Vol.56, No.9.

64. Smith, Delores (1994), Relationship between Jamaican Adolescent Drinking Partners and Self-Image Adolescence, V.28, No, 114, p.429-37.
65. *Shukla; Kiran (1992),* "A study of development of social competence as a Junction of parental, behaviour and free interaction". *Sic - Ravishankar University P.l 024.*
66. Shulman, Shmuel (1993), Close Relationship and Coping Behaviour in Adolescence, Journal of Adolescence, V.16, No.3, p.267-83.
67. *Thapliyal D.P (1981),* "A Study of Classroom Morale, its factors and Relationship with students Academic Achievement". *Third Survey of Research n Education, by .M.B. Butch.* Tolliver and Joel (1995), Dissertation Abstract InternationalVolo.56. No.9.
68. *Verma B.P.* (1992), Relationships between temperament Academic achievement Indian Educational Review" *Vol.27(3). P 95-101*
69. O.Whana (1982), "The influence of the social Problems of the
70. Community on the Academic achievement of pupils with special reference to Soweto". Dissertation Abstracts International Feb 1984. V 01-44.
71. *Pardhan .C., (1992).* "Effect of school Organisational Climate on the Creativity, adjustment and academic achievement of Secondary Schools of
72. "*Orisa*" Educational Vtkal University. Fifth Survey ofTSRE by Buch. Ram Nath Sharma (1975) "*introductory Sociology*", Rajahs Prakashan Mandir, Educational Publishers, Meerut, UP P.250-255.
73. Wardle, Francis (1995), Building self image, Child Care Information Jul- Aug. pp
74. Walberg, H. J (1989) student aspiration, National and International perspectives. In Quaglia (ED), Research in rural Educcation, 6(2) 1-9.
75. Weber, Elizabeth, C., (1994) Enhance Social Skills with Peer Recommended Books, Day-Care & Early - Education, V.21, No.4, p.20-24.
76. Watts, W, (1992) Drug Abuse and Eating Disorders, Journal of Drug Education, V.22, No.3, p.223-40.
77. *Whister José* (1992), "Mid- continent Regional educational lab", Aurora, 1992
78. Youngblade-Lise, M. (1992), Parent Child Antecedent of 5 years old Close Friendship : A Longitudinal Analysis, Developmental Psychology, V.28, N.4, p.700-13.
79. Alex h. S. Harris,, fredericluskin, *et al.,*(2006) effects of a group forgiveness intervention on forgiveness, perceived stress, and trait-anger, vol 10 (2).

80. Berry, jack w.; worthingtonjr., everett (2008), Forgivingness, relationship quality, stress while imagining relationship events, and physical and mental health. Journal of counselling psychology, vol 48(4), 447-455.

81. Burckhardt c.s&andersonk.l *et al.,* (2003) the quality of life reliability,validity and utilization health and quality of life out comes, vol.60 (1)

82. Daniela c wilks1felixnetostellamavroveli et al., (2009) trait emotional intelligence, forgiveness, and gratitude in cape verdean and portuguese students. Department of psychology, university of maryland, college park.

83. Ferrans, carol *et.al.,* (2014) quality of life index: development and psychometric properties.

84. Jo anntsang, Matthew, Stanford, *et al.,* testing underlying mechanisms of forgiveness: need for closure and accessibility; Department of psychology and neuroscience, baylor university.

85. Lin ky,huyt, changkj, linhf, tsauojy. *et al.,* (2011) Effects of yoga on psychological health, quality of life, and physical health of patients with cancer: a meta-analysis. Introduction obstetrics and gynaecology international, vol 74.

86. Luke a.Egan, natasha *et al.,* forgiveness as a coping strategy to allow school students to deal with the effects of being bullied: theoretical and empirical discussion

87. Mary katelaw parker, et al.,(2008) the relation between hostility and social support: investigating potential mediation or moderation by trait forgiveness, attribution style, and trait empathy (proquest information & learning). *Dissertation abstracts international: section b: the sciences and engineering, 69* (1-b), 691.

88. Parviz asgari1, khadijehroshaniet. al.,(2013) validation of forgiveness scale and a survey on the relationship of forgiveness and students' mental health, department of psychology.

89. Robyn westmacott, phd; daunemacgregor,rand askalan, gabrielledeveber, et al., emergence of cognitive deficits after unilateral neonatal stroke author affiliations from the children's stroke program, the hospital for sick children division of neurology, department of pediatrics, faculty of medicine, university of toronto, on, canada.

90. S. Farooq, Chaudhry, Shafiq, Berhanu et al.,(2011) factors affecting students' quality of academic performance: a case of secondary school level; university of the punjab,journal of quality and technology management volume vii, issue ii.

91. Sampogna f, tabolli; et al., quality of life impairment and psychological distress in elderly patients with psoriasis. Italian multipurpose psoriasis research on vital experiences study group
92. Zurich frank anddaniel et al.,(2007) The role of trait forgiveness and relationship satisfaction in episodic forgiveness matthias allemande, irina ambers, zimprich university of. Finchamflorida state university journal of social and clinical psychology, vol. 26, no. 2, pp. 199–217
93. Aanu, E. M. and Olatoye, R. A. (2011): Use of library resources, study habit and science achievement of junior secondary school students. Educational Research, 2(7), 1265-1269.
94. Abid Hussain. Ch. (2006): Effect of Guidance Services on Study Attitudes, Study Habits and Academic Achievement of Secondary School Students. Bulletin of Education & Research, 28(1), 35-45.
95. Adegbile, J. (2000): A study of the reading habits of secondary school students in Nigeria. African Journal of Research in Education, 1(1), 153–159. 170
96. Aggarwal, Y. P. and Saini, V. P. (1969): Patterns of study habits and its relationship with achievement and parent economic and educational status, Journal of Educational Research and Extension, 5(4), 158-164.
97. Agulanna, G. G. (1999): Family structure and prevalence of behavioral problems among Nigerian adolescents, The Counselor, 17(1), 154-154.
98. Ahmann, J. S., Smith, S. and Glack, M. D. (1958): Predicting academic success in college by means of a Study and Attitudes Inventory. Educational Psychology Measurement, 18, 853-857.
99. Akinboye, J.O. (1974): Study habits modification, study attitude change and academic performance, Un-published Master's Thesis, University of Ibadan, Ibadan.
100. Akinboye, J.O.(1980), How to study and pass important examinations; A psychological approach, Ibadan, Maritime Printers.
102. Aluede and Onolemhemhen (2001): Effect of study habit counseling on the academic performance of secondary schools students in English language. J. Edu. Res. Ext., 38(3), 17-26.
103. Anamoze, L. M. (1999): A study of secondary school students' study skills, Special end of Century International Conference, Nigerian Association of Educationists for National Development, Kaduna Polytechnic.
104. Andreou ,Chrisoula. "Understanding Procrastination." Journal for the Theory of Social Behavior37. 2 (2007): 183-193. Print.
105. Ansari, Z. A. (1980): Study Habits and Attitudes of Students: Development and Validation of Questionnaire Measures. Islamabad: National Institute of Psychology.

106. Baer, R. A. (Ed.). (2006). Mindfulness-based treatment approaches: Clinician's guide to evidence base and applications. San Diego, CA: Elsevier Academic Press.
107. Blankstein, Kirk R., Paul L. Hewitt, Spomenka Koledin, Gordon L. Flett. "Components of Perfectionism and Procrastination in College Students
108. Brophy, J. (1998): Motivating students to learn, Usa: McGrow Companies No. Broussard, S. C. and Garrison, M. E. (2004):
109. Chauhan, S. S. and Singh, H. (1982):. Indian Education Review NCERT, New Delhi, 22(1), 92-96.
110. Chauhan, S. S. (2003): Advanced Educational Psychology, Sterling Publisher, New Delhi.
111. Didonna, F. (Ed.). (2009). Clinical Handbook of Mindfulness. New York: Springer.
112. Ferrari, Joseph R. "Procrastination and Attention: Factor Analysis of Attention Deficit, Boredomness, Intelligence, Self-Esteem, and Task Delay Frequencies." Journal of Social Behavior & Personality 15.5 (2000): 185-196. Print.
113. Germer, C. K., Siegel, R. D., & Fulton, P. R. (Eds.). (2005). Mindfulness and psychotherapy.New York: Guilford Press.
114. Gunuratana, B. H. (2002). Mindfulness in Plain English. Somerville, MA: Wisdom Publications.
115. Haycock, Laurel A., Patricia McCarthy, and Carol L. Skay. "Procrastination in College Students: The Role of Self-Efficacy and Anxiety." Journal of Counseling & Development 76.3 (1998): 317-323. Print.
116. Hayes, S. C., Follette, V. M., & Linehan, M. M. (Eds.). (2004). Mindfulness and acceptance: Expanding the cognitive-behavioral tradition. New York: Guilford Press.
117. Hsin, Angela, Chun Chu, and Jin Nam Choi. "Rethinking Procrastination: Positive Effects of "Active" Procrastination Behavior on Attitudes and Performance" Journal of Social Psychology 145.3 (2005): 245-264.
118. Klassen, Robert M. et al. 'A Cross-Cultural Study Of Adolescent Procrastination'. Wiley online lirary. N.p., 2009. Web. 14 Jan. 2015.
119. Orsillo, S. M., & Roemer, L. (Eds.). (2005). Acceptance and mindfulness-based approaches toanxiety: Conceptualization and treatment. New York: Springer Science.
120. Procrastination and Task Avoidance: Ferrari, Joseph R., Judith L. Johnson, and William G. McCown. Procrastination and Task Avoidance

Theory, Research, and Treatment. New York, New York: Plenum Press, 1995.

121. Roemer, L., & Orsillo, S. M. (2009). Mindfulness- and acceptance-based behavioral therapies in practice. New York: Guilford Press.
122. Sapadin, Dr. Linda. It's About Time! The 6 Styles of Procrastination and How to Overcome Them. NewYork, New York: Penguin Group, 1996.
123. Segal, Z. V., Williams, J. M. G., & Teasdale, J. D. (2002). Mindfulness-based cognitive therapy for depression: A new approach to preventing relapse. New York: Guilford Press.
124. Seo, Eun Hee. "Cramming, Active Procrastination, And Academic Achievement." Social Behavior & Personality: International Journal 40.8 (2012):1333-1340. Print.
126. Sirois, Fuschia M. "Procrastination and counterfactual thinking: Avoiding what might have been."British Journal of Social Psychology 43.2 (2004): 269-286. Print.
127. UK essays,. 'Academic Procrastination And Academic Achievement Psychology Essay'. N.p., 2015. Web. 13 Jan. 2015.

❏❏❏